Freedom and Solidarity

FREEDOM AND SOLIDARITY

SOLIDARITY

Toward New Beginnings

FRED DALLMAYR

UNIVERSITY PRESS OF KENTUCKY

Scholarly publisher for the Commonwealth,
serving Bellarmine University, Berea College, Centre College of Kentucky,
Eastern Kentucky University, The Filson Historical Society, Georgetown
College, Kentucky Historical Society, Kentucky State University, Morehead
State University, Murray State University, Northern Kentucky University,
Transylvania University, University of Kentucky, University of Louisville,
and Western Kentucky University.

Editorial and Sales Offices: The University Press of Kentucky
663 South Limestone Street, Lexington, Kentucky 40508-4008
www.kentuckypress.com

Cataloging-in-Publication data is available from the Library of Congress.

ISBN 978-0-8131-6578-3 (hardcover : alk. paper)
ISBN 978-0-8131-6579-0 (epub)
ISBN 978-0-8131-6580-6 (pdf)

Member of the Association of
American University Presses

To friendship everywhere

Behold, I am doing a new thing,
Even now it is springing to light.
—Isaiah 43:19

There is something in me that is of tomorrow and the day
after tomorrow and time to come.
—Friedrich Nietzsche,
Thus Spoke Zarathustra

Absolute freedom mocks at justice; absolute (totalizing)
justice denies freedom. To be fruitful, the two ideas must
find their limits in each other.
—Albert Camus,
The Rebel

It is within a social and political ecology that we can take
into account the complementarity between individual
and community, economic goals and the aspiration to
meaning, the desire for independence and the need for
attachment.
—Tzvetan Todorov,
The Inner Enemies of Democracy

Contents

Preface   xi

Introduction: Reenvisaging Freedom and Solidarity   1

1. Twilights and New Dawns: Revaluation and De(con)struction   17

2. Letting-Be Politically: Heidegger on Freedom and Solidarity   39

3. The Promise of Democracy: Nonpossessive Freedom and Caring Solidarity   65

4. Markets and Democracy: Beyond Neoliberalism   79

5. Rights and Right(ness): Humanity at the Crossroads   97

6. "Man against the State": Community and Dissent   115

7. Faith and Communicative Freedom: A Tribute to Wolfgang Huber   135

8. Between Holism and Totalitarianism: Remembering Dimitry Likhachev   153

9. Freedom as Engaged Social Praxis: Lessons from D. P. Chattopadhyaya   169

10. Freedom and Solidarity (Again): Reimagining Social Democracy   183

Notes   197

Index   225

Preface

What is most startling, a great philosopher once said, is that there is something rather than nothing. This means that the "something" is a source of marvel, astonishment, and wonder, at least for philosophical eyes—which are rare. For the great majority of people, the world of "somethings"—even if initially strange or exotic—quickly turns into commonplace. The great social thinker Max Weber at one point talked about the "routinization of charisma"—that is, the steady transformation of innovative ideas and practices into generally accepted conventions and routines. Even revolutionary breakthroughs, he held, over time settle into the stability of commonly shared habits, into the comfort of a dominant worldview sustained by public institutions and a standard vocabulary. Expressed in non-Weberian language, the worldview might be called a reigning "paradigm" or frame of significance or, in still different terminology, a prevailing "social imaginary."

For people living in the West today—and even for many living outside the West—the dominant paradigm or worldview is that of Western modernity with its focus on individual liberty, secularism, and scientific control of nature. The paradigm emerged as the result of a break or rupture with the medieval and classical past—a break epitomized by Descartes's radical "doubt." What was left in the wake of this doubt was a thoroughly bipolar outlook pitting against each other the solitary mind (*ego cogitans*) and the rest of the world (*res extensa*) comprising society and nature. Although repeatedly modified or reformulated, this dualist structure was never abandoned. Under the influence of a sequence of "liberal" thinkers (from Thomas Hobbes and John Locke to Jean-Jacques Rousseau), the individual self turned increasingly into the linchpin of the modern Western paradigm; in fact, the freedom or liberty of nonsocial individuals was celebrated as the "natural" human condition (in the "state of nature"), whereas involvement in society and nature was treated as secondary and subsidiary (even artificial).

As one should note, the bipolar structure of the modern world-view is not socially or politically innocuous. Although the structure seemingly balances two sides—mind/matter, subject/object, ego/society—a primacy is clearly granted to the first of the paired terms. In accordance with the Baconian formula "knowledge is power," the knowing or rational mind in modernity has endeavored to bring matter and the entire world under its control. As a result, modern life has unleashed the utopia (or dystopia) of "total knowledge" and a gigantic "superbrain" where all information would be known and stored (by people controlling the system). What is termed scientific or technological advancement is basically the transformation of all things or "objects" in the world into pliant targets for specialists or knowing "subjects." It is mainly in the binary relation of ego/society that problems emerge. Although preferring to treat the individual as primary or "natural" and society as derivative, the worldview cannot consistently maintain this primacy in case of crisis or danger (as Thomas Hobbes clearly foresaw). Thus, a dilemma or conflict emerges in crisis situations—a conflict pitting sovereign power against dissenting individuals who claim their freedom. To camouflage this conflict, an effort will be made to present the public community as a higher form of subjectivity and national interest as a sublimation of self-interest—an effort hardly persuasive or consoling to persecuted dissenters.

The implications of the sketched paradigm have played themselves out in recent centuries and continue to play themselves out today both domestically and globally. In terms of dominant political ideologies, the past century was overshadowed by the conflict between liberalism and socialism, the former focused on individual "freedom" and the second on social "solidarity"—but a solidarity often imposed by sovereign power and totalitarian control. Merged with the economic rivalry between capitalism and communism, the freedom/solidarity antimony culminated finally in nearly half a century of "cold war." Although the Cold War officially ended some two decades ago, its rhetoric and ideological slogans have by no means retreated into the background or ceased to maintain their grip on people's imagination. Here again, the Weberian insight holds true in the sense that old clichés are still widely treated as self-evident truths.

Fortunately, the sketched paradigm is no longer uncontested; in fact, there is today a growing chorus of voices calling into question the dominant worldview together with its binary oppositions. What critical voices of this kind herald or seek to herald are new horizons or new beginnings of thought and practice—that is, a transition to a new paradigm and even a new "Axial Age." Transition here means a movement or transit from the Western-centric perspective to a more global or cosmopolitan constellation in which the polarity between ego and external world, between freedom and social solidarity, is overcome or reconciled. In its own way, the present book seeks to pave the way toward this overcoming or reconciliation. Although not directly spelling out the contours of a new "Axial Age," its chapters seek at least to lay the groundwork for a possible paradigm shift.

In the nature of things, such a shift is difficult. Because the prevailing worldview is routinized and accepted as commonplace, considerable effort is needed to loosen its bonds and to unsettle its taken-for-granted assumptions. This process is what Friedrich Nietzsche called the "revaluation of values" and what Martin Heidegger (and Jacques Derrida) later termed "de(con)struction." Without this effort, there would be no possibility to gain access to new horizons and to marvel again at the world—today a global world—with fresh eyes. Yet paradigmatic innovation, although exciting, is also hazardous: the unsettling of established ways of life can bring to the fore strange or dangerous "remedies." Thus, the overcoming of the modern paradigm can conjure up the chimera of a wholesale return to "premodern" times; above all, the widespread abuse of the modern idea of individual freedom can lead to the rejection of freedom in favor of unfreedom, submissiveness, and heteronomy. This remedy for modern ills is sometimes aided and abetted by the resurgence of organized religion (as distinguished from religious faith) in our time. In the eyes of some supporters, this resurgence has the benefit not only of restoring clerical and public authority but also of fostering a tightly knit social community (as an antidote to modern individualism).

In these and related instances, the proposed "remedy" may be worse than the ills to be cured. With reference to communalism or tight communitarianism, the memories of fascist-style "folk community" and Stalinist-style collectivism are still too fresh not to provide cause for concern. What this means is that human freedom is not relinquishable—although it may have to be rethought and redefined. In the aftermath of Western modernity, whatever community or "solidarity" is to be sought cannot be the antithesis of human freedom but only its higher fulfillment. In this context, it is well to remember Nietzsche's words in *Beyond Good and Evil* denouncing the "common good" as an oxymoron because what is "common" (*gemein*) is not good and what is "good" is not common. In line with Nietzsche's teachings, any viable democratic community in our time has to resist the type of conformism and "herd mentality"—fostered by the media and some political leaders—that seeks to "dumb down" every excellence to the lowest common denominator. Contra some of Nietzsche's more elitist statements, however, one can also say that excellence—achieved through restraint and self-cultivation—does not need to be antisocial but can foster a kind of engagement that uplifts social life (as illustrated by the examples of Mahatma Gandhi, Martin Luther King Jr., and Nelson Mandela).

In my view, what is needed in our time is not a simple exit from modernity but rather the endeavor to reinterpret the meaning of its constituent terms—above all the terms *freedom* and *solidarity*. What this rethinking has to bring into view is a holistic, nonpossessive or relational kind of freedom as well as a noncoercive and emancipatory kind of solidarity. Perhaps terms such as *social liberty* and *liberal solidarity* might serve the purpose. But, of course, the real issue is not the labeling but the substance of the new orientation. The philosopher Alasdair MacIntyre stated at one time that what is demanded today is "another St. Benedict." There is more than a kernel of truth in this assertion—although it needs to be carefully construed. There is surely no need to reestablish a religious order that already exists. But there is an urgent desire for an exemplary community of free people wholly committed to the search for truth, goodness, and justice.

Such an exemplary community today cannot, or can only in the rarest instances, be directly linked with governments or governmental institutions, given the character of most modern states as bloated bureaucratic apparatuses of physical and mental control. The focus today has to be rather on civil society and vibrant institutions of nongovernmental life. Gandhi, at the time of Indian independence and just before the erection of the new Indian government, proposed an intriguing formula that he called "Loka Sevakh Sangh"—that is, Association for Service to People. This association, in Gandhi's view, was to be composed of independent civic leaders drawn from different ethnic and religious backgrounds and entrusted with the task of monitoring and curbing the power lust of governmental officials by cultivating moral and civic vigilance among people. In many societies, religious institutions have traditionally been entrusted with a similar task, but churches have too often been co-opted and served as accomplices of state power. Against this background, MacIntyre's call for a new St. Benedict clearly looks for a non-co-opted alternative; from another angle, Dietrich Bonhoeffer's search for a *communio sanctorum* (as an antidote to totalitarianism) points in a similar direction. My friend Richard Falk has coined an inspiring and potentially globally relevant term: *citizen pilgrims*. Perhaps one might also think of these pilgrims as the friends of a friendly and gentle Zarathustra, who said, "Let the future and the farthest be for you the cause of your today: in your friend you shall love the overman as your motive."

In recent years, I have been involved in a sort of Loka Sevakh Sangh: the World Public Forum—Dialogue of Civilizations, an international nongovernmental organization that brings together distinguished people from many different countries, many different religions, and many different professions and occupations. The society's basic aim is to serve as a global arena where pressing issues or crises—geopolitical, economic, environmental, cultural, and religious—can be discussed openly and fairly in the hope of promoting transparency, civic responsibility, and social justice. I am very grateful to many forum participants for their intellectual stamina and, above all, for extending to me their personal friendship, including Vladimir Yakunin, Richard Falk, Chandra Muzaffar, Hans Köchler, Marietta Stepanyants, Johan Galtung, and the great champion of Gandhi's legacy Jagdish Kapur (who passed away too soon)—to name just a few.

As it seems to me, language is often more astute than philosophical doctrines. In the German language, the term *Freier* refers to a "free person" but also to a suitor, a person seeking love or companionship. This combination of freedom and companionship is precisely at the heart of friendship. For the cover of this book, I have chosen Pablo Picasso's painting *L'Amitié* because genuine friendship, in my view, displays the perfect harmony of freedom and solidarity. In the Daoist classic *Zhuangzi,* one finds this story (in chapter 6): "Three men, Master Sanghu, Meng Zifan, and Master Qinzhang were talking to each other, asking, 'Who is able to be with others without being with others, be for others without being for others? Who is able to climb the skies, roam the mists, and dance in the infinite, living forgetful of each other without end?' The three men looked at each other and smiled, none opposed in his heart; and so they became friends."

As I wrote this book, several other people, in addition to those mentioned earlier, have been my steady intellectual companions and deserve my thanks—again just a few names: Charles Taylor, Douglas Allen, Ashis Nandy, Michiko Yusa, and Tu Weiming. Most important for me, of course, has been my small *sangh*: my wife, Ilse, and our children and grandchildren. Without them, nothing.

Notre Dame, October 2014

Introduction

Reenvisaging Freedom and Solidarity

> The new way, the "different thinking," does not mean going further along the lines of the old.
> —Karl Jaspers, *The Future of Mankind*

Our world is changing fast—not just in details but as a whole. An era anchored in Europe and the West is coming to a close, giving way to new global and even cosmological horizons. Although historical evolution usually proceeds a step at a time, changes sometimes aggregate or bundle up to produce a new framework or constellation. This seems to be our situation today. Analysts use different terms to designate cumulative or holistic modes of transformation. In *The Origin and Goal of History*, the philosopher Karl Jaspers reflected on the course and meaning of human history seen from a (more or less) global perspective. Following in the footsteps of Spengler and Toynbee, Jaspers detected in human history a limited number of cumulative shifts or turning points, among which he singled out as most important the so-called "Axial Age" occurring in the Occident and Asia roughly between 800 and 200 B.C.E. Carried forward by some speculative thinkers as well as by founders of major world religions, the Axial Age for Jaspers involved a breakthrough to entirely new depths of human consciousness—that is, a process of human "spiritualization" that circled the entire globe (even in the absence of direct cultural interconnections). In his words, the Axial period "gave birth to everything which, since then, humans have been able to be, the point most overwhelmingly fruitful in fash-

1

ioning humanity. . . . From it world history receives the only structure and unity that has endured—at least until our own time."[1]

Given the cumulative changes occurring globally in the world today, it is tempting to establish a parallel between our era and Jaspers's Axial period. In fact, going beyond the notion of a loose analogy, some prominent contemporary authors have portrayed our time as a replica or renewal of Axial Age spiritualism or "spiritualization."[2] What renders the comparison partly plausible is the global sweep of present-day transformations (a sweep, however, that is shared by the expansion of markets and communications networks). An additional support comes from the undeniable resurgence of traditional religion in many parts of the world. Nevertheless, the parallel suffers from numerous drawbacks. There is, first of all, the enormous gap separating the Axial Age from our own. Jaspers himself recognized another historical turning point or watershed—namely, the rise of "the scientific-technological age" whose remolding effect "we are experiencing in ourselves." For Jaspers, the latter age started around 1500 in the West; carried forward by people such as Galileo, Bacon, and Descartes, it introduced new standards of knowledge and new forms of individual freedom that coalesced into a distinctive historical constellation.[3]

More serious are drawbacks deriving from the philosophy- and religion-founding character of the original Axial Age. Philosophy today is an ongoing discipline and cannot be restarted from scratch (bypassing current issues). Likewise, the rise of religion—especially of the great world religions—was a hapax phenomenon in the ancient world that cannot readily be duplicated today. What is possible and even urgently required in our time is a rethinking and reinvigoration of what it means to think and to be religious in a genuine way. Such a renewal, however, can no longer be restricted, as it was in antiquity, to religious "founders" and exemplary spiritual "personalities" but has to find expression more broadly in popular experience and sentiments.[4]

Thus, if a parallel is to be drawn with the Axial Age, it can be drawn only in the radical quest for new beginnings or a new grounding, in the intensive search for the meaning of human being in the world. The world in which this search occurs, however, is not the world of ancient empires and civilizations, but the world of "modernity" that coincides to a large extent with what Jaspers called "the scientific-technological age" and that reached its culmination in Western Enlightenment. It is for this reason that most radical questioning in our time revolves around the status of modernity, the "crisis" of modernity, and the role of modern science and technology; ancillary questions deal with multiple modernities, contending modernities, the end of modernity, and even the "end of history." Despite complex internal variations, the modern age (so called) exhibits a coherent paradigmatic structure whose philosophical contours were first pinpointed with great lucidity by René Descartes—his work derived in turn from the intense cultural ferment permeating the Renaissance period. After having challenged all the major premises of Scholastic philosophy and metaphysics, Descartes arrived at last at (what he considered) the unshakeable foundation of inquiry: the inquiring mind or internal mental substance (*res cogitans*) in relation to which all nonmental phenomena appear as externalities or as ingredients of an external material world. With this bold hypothesis, the French thinker launched or set in motion a whole array of dilemmas and antinomies whose interplay came to preoccupy the ensuing centuries: the interplay of mind and matter (or nature), of subject and object, of internality and externality. It is this basic structure that radical questioning today seeks to challenge in the hope of paving the way for a paradigm shift or new intellectual beginnings.[5]

Not only is the paradigmatic structure just mentioned an intellectual constellation, but it also has had distinct repercussions in social and political life, especially in the relations between self and others, between individual and society. Given the primacy accorded to the internal mind (or *ego cogitans*), fellow human beings were tendentially reduced to external objects on a par with the objects of material nature—objects that, in principle, are there to be either appropriated or else manipulated and controlled. The same primacy of the inner self had a decisive effect on the notion of human "freedom" or "autonomy"—a notion that became the linchpin of modern life.[6] Basically, by contrast to earlier cosmological conceptions, freedom in modernity came to be seen as a human faculty or property whose promotion or enhancement was regarded as the goal of all human endeavors. Given the placement of the self in an external social context, however, freedom in modernity assumed a characteristic dualistic and eventually "dialectical" structure. On the one hand, to the extent that the external environment proved to be pliable or susceptible to influence or control, freedom meant the pursuit of a distinct "project" to be actively implemented in the world; this is what is typically meant by "positive freedom." On the other hand, where the environment proves to be recalcitrant or stubborn, the remaining strategy is to retreat into the shelter of internal privacy—an option usually designated "negative freedom." To escape from the narrowness of individual life, the accent is sometimes placed on social collectivities and the pursuit of collective projects or goals; in this case, the role of individual freedom evaporates, although its character as property is rarely called into question.[7]

To be sure, at least in its initial phases, Western modernity (as a paradigm) signaled a momentous breakthrough to new and deeper levels of human consciousness and self-awareness. Thus, despite great internal variations, the European Renaissance made room for the flourishing of personal freedom and individuality that had lain dormant under thick layers of medieval conventionalism. In turn, the Protestant Reformation paved access to recessed layers of religious inwardness, largely removed from clerical control—while also celebrating the sanctity of "ordinary" life (outside monastic retreats). Finally, the period of the European Enlightenment ushered in a process of human liberation from external (political and clerical) controls, a process that reached its culmination in a series of revolutions and radical reforms. It was only in the course of these Enlightenment and post-Enlightenment developments that the initially promising and uplifting features of modernity began to reveal their darker underside: the collusion of liberation with domination, of enlightened rationality with public power.[8] Basically, what happened was that promising social horizons were increasingly transformed into ideological doctrines, and emancipatory formulas into emblems of social privilege. Differently phrased, human rationality and individual liberty were increasingly removed or "disembedded" from sustaining social, political, and ethical contexts. This process of "disembedding" was most pronounced in modern economics, where laissez-faire liberalism (or capitalism) progressively obliterated all considerations not compatible with the calculus of individual or corporate profit.[9] As a result of these and related developments, human freedom—the signature value of Western modernity—was increasingly turned into a shibboleth, a synonym of individual or corporate narcissism.

Combined with military and technological corollaries, the sketched developments are at the heart of the so-called crisis of modernity—a crisis that has given rise to steadily more virulent critiques. Critical assessments frequently take aim precisely at the role of freedom in modern life, given its pivotal status in Western modernity. In the eyes of intellectual or religious traditionalists, modernity and modernization are often seen as nothing but derailments, a deplorable slide from the heights of premodern "holism" or "embeddedness" into the chaos of particular pursuits and the squalor of modern vices.[10] The same outlook can also be found in forms of contemporary "communitarianism," where collectively shared "values" are celebrated with little or no regard for the demands of social pluralism and democratic rights or freedoms. Even venerable notions such as the "good life" or the "common good" are sometimes turned by public or religious leaders into instruments of collective oppression or manipulation. What tends to be often forgotten is the fact that the primacy of shared values can also be enlisted in the service of aggressive nationalistic, sectarian, or ethnic agendas—as the past hundred years have so dramatically and devastatingly demonstrated. Even apart from traditionalists hankering for the comforts of a (presumably) stable past, modernist intellectuals and movements can also succumb to the lure of radically collectivist and antiliberal programs—communism being the most prominent example. Thus, under the banner of a shared attack on liberal freedom, ethical traditionalists and progressive "materialists" can converge (without coinciding) in the pursuit of "totalitarian" ventures.[11]

What is demanded in our present situation—it seems to me—is neither the dismissal nor the doctrinaire embrace of freedom or autonomy in the modernist sense of these terms. Rather, what our time calls for is a more difficult task: the radical rethinking of human freedom and its constitutive relation to the surrounding (social and natural) world. The difficulty of the task is immensely increased and complicated by the fact that modern freedom is not an isolated, decontextualized notion but forms part and parcel of a broader frame of reference or paradigmatic constellation. Thus, any rethinking of the term becomes embroiled in deeper, subterranean currents: the ongoing paradigm shift characterizing our time. Importantly, the shape of the impending paradigm cannot be readily grasped or predicted on the basis of preceding categories. This means that the shift cannot be willfully constructed or engineered; thus, it transgresses the confines of modern "positive" freedom. Nor is the shift merely an external fate passively or "negatively" to be endured because new possibilities arise embryonically from the contradictions of the past. To this extent, paradigm shifts always signal breakthroughs or rupturing events—without necessarily being eschatological disruptions canceling temporality or human historical experience.

Given their comprehensive character, paradigm changes are unsettling and often traumatic episodes; emerging conditions of human life are not yet cognitively surveyed, worked over, or domesticated. In a way, "being" (in every sense) erupts anew or takes a fresh start—testifying to the untamed potentialities of what the Spanish Indian thinker Raimon Panikkar has called the "rhythm of being." In a similar vein, the French philosopher Maurice Merleau-Ponty speaks of a "brute or wild being" (*être brut ou sauvage*), an "amorphous" precognitive world "which contains no mode of expression and which nonetheless calls them forth and requires all of them."[12] With this amorphous world, what comes into view is a novel form of human freedom not subsumable in any way under its modern conceptualizations: freedom seen as a radical "openness" to new experiences, as a willingness to shed habitual preconceptions in favor of a return to ignorance, and as a gateway to new "disclosures"—disclosures of the world, of other human beings and cultures, and of nature. This means that freedom here is no longer autonomy as proprietary self-possession. In the words of Merleau-Ponty again, we interrogate our experience "precisely in order to know how it opens us to what is not ourselves. This does not even exclude the possibility that we find in our experience a movement toward what could not in any event be present to us in the original and whose irremediable absence would thus count among our originating experiences."[13]

As indicated earlier, moving between paradigms is usually an unsettling and wrenching experience; it is also marked by high risks or dangers. Abandoning the safe harbor of settled conventions and conceptual categories opens the path to a pristine wildness pregnant with both enabling and destructive consequences. The philosopher Gilles Deleuze has coined the felicitous expression *chaosmos* to capture the process of "creative disorder"—more precisely, the fact that order or cosmos arises always out of precognitive disorder and requires the energizing impulses of "chaos" to maintain itself over time.[14] Using a different idiom, one might say that the sustaining "ground" of being is always also an unground or abyss (*Abgrund*). What renders the conjunction of chaos and order so eminently risky is the possible abuse or instrumentalization of the constitutive terms. Thus, attracted by the lure of wildness, people may (mis)construe chaos as a personal or collective agenda or "project," thereby unleashing immense social mayhem and catastrophes. What is bypassed in this abuse is the unavailability of "brute being," the fact that paradigmatic constellations cannot be targets of unilateral human control. This insight bestows a benign and noncoercive quality on "chaosmos," especially on the order emerging out of disorder. Given its holistic equality, such order carries with it the connotation of wholeness, the prospect of making whole or of healing earlier diremptions. In Merleau-Ponty's words (paraphrasing Heidegger), "*Grund* is *Abgrund*. But the abyss one thus discovers is not such by a simple *lack* of ground: it is the upsurge of *Hoheit* which supports from above (*tient par le haut*)."[15]

Paradigm shifts or transitions usually are quiet or reticent happenings, far removed from political platforms or ideological manifestos. Because of their sheltered status, awareness of them requires witnesses or resonance chambers endowed with unusually sensitive antennae. During the transition from the "modern" paradigm to the onset of new horizons, Western culture produced two preeminent figures capable of witnessing the change with relentless intensity: Friedrich Nietzsche and Martin Heidegger (to both of whom chapter 1 is devoted). Nietzsche's work is well known for his emphasis on the needed "revaluation of all values," an emphasis that resolutely zeroes in on the inevitable decay of traditional "values" when they are transformed from dynamic challenges into cognitive doctrines and routinized formulas. In a similar vein, Heidegger's work revolves around the "overcoming" of traditional metaphysics and the relentless search for a "new beginning" (*anderer Anfang*) obstructed by the weight of cognitive presumptions. In particular, his notion of *Destruktion* (deconstruction) stresses the need to uncover the "unthought" or precognitive underpinnings in the thought systems of the past. More than other thinkers, Nietzsche and Heidegger have been the targets of an unusual barrage of vituperation (even demonization) by the guardians of established paradigms. Unwilling to acknowledge novelty, the same guardians also have foisted on both thinkers a large number of misleading labels or descriptions (borrowed from the past), such as *irrationalism* or *antirationalism, antiliberalism, mysticism,* and *amoralism.*

To exit from misleading labels, a crucial requirement—as indicated earlier—is the rigorous rethinking of traditional categories and concepts. Among the latter, the pivotal category of Western modernity is the idea of human freedom anchored in the cogito and typically identified with a self-possessed autonomy or proprietary quality. However, given the unified character of the modern constellation, freedom is entangled with a host of other notions—which likewise need to be rethought. A major issue, given freedom's traditional linkage with self-possession, is how freedom can be reconceived and rendered compatible with the notion of solidarity (which, in many ways, straddles the mottos of equality and fraternity).[16] During recent times, many thinkers have wrestled with the task of such reformulation; however, the most resolute effort to extricate the ideas from their older moorings has been undertaken in the writings of Heidegger (the topic of chapter 2). In line with his post-Cartesian and postsubjectivist construal of human existence, Heidegger has relocated freedom from the arena of human possessiveness to a deeper "ontological" level, where it comes to mean the emblem of a transformative quest or search: the search for truth and the "good life" in a worldly context. As seen from this angle, truth and goodness cannot be identified with finished doctrines or dogmatic formulas but are challenges and guideposts in an uncharted journey that channels and transforms human lives. In the same way, solidarity cannot just designate an empirical togetherness or collectivist project—something Nietzsche denounced as a synonym for "herd mentality" and Heidegger described as "*das Man*" (the They), designating an amorphous and anonymous collectivity. The task for Heidegger (as for Nietzsche) was to find a place of freedom in the midst of sociality; he designated this place "authentic" co-being or solidarity. Far from coinciding with heavy-handed communalism, "authentic" solidarity for Heidegger means a social bonding in which all participants remain freely open to their own possibilities—a bonding that some have described as a "community without communalism" or a "community of those without [totalizing] community."[17]

Heidegger's writings show a preeminent way of reconnecting or reconciling freedom and solidarity on a novel (postmodern or transmodern) basis, thus bypassing or overcoming the deep antinomies besetting modern life. What remains to be done, however, is the translation of some of his teachings into a more overtly political idiom, especially an idiom compatible with the basic features of democracy. Unhappily, such translation is greatly hampered by the ideological controversies surrounding his work. I have tried to penetrate this dense ideological fog repeatedly in other contexts; at this point, I can only refer well-intentioned readers to these discussions.[18] For present purposes, I include the testimony of a number of other thinkers—some influenced by Heidegger—to elucidate what I call the "promise of democracy" (which is the topic of chapter 3). To make headway in this domain, I enlist the support of democratic thinkers such as John Dewey and Maurice Merleau-Ponty for whom democracy was not just a formal procedure but the emblem of an open-ended quest, a dynamic practice and shared way of life. This accent on dynamic practice entails that democracy can never be fully stabilized or actualized but is always marked by potentiality or by what Sheldon Wolin terms its "fugitive" character—a character that requires constant cultivation and renewal, especially the cultivation of genuine freedom (discussed further in chapter 3).

Potentiality also means that democracy as a regime cannot be appropriated, monopolized, or "owned" by any given elite or social faction. In the words of French philosopher Claude Lefort, the structural unity that in previous ages had been entrusted to monarchs or princes is left vacant or "empty" in modern democracy—with the result that empirical actuality is always haunted by a kind of "non-being," self-transcendence, or open horizon.[19] In the eyes of some interpreters, this openness of the regime entails that democracy is inhabited by a permanent clash or antagonism between factions or groups—an interpretation that, though empirically largely correct, neglects a crucial aspect of struggle—that it occurs not just for its own sake but in the pursuit of social justice and solidarity (however elusive they may be). To limit the role of struggle, other interpreters rely on rational argumentation or deliberation—giving perhaps too much credit to cognitive rationality and not enough credit to practical experience. Modifying these interpretations, chapter 3 advances the notion of a "caring democracy" that, while acknowledging the role of conflict and deliberation, integrates both into the broader matrix of a shared learning experience and engaged praxis.

One of the requirements of a "caring democracy"—and of any genuine democracy, for that purpose—is that self-seeking and especially the quest for private profit be subordinated to the demands of a shared public life. This means that the economic market cannot be left entirely to its own devices (a point underscored in chapter 4). In premodern times, economic exchanges—the affairs of the *oikos* (household)—were still closely enmeshed in the polis, or the broader social and political fabric. As economic historian Karl Polanyi has persuasively shown, the entire development of economics in modernity can be grasped as a relentless process of "disembedding"—that is, the "liberation" of private profit seeking from all social and ethical constraints. Although Adam Smith was still fully cognizant of such constraints in the eighteenth century, subsequent developments— from the French Physiocrats and laissez-faire liberals to the Austrian and Chicago Schools—led to the eventual triumph of the market and its growing colonization of all other social domains, including the domain of democracy. It is this kind of triumphalism that triggered repeated economic breakdowns, culminating in the financial "meltdown" of 2008–2009 that pushed several Western democracies to the brink of disaster. The meltdown has provoked powerful reactions, both on the popular level (the Occupy Movement) and in professional circles, with some leading Nobel Laureate economists denouncing neoliberalism as corrupt and corrupting and urging a "reembedding" of markets in social and political contexts. In addition, some political thinkers have reaffirmed the need for public philosophy and for a politically and ethically governed market. Only a socially limited and responsible market, it is held, can rescue democracy from plutocracy and the religion of private wealth.[20]

In addition to the curbing of market triumphalism, modern democracy requires attention to the idea of "human rights," which in many ways is a corollary of the pivotal status of modern freedom. The question here is whether human rights, just like freedom, have a possessive or proprietary character, which reduces them to adjuncts of anthropocentric self-enclosure. Undeniably, in its early modern formulation, the idea of human rights was closely tied up with the rise of "individualism" and construed as a protective shield against political and clerical domination. However, apart from being historically dated, this conception also reveals a Western bias—as several recent thinkers (discussed in chapter 5) have noted. Thus, in an important essay Raimon Panikkar has raised the question whether the notion of human rights—in its current or predominant understanding—is basically a Western concept or tied up with the modern Western paradigm. As he shows, the linkage is clearly revealed in the individualistic and "anthropocentric" tenor of the currents rights discourse—a tenor that differs sharply from the holistic and cosmological orientation of traditional Indian culture and philosophy. Without counseling a simple return to the past, Panikkar carefully seeks to steer a course beyond both traditional "cosmocentrism" and modern "anthropocentrism" in the direction of a balanced or "cosmotheandric" vision reconciling holism and human rights—a reconciliation that is also endorsed by Chinese American philosopher Tu Weiming in the Confucian context. Given Islam's traditional "theocentric" focus, the notion of human rights is most strenuously contested in Islamic thought—a contestation, however, that in turn is challenged by a number of progressive Muslim thinkers determined to rescue human rights from the tentacles of both clerical traditionalism and Western individualistic modernism, thus lending credit to the issue of the "rightness" of human rights.

What chapters 1 through 5 in this book explore is the possibility of a transition from the modern paradigm—presently in a state of decay or disarray—toward new beginnings or new modes of life where freedom and solidarity would be reconciled, thus making possible a new flourishing of humanity on a global scale. It must be recognized, however, that antinomies of the past cannot quickly be exorcised by philosophical writings, no matter how probing and future oriented they may be. On the contrary, one has to accept that precisely at the twilight of the modern paradigm, its inherent conflicts—between freedom and solidarity, ego and society—may surface in the most virulent forms. Under the title "Man against the State," chapter 6 examines some variations of these festering conflicts. The formula goes back to Herbert Spencer and his advocacy of a radical laissez-faire liberalism (or libertarianism) during the nineteenth century. Relying on Hobbesian and Lockean ideas, Spencer argued that in the "state of nature" individuals are endowed with complete liberty, especially the freedom to acquire property—whose protection is the sole objective of government. In some formulations, this argument was linked with biological evolutionism, leading to the doctrine of "social Darwinism" and the motto "survival of the fittest." In opposition to this "possessive" or property-centered idea of freedom, chapter 6 turns to more ethically grounded conceptions of individual freedom and their role in civil disobedience and dissent— conceptions articulated especially in the works of Henry David Thoreau, Mahatma Gandhi, and Albert Camus. Far from associating disobedience and dissent with motivations of selfish gain, their views cast a very different light on the possible antagonism between individual and society, presenting the radical dissenter as an agent seeking to raise social or community life to a higher ethical level. To underscore the ethical legitimacy of such dissent, I invoke finally the examples of Socrates and the resistance movement against the Nazi regime in Germany, including especially Count Claus Schenk Graf von Stauffenberg and Pastor Dietrich Bonhoeffer.

As I see it, the cited dissenters are exemplary mentors whose life and death—at the hands of ruling powers—should be a steady source of political reflection and a beckoning call to vigilance. Chapters 7 through 9 offer individual case studies that illustrate, in different contexts, the difficulties involved in overcoming modern antinomies, especially the tension between freedom and solidarity. The cases are taken, respectively, from contemporary Protestant theology in its quest to reconcile human freedom with the Christian community of believers; from Russian intellectual history in its difficult journey from traditional holism via totalitarianism to a precarious democratic freedom; and from recent Indian philosophy as it tried to situate itself vis-à-vis traditional Hindu cosmology in its search for a viable democratic path in postcolonial India.

The first case study takes off from the discussion of the conflict between religious community and dissent. In many ways, the teachings of Pastor Bonhoeffer have been carried forward in recent times by the German Protestant theologian Wolfgang Huber (discussed in chapter 7). Like Bonhoeffer, Huber has been deeply influenced by Karl Barth's "dialectical theology"; again like Bonhoeffer, he takes his point of departure from the so-called Barmen Declaration of 1934 drafted by Barth, which denounced the co-optation of Christian churches by the fascist totalitarian state while at the same time vindicating faith as a source of freedom and as a leaven in the cultivation of genuine social solidarity. Unlike his predecessors, Huber has been willing to embrace some philosophical and intellectual innovations of recent times, especially some of the teachings of critical social theory and the idea of a pervasive "linguistic turn." Linked with reliance on basic Lutheran teachings on Christian liberty, this embrace has led Huber to the formulation of the principle of a "communicative freedom," wherein human freedom emerges in engaged communication or dialogue with others without being submerged in a mindless collectivism. Most importantly, freedom here does not coincide with a stubborn, self-possessed autonomy but rather denotes a communicative openness to society, world, and the community of believers.

The tension between freedom and solidarity has been not only a concern for Western intellectual and religious leaders but also a source of searching reflections among Russian intellectuals, especially those close to Orthodox religion and spirituality (such as Nikolai Berdyaev, Sergei Bulgakov, and others). In chapter 8, I lift up for remembrance the life and work of Dimitry Likhachev, the great cultural and literary historian of the past century (and, like Boris Pasternak, a gulag survivor). As a cultural historian, Likhachev was keenly aware of the growing individualism and fragmentation of modern social life, a tendency deriving in large measure from Western liberal ideas and practices. To profile this tendency more sharply, he turned to the study of medieval Russian literature, which, in his view, faithfully captured the solidarity and holistic spirit animating social life in "Old Rus." Yet his fondness for medieval wholeness—as a counterpoise to atomistic individualism—never prompted Likhachev to advocate a restoration of the past, especially not through political coercion. His painful experiences with Soviet-style totalitarianism protected him against any flirtation with state-imposed forms of community or solidarity. Thus, his intellectual trajectory led him in the end to endorse a kind of "communicative freedom" (in Huber's sense) or else a solidarity based on the freely granted recognition of individual or group differences in both domestic and global contexts.

The final case study is taken from Indian intellectual history, more specifically from the time of postindependence India. The focus of chapter 9 is the distinguished philosopher Debi Prasad Chattopadhyaya, longtime chairman of the Indian Council of Philosophical Research and more recently director of the Center for the Study of Civilizations in India. Trained by some of the best teachers and having taught in prominent Indian and Western universities, Chattopadhyaya is thoroughly acquainted with both Western and Indian (or Asian) traditions of philosophical and religious thought. His writings provide ample evidence of his familiarity with these traditions; some of them, discussed selectively in chapter 9, pay specific attention to the freedom–solidarity correlation. As he shows, freedom in the modern West is anchored in the thinking ego and/or subjective agency, thus leading to the equation of the term *freedom* with the liberation of the self or subject. By contrast, in the Indian (and Asian) tradition, freedom is linked with the striving for self-transcendence—that is, with the overcoming of and liberation from the self or subject. As it happens, however, this striving can no longer be grasped in purely cognitive or epistemic terms, for who or what is being liberated in the overcoming of the self? According to Chattopadhyaya, this dilemma can be resolved only by a move from cognition (or the cogito) to the realm of engaged social praxis—a move that brings to the fore freedom's intimate relation with solidarity.

The concluding chapter returns to the central theme of this book: the issue of a reconnection of freedom (in the Western sense) with social engagement. Although stressing the need for new beginnings or departures (beyond the dominant modern paradigm), the book at no point claims that these innovations are entirely unprecedented or disconnected from the past. To illustrate the historical preparations for or anticipations of the suggested paradigm shift, chapter 10 returns to the work of John Dewey, highlighting especially his emphasis on the needed rethinking of the meaning of "individualism" and on the required reconstitution of the "public sphere" as the arena in which a social agent can legitimately and responsibly be engaged. From Dewey's work, the chapter turns to more recent political philosophy, showing how a series of prominent social and political thinkers have pursued and innovatively reformulated some of Dewey's leads. One of these reformulations—under the heading "hermeneutic communism"—illustrates how the creativity of interpretive freedom can find a partner in a Marxism cleansed of "metaphysical" dogmatism and recast along the lines of a democratic and ethically nurtured socialism.

By way of conclusion, this chapter takes up again the possible derailments of freedom and solidarity, respectively, into selfish narcissism and ethnocentric collectivism. The solution to these derailments consists in the conception of solidarity as an open-ended, differentiated "public" and the conception of freedom as "authentic" guardianship. Instead of seeking personal power or privilege, authentic guardians—such as Mahatma Gandhi—are able to rescue societies from myopic impulses, thus steering them in the direction of justice and peace.

1

Twilights and New Dawns

Revaluation and De(con)struction

Are you co-conspirators in the current folly of nations who
want . . . to be as rich as possible?
——Friedrich Nietzsche, *The Dawn*

Guiding humankind back into the dawn of another beginning.
——Martin Heidegger, *On the Way to Language*

An old adage holds that "times change and we ourselves change with
them" (*tempora mutantur et nos mutamur in illis*). This means that
even in the ordinary course of things, temporal changes require participants to adjust and to modify their attitudes and beliefs accordingly.
This requirement or challenge is immensely increased in extraordinary
times, especially in what I have called times of paradigmatic or holistic
shifts. In these situations, not only partial facets but an entire constellation of ideas and practices are in flux and in process of giving way
to a new configuration of life. For people caught in transit or in the
transition between paradigms, the change involves an unusually heavy
burden fraught with all kinds of derailments and misunderstandings.
Above all, such people need to distance themselves from or loosen the
hold of traditional conceptions or categories—without having available to them ready-made substitutes. There is often the temptation to
misconstrue new possibilities simply as aggravated forms of older perspectives; at other times, novelty may be identified with iconoclasm,
and open horizons confused with anarchistic or destructive impulses.

Importantly, misconstrual or mislabeling is not only the work of onlookers; rather, people undergoing the transition—perhaps undergoing it most intensely—likewise do not have a superior standpoint and thus may flounder in their self-descriptions.

Among Western thinkers deeply embroiled in the most recent transition, two stand out from the rest: Friedrich Nietzsche and Martin Heidegger, the former serving in a way as precursor or pacemaker of the second. Although clearly anticipating and foretelling a new era, Nietzsche's work was still embedded in many ways in the constellation of nineteenth-century thought: its anti-idealism and tendential natural scientism. Although straining against Enlightenment rationalism, his thought often preserved remnants of Cartesian binary dilemmas: the binaries of mind and matter, of cogito and world. Although critical of Cartesian individualism, his writings often celebrate a radical solitude uncontaminated by worldly intrusions (thus seemingly endorsing a "negative" concept of liberty). At the same time, however, in the teeth of a relentless denunciation of modern democracy as a form of "herd mentality," his work adumbrates a higher form of human community: the ideal of an undomesticated solidarity of genuine friends and spiritual seekers. The endeavors launched by Nietzsche were pursued and intensified by Heidegger in the changed twentieth-century context—a context marked by the rise of phenomenology, existentialism, and hermeneutics. Due to his long apprenticeship with Edmund Husserl, Heidegger from the beginning charted a way beyond the modern Cartesian binaries of mind/matter and subject/object. What he found beyond these binaries was the Aristotelian notion of "being"—to be sure, a notion that had to be thoroughly rethought and reconstituted and thus to be cleansed of the heavy dust of traditional metaphysics. As is well known, of course, Heidegger also did not escape the mislabeling of his efforts—both by himself and by others. In this chapter, I want to illustrate these two thinkers' anticipatory outlook by focusing on a limited number of their writings.

Revaluation of All Values

Among Nietzsche's voluminous texts, many seem to be composed for all times and places. In some cases, however, the title already discloses a futuristic perspective. This is particularly true of *Beyond Good and Evil*, subtitled *Prelude to a Philosophy of the Future*. The book is easily one of Nietzsche's most notorious and contested writings. It has been wildly greeted and extolled by so-called free spirits—unconcerned with any notion of "freedom" not reducible to self-interest. It has been harshly deplored and rebuked by custodians of "tradition"—unconcerned about the heavy patina covering traditional moral doctrines. No doubt, both reactions find ample support in many passages of the text—a text that refuses to proceed in linear fashion, preferring instead a style of continuous innovation and anticipation. This innovation—one cannot fail to recognize—is carried forward by a moral pathos, notwithstanding the harsh denunciation of dominant moralities or moralisms. In Nietzsche's words, "Whether it is hedonism or pessimism, utilitarianism or eudeamonism—all these ways of thinking that measure the value of things in accordance with *pleasure* and *pain* . . . are ways of thinking that stay in the foreground and naivetés on which everyone conscious of *creative* powers and an artistic conscience will look down not without derision, nor without pity." Seen against this background, the "overcoming of morality" and even the "self-overcoming of morality" are for him the name of "that long secret work" that has been "saved up for the finest and most honest" to serve eventually as "living touchstones of the soul."[1]

The work to which Nietzsche here refers is the transformation of philosophy in general, including moral philosophy, and of prevailing ways of life. It is to the transformation of philosophy that some of the most eloquent passages of the text are devoted. Appealing to a "new species of philosophers" that is coming up, he describes them as a species no longer tied to fixed dogmas or doctrines: "As I unriddle them, insofar as they allow themselves to be unriddled . . . these philosophers of the future may have a right (it might also be a wrong) to be called 'attempters' (*Versucher*). And this name itself is in the end a mere attempt (*Versuch*) and, if you will, a temptation (*Versuchung*)." One of the main things the new philosophers have to do is to disentangle themselves from prevailing schemata and formulas and to open themselves to the advent of new possibilities and horizons. As Nietzsche indicates, our hope and aspiration have to reach out "toward spirits strong and original enough" to escape from inveterate habits of thought—that is, "to provide the stimuli for opposite values and to revalue and invert 'eternal values.'" Differently put, the hope goes out "toward forerunners (*Vorläufer*), toward men of the future who in the present tie the knot and constraint that forces the will of millennia upon *new* tracks." These precursors or anticipatory thinkers will be able "to teach man the future as *his will*, and to prepare great ventures and overall attempts (*Versuche*) of discipline and cultivation by way of putting an end to that gruesome dominion of nonsense and accident that has so far been called 'history'—the nonsense of the 'greatest number' being merely its ultimate formula."[2]

The schemata from which future thinkers are supposed to extricate themselves are mainly (though not exclusively) the binary divisions bequeathed by Cartesian philosophy: the binaries of subject and object, mind and matter, cogito and world. The very opening of *Beyond Good and Evil* casts doubt on the basic premise of modern Western philosophy, Descartes's radical doubt: "It has not even occurred to the most cautious [modern thinkers] that one might have a doubt right here at the threshold where it was surely most necessary—even if they vowed to themselves '*de omnibus dubitandum.*'" A central premise of Cartesian doubt is the *ego cogitans,* the availability of an "I" that thinks, but this availability is far from clear. There may be some "harmless" observers, Nietzsche comments, who still believe in "immediate certainties," for example, "in the 'I think' (or as the suspicious Schopenhauer put it 'I will')—as though cognition here got hold of its object purely and nakedly as a 'thing in itself' without any falsification on the part of either the subject or the object." But this assumption does not hold up to scrutiny. "When I analyze the process that is expressed in the sentence 'I think,'" Nietzsche continues, "I find a whole series of daring assertions that would be difficult, perhaps impossible to prove; for example, that it is *I* who thinks, that there must necessarily be something that thinks, that thinking is an activity and operation on the part of a being who is thought of as a cause, that there is an *ego* and, finally, that it is already determined what is to be designated by thinking—that I *know* what thinking is." Observations of this kind lead Nietzsche finally to a daring postsubjectivist formulation (which in some ways anticipates Heidegger's later thought). "I shall never tire," we read, "of emphasizing a small terse fact which superstitious minds hate to concede—namely, that a thought comes when 'it' wishes, and not when 'I' wish, so that it is a falsification of the facts of the case to say that the subject 'I' is the condition of the predicate 'think.' Rather, *it* thinks; but that this 'it' is precisely the famous old *ego* is, to put it mildly, a supposition, an assertion, and assuredly not an 'immediate certainty.'"[3]

The critique of the Cartesian cogito leads Nietzsche also to remonstrate against the modern conception of free will and free action that portrays the self as the autonomous cause of effects. For Nietzsche, this portrayal is due largely to a "grammatical habit" that holds: "every activity requires an agent; consequently . . ." It is above all the infusion of "the synthetic concept 'I'" into acting and willing that has led to "a whole series of erroneous conclusions"—to such a degree that "he who wills believes sincerely that willing *suffices* for action." Ever since the onset of modernity, the notion of "freedom of the will" has in fact been the linchpin of philosophical thought. For Nietzsche, the desire for such freedom—in the "superlative meta-physical sense"—still "holds sway unfortunately in the minds of the half-educated." Rigorously pursued, it reflects a desire "to bear the entire and ultimate responsibility for one's actions, to absolve God, the world, ancestors, chance, and society," and thus to emerge ultimately as the *causa sui* capable "with more than Münchhau-sen's audacity, to pull oneself up into existence by the hair, out of the swamp of nothingness." What is neglected in this conception is the deep complexity of such notions as will and free will, the fact that the latter is "the expression for the complex state of delight of the person exercising volition," a person who commands and at the same time obeys the willed order. Above all, what is sidelined is the awareness that the body is not an instrument of the cogito but rather "a social structure composed of many souls."[4]

As one should note, Nietzsche, in critiquing the customary notion of freedom as causation, does not endorse the opposite notion of unfree will or substitute heteronomy for autonomy, deter-minism for freedom. The basic point is that notions such as cause and effect, sequence, freedom, and purpose are *interpretations,* not empirical explanations; but when we treat this arsenal of concepts like an objective reality, "we act once more as we have always—mythologically." Generally speaking, while distancing himself from

the cogito, Nietzsche does not simply take the side of the opposite pole of "extended matter"; to this extent, his attitude, although
friendly toward science, is ambivalent regarding claims of scientific "objectivity." With considerable vehemence, *Beyond Good and
Evil* denounces the vogue of scientific "positivism" that at the time
(the 1880s) was sweeping Europe. Nietzsche speaks of the ascent of
"hodgepodge scholars who call themselves 'philosophers of reality'
or 'positivists'" and who suffocate young scholars' talents for creative thinking. As a result, "science is flourishing and her good conscience is written all over her face," but philosophy has been reduced
to "theory of knowledge" or epistemology that is no more than a
"timid epochism and doctrine of abstinence." For Nietzsche, there
is some gain but mostly a loss in this change of academic fortunes.
He writes: "However gratefully we may welcome an *objective* spirit—
and is there anyone who has never been mortally sick of everything
subjective and his accursed ipsissimosity [self-centeredness]—in the
end we also have . . . to put a halt to the excessive manner in which
the 'unselfing' [othering] of the spirit is being celebrated today as if
it were the goal itself and redemption."[5]

A central feature of modern science bemoaned by Nietzsche
is its penchant for dissecting analysis and ultimately its "atomism"
neglectful of connections. As he writes, one must declare war, even
"relentless war," against the "atomistic need" that surfaces in places
where one least expects it. In this battle, one must also give a "finish-
ing stroke" to the kind of atomism bequeathed by Christian religion:
the "atomism of the soul," which regards the latter as "indivisible, a
monad, an *atomon*." In exorcising this legacy, he cautions, it is not
at all necessary to get rid of the "soul" itself and thus to renounce
one of "the most ancient and venerable hypotheses"—as happens frequently "to clumsy naturalists [positivists]." Rather, what is needed
is a rethinking and reinterpretation of the "soul-hypothesis," which
leads to such notions as "mortal soul" or "soul as subjective multiplicity" or "soul as social structure of drives and affects." This line of
thought leads Nietzsche to one of his most important insights: that
far from atomistic dispersal, concepts, ideas, and words form part
of a coherent grammar of thought, of an interconnected paradigm
or constellation: "Individual philosophical concepts are not anything
capricious or autonomously evolving, but grow up in connection and

relationship with each other; however suddenly and arbitrarily they seem to appear in the history of thought, they nevertheless belong just as much to a system as all the members of the fauna of a continent." The same connectedness also prevails among diverse philosophers or philosophies of a period. As under an "invisible spell," they always "revolve in the same orbit"; in fact, their thinking is far less a discovery than "a recognition, a remembering, a return and a homecoming to a remote, primordial, and inclusive household of the soul."[6]

Just because of the internal cohesion of paradigms, transition from a present paradigm to an impending paradigm is exceedingly difficult—to some extent perhaps impossible. The latter restriction applies also to Nietzsche's work. Despite strenuous efforts to overcome modern philosophical binaries or dualisms, he embroiled himself in some other binaries (which were not always an improvement over those left behind). As far as I can see, there are especially two binaries structuring his thought: those of higher versus lower rank and of solitude versus mass society (the two being closely interconnected). His commitment to rank order—even caste order—is emphatic and sometimes even taken as the key tenet of his thought. As *Beyond Good and Evil* proclaims, "Every enhancement of the type 'man' has so far been the work of an aristocratic society, a society that believes in the long ladder of an order of rank and differences in value between man and man, and that needs slavery in some sense or other." Rank order for Nietzsche involves a "pathos of distance," an "ingrained difference between strata" where the ruling caste "looks afar and looks down upon subjects as instruments." The order of rank is closely connected with the famous (or notorious) distinction between "master morality" and "slave morality" that gives rise to the difference between "good" and "bad" or between "noble" and "contemptible" (not to be confused with the dichotomy of "good" and "evil"). As Nietzsche elaborates, master morality "in the severity of its principle" dictates "that one has duties only to one's peers, that against beings of a lower rank, against everything alien, one may behave as one pleases or 'as the heart desires,' and in any case 'beyond good and evil.'" Where this principle is rejected or mitigated—as happened in late-modern Europe—the result is bound to be calamitous, leading to "the *denial* of life itself" and to the "disintegration and decay" of society.[7]

Statements of this kind are startling in their doctrinaire flavor. They are hardly persuasive to people not members of higher castes. More importantly, they collide with the central tenor of Nietzsche's own work: its tentativeness and rebellion against fixed doctrines. In a text opposed to Platonic essentialism, what is one to do with the assertion that "life itself is *essentially* appropriation, injury, overpowering of what is alien and weaker, and, at least, exploitation"?[8] Where does this harsh "realism" come from in a work celebrating multiplicity and interpretation? Closely linked with this higher/lower division is the opposition between noble solitude and the human "herd"—another supposed trademark of Nietzscheanism. Despite the opening criticism of the *ego cogitans,* "I think," *Beyond Good and Evil* in its later sections launches a paean to the ego and egoism—to be sure, the egoism of the higher caste. "At the risk of displeasing innocent ears," Nietzsche writes, "I propose: egoism belongs to the nature of a noble soul—I mean that unshakable faith that to a being such as 'we are' other beings must be subordinate by nature and have to sacrifice themselves. The noble soul accepts this fact of its egoism without any question mark." A corollary of nobility here is the pathos of distance, the awareness that greatness entails "wanting to be by oneself, being able to be different, standing alone and having to live independently." From this angle, the highest and most noble person is he "who can be loneliest, the most concealed, the most deviant, the human being beyond good and evil, that is overrich in will." Opposed to this solitary greatness stands the "herd animal," the member of modern mass society—a society ultimately identified with democracy and its egalitarian creed: "To us, the democratic movement is not only a form of the decay of political organization but a form of decay, namely the diminution, of man making him mediocre and lowering his value."[9]

Again, one may ask about the plausibility of this opposition—not just for political but also for philosophical reasons. Why this stress on distance and radical separation in a text that earlier celebrated the interconnectedness and paradigmatic correlation of elements—even to the point of speaking of an "inclusive household of the soul"? Where is the warrant for the simple equation of democracy with mass society and herd mentality? Are there not ample examples of the proper recognition of merit and achievement in distinctly democratic contexts? Moreover, is there not the possibility of a genuine community of free spirits—beyond the confines of a stifling communalism fostering bland mediocrity? As it happens, such a community is precisely invoked or anticipated in the "Aftersong" attached to *Beyond Good and Evil*, where we read, "Looking all day and night, for friends I wait: for new friends. Come, it's time; it's late."[10] One of the most dubious and contestable claims of this text is the equation of nobility or high rank with "will to power"—an equation asserted in the statement (among many others) that "exploitation . . . belongs to the *essence* of what lives, as a basic organic function; it is a consequence of the will to power, which is after all the will to life."[11] How can one not be startled by this blunt thesis—given the earlier portrayal of will and willing as "something *complicated*, that is a unit only as a word"? Would the "will" to power not also fall under this verdict of complexity—and thus require nuanced interpretation (beyond the level of an "organic function")? And would the same verdict not also apply to such notions as "power" and (especially) of "life" itself?

The noted predicaments persist and are even aggravated in other Nietzschean writings, especially in the posthumously published text *The Will to Power*, subtitled *Attempt at a Revaluation of All Values*. There is some controversy among scholars concerning the authenticity of some passages and especially concerning the editorial role of Nietzsche's sister. Leaving those issues aside, however, central claims of the text are clearly Nietzsche's own because they recur so frequently in his other writings. Foremost among these claims is the need for an innovative reversal of values, to be accomplished under the aegis of the will to power. The preface to the book states in forceful language the reason for the required reversal: the progressive devaluation and erosion of traditionally reigning values because of their loss of metaphysical grounding, hence their evaporation into nothingness or "nihilism"—which, in turn, generates the demand for a radical revaluation of values anchored in a domineering will to power. According to the preface, the book seeks "to recount the history of the next two centuries to describe what is coming, what can no longer come differently: namely, the advent of nihilism"—an advent that "speaks even now in a hundred signs" and "announces itself everywhere." At the same time, the book is meant to offer a "gospel of the future" (*Zukunfts-Evangelium*). Its very title gives expression to a "countermovement," a movement that "in some future will take the place of perfect nihilism" (while recognizing the latter as its precondition).[12]

The basic guideposts of this countermovement or this attempted "revaluation of all values" are discussed in successive chapters of the book. Thus, after a detailed analysis of the background and meaning of "European nihilism" and a critique of the traditionally "highest values," the study turns to the guiding principles of the "new evaluation" and finally to a celebration of the desired rank or caste order buttressed by "discipline and breeding." Among the guiding principles of revaluation, the will to power is again seen as preeminent in all domains of life. "The organic functions," we read, "translate back to the basic will, the will to power—and are understood as its offshoots"; that will specializes as "will to nourishment, to property, to tools, to servants (those who obey) and masters." In the human and social domain, individualism and egocentrism manifest this will: "Basic error: to place the goal in the herd and not in single individuals. The herd is a means, no more! . . . The 'ego' subdues and kills; it operates like an organic cell: it is a robber and violent." The concluding chapter on rank and discipline offers statements such as the following (among other more nuanced formulations): "What determines rank, sets off rank, is only quanta of power, and nothing else" and, regarding the impending "masters of the world" (*Herren der Erde*), "The same conditions that hasten the evolution of the herd animal also hasten the evolution of the leader-animal (*Führer-Tier*)."[13]

De(con)struction

As the preceding discussion shows, Nietzsche was clearly—and saw himself as—a thinker between ages, a sojourner between paradigmatic constellations of ideas and ways of life. In many of his writings, he mounted an astute critique of some of the dilemmas, antinomies, or binaries besetting modern Western thought. At the same time, many passages of his works—especially those relating to Zarathustra and the "coming new friends"—adumbrate an exhilarating vision of new or future possibilities of human life. Unhappily, as has also been shown, the access route to these vistas was impeded by the weight of older conceptions, the debris of binary dilemmas, resentments, and prejudgments. In this respect, his outlook shows a resemblance to Heidegger's work—although some roadblocks were in that later era beginning to be removed. An important affinity resides in the assessment of modern democracy, which both thinkers tended to equate (unfairly) with a slide into mediocrity. However, in Heidegger's case, the remedy for this tendential slide was found not in the "will to power"—which he came to denounce increasingly over the years—but in the trust in an "other beginning" linked with an overcoming of anthropocentrism.[14] The access route toward the new beginning and the removal of roadblocks were at the same time facilitated by Heidegger's apprenticeship with Edmund Husserl, the founder of "phenomenology," which offered a new way of "seeing" the world together with a new stress on interpretation.

The closest parallel between Nietzsche and Heidegger resides in their critique of the antinomies of the modern philosophical paradigm and their commitment to an "overcoming" of traditional metaphysics in a broad sense. The central feature of *Being and Time*—the portrayal of human existence (*Dasein*) as "being-in-the-world"—signals a radical turning away from the Cartesian binary of cogito and world. For Heidegger, the Cartesian formula was beset with numerous defects. First of all, the French thinker, following the line of the Scholastic tradition, construed both self and the world as "substances" and hence as static (and separate) essences. As Heidegger writes, "With his opposition of *cogito* and '*res extensa*' [world], Descartes wanted not only to pinpoint the problem of 'I and world' but to solve their relation in a radical manner. But by taking his orientation from traditional sources . . . he inevitably obstructed his view of the phenomenon of 'world' and made it possible for the latter to be reduced to a set of empirical entities." This defect also had an impact on the status of the cogito and on the understanding of human existence (*Dasein*). In a passage reminiscent of some of Nietzsche's arguments, *Being and Time* calls into question the foundational status of "I" and "I think." Regarding the notion of "I think," we read, "The 'I' must be taken only as a 'formal indication' of something which, on closer inspection, may reveal itself precisely as its opposite. In the latter case, 'not I' does not necessarily designate a phenomenon lack-

ing any *ego*-quality, but may mean a mode of existence 'lost' to itself."
The upshot is that one needs to take a wholly different approach to
the issue: in starting from "being-in-the-world" and clarifying its
status, we find "that there is never, nor could there be, a bare subject
[ego] without world. In the same way, we do not in the end find an
isolated subject without others."[15]

Where Heidegger departs from and moves beyond Nietzsche's
texts is in his effort to trace carefully the steps leading from the modern paradigm to a new constellation or different horizons. It is here
that his phenomenological training as well as his ontological sensi-
tivity reveal their crucial importance. One of the opening sections of
Being and Time deals with "the task of the destruction (*Destruktion*)
of the history of ontology/metaphysics"—although the task might
better be described as one of "deconstruction" because it involves a
linkage of temporalities, a critical look back to the past and an anticipatory glance toward the future. In Heidegger's words, "Human
Dasein in its factual existence is how and what it has been. It *is* its
past, whether explicitly or not." But this is not the whole story: "It is
not merely that the past, as it were, is pushing it along from behind,
and that *Dasein* hence possesses its past as an available property."
Rather, something else is at work: "*Dasein* is or has its past in the
mode of a being which, roughly stated, happens from out of the
future." This means, to be sure, that *Dasein* has grown up in a "traditional mode of self-interpretation" or a given paradigmatic context;
it is in terms of this context that it habitually understands itself and
gauges the possibilities of its being. However, and here is the rub, "its
own past—and this always means the past of its 'generation'—is not
something which *follows along* behind *Dasein,* but something which
is impending or moves already *ahead* of it."[16]

The temporal "historicality" of *Dasein* and its slant toward the
future may be ignored or sidelined in some circumstances; however,
it may also be explored and purposely cultivated. Heidegger speaks
in this case of the cultivation of "tradition" in the sense of transmission: "The exploration of tradition and the disclosure of what
and how it 'transmits' can be grasped as a task in its own right. At
this point, *Dasein* launches itself in a mode of historical questioning and inquiry." What needs to be noted, however, is that tradition
and historical inquiry can also be a temptation or a lure to self-

abandonment. However important tradition and a given "world-context" may be, *Dasein* has the tendency "to succumb to this world-context and to understand itself in its terms." In the same way, *Dasein* can "fall prey to its more or less consciously grasped tradition"; the latter in that case "appropriates and usurps *Dasein*'s own searching and choosing." At this point, the transmission of tradition malfunctions or misfires: "When tradition becomes dominant in this way, the result is that what it 'transmits' is not only rendered inaccessible but actually concealed or covered over. The past is submerged in self-evidence." By way of a triumphant traditionalism, tradition surrenders historical origins to oblivion. Heidegger goes so far as to say that traditionalism of this kind "uproots the historicality of *Dasein*." What is needed to counteract this tendency is a "return to the past in the sense of a productive rethinking and [a] reappropriation" of its possibilities."[17]

The tendency of past inquiry to decay into self-evidence can be illustrated by reference to the history of Western philosophy. Ontology in a deep metaphysical sense was initiated by the pre-Socratics and continued by Plato and Aristotle. The Greek ontological paradigm was taken over by Scholasticism in the Middle Ages, at which point it congealed into a fixed, established doctrine (despite variations over time). The Scholastic legacy was reformulated by Suarez and the Spanish school until it reached the onset of Western modernity in the Cartesian notions of *ego cogitans,* extended matter, and reason. These notions in turn were refined in the Enlightenment and in the German idealist philosophy focused on "subjectivity" and "spirit." If today, Heidegger comments, philosophical inquiry is to be restarted and the question of *Dasein* and its mode of being to be posed anew, then what is required is "a loosening of congealed tradition and the removal of its accumulated patina." This task, he adds, we understand as "the destruction (*Destruktion*) of the transmitted content of ancient ontology and the recovery, guided by the question of the meaning of being (*Seinsfrage*), of the original experiences giving rise to it in the first place." To guard against the impression of a pure demolition, *Being and Time* adds soberly: "Destruction does not have the merely *negative* sense of a dismissal of the ontological tradition. On the contrary, the attempt is to uncover and pinpoint the *positive* possibilities and hence also the limits of tradition which emerge in a given field of inquiry." If there is a "negative" aspect in destruction, it is that the latter refers not so much to the past itself but rather to "the present and the presently dominant treatment of the history of ontology."[18]

As the preceding comments on "destruction" show, the renewal of the question of being (*Seinsfrage*) cannot happen through a mere rehearsal or regurgitation of traditional ontology. Rather, a new approach is needed, and this approach is precisely provided by phenomenology (or a conjunction of phenomenology and hermeneutics)—as long as the latter is not misconstrued as a standpoint or fixed doctrine. Heidegger observes that "the term 'phenomenology' denotes primarily a certain approach or method; it does not indicate the 'what' or substantive content, but rather the 'how' of inquiry." According to its founder's (Husserl's) formulation, modern phenomenology involves a move "to the things themselves" (*zu den Sachen selbst*)—and this means away from "free-floating constructions, accidental findings, seemingly stable concepts, and pseudo-problems." If we go back to the Greek roots of this type of inquiry, we find that the term *phenomenon*—in Heidegger's portrayal—means something that shows itself, manifests or discloses itself prior to any derivative cognitive formulation. Accordingly, one can say that *phenomena* refers to the totality of what is manifest or can be brought to light—what the Greeks sometimes identified simply with "all beings (*ta onta*)." To be sure, as Heidegger immediately acknowledges, beings do not always manifest or show themselves as what they are. Indeed, there is always the possibility of "semblance" (*Schein*) or mere "appearance" (*Erscheinung*) where beings show themselves as what precisely they are not. What is important, however, is the primacy of self-disclosure over semblance and appearance in the sense that the latter are possible only on the basis of the former: "Only when something is basically capable to manifest itself, that is, to be a 'phenomenon,' is there also the possibility that it shows itself as what it is *not*" and hence as semblance. In the same way, appearance is possible only on the basis of self-disclosure.[19]

Precisely because the disclosure of phenomena is complicated and not always straightforward, a special inquiry into their meaning is necessary, which is the task of phenomenology. Because in the course of history the meaning of phenomena is covered over by a thick patina of concepts and cognitive constructions, the approach of phenomenology is needed to uncover the way in which phenomena manifest or show themselves forth. Hence the motto cited earlier: "To the things themselves!" Yet what is phenomenology as an inquiry trying to uncover? What does it allow to "show itself forth"? Clearly, the inquiry is needed most urgently when the meaning of a phenomenon does not show itself forth but is in some way hidden or concealed. In terms of *Being and Time,* deliberate effort is required especially when inquiring into something "which does not usually or immediately show itself, what by contrast to what shows itself, remains hidden or covered over—and yet what belongs essentially to what usually or immediately manifests itself as its sense and ground." Borrowing a leaf from the Aristotelian tradition, Heidegger states that what is usually covered over in phenomena is their being-status or the sense of being that allows them to be: "But what remains hidden in an egregious sense, or what tends to be covered over and to show itself only 'in disguise,' is not this or that entity but rather the 'Being of beings' (*das Sein des Seienden*)," which prompts the renewal of the being-question (*Seinsfrage*).[20]

What needs to be noted here is that the latter is precisely a "question" and not a doctrine about a fixed entity. This means that the meaning of "Being" and of all beings (including the sense of *Dasein*) is a target of inquiry and interpretation that needs to be renewed ever again as a horizon of possibilities. In Heidegger's words, "Phenomenology is our access route to and our way of bringing into focus the theme of ontology. Differently stated: ontology for us is possible only as phenomenology." The emphasis on inquiry and the denial of a fixed doctrine do not entail that the way phenomena show themselves is purely arbitrary and that the access route is a matter of willful construction. Phenomena themselves are not misleading and do not hide something else behind their backs, but their meaning can be covered over or obstructed, which precisely warrants phenomenological inquiry. The upshot is that the mode and meaning of being(s) must be investigated in a methodical way; invoking the teachings of Husserl again, Heidegger at this point refers to the process of an "originary" and "intuitive" grasping and explication of phenomena (in contrast to a purely accidental and unreflective approach). From this angle, phenomenology means

the rigorous pursuit of what shows itself forth in and through phenomena. Phenomenological inquiry hence denotes the employment of all methods needed for the disclosure and explication of
phenomena, including an appropriate terminology and conceptual arsenal. "If our analysis is to be authentic," *Being and Time*
adds, "the prior task of assuring ourselves 'phenomenologically' of
a given phenomenon is inscribed in the goal of our inquiry from
the beginning."[21]

Going somewhat beyond Husserl's teachings, *Being and Time*
links phenomenology closely with the "being-question" and hence
with ontology—again not as a substantive doctrine but as an ongoing search or quest. "In terms of content," we read, "phenomenology
is the science of the Being of beings, hence ontology." However, in
view of the focus of the text on the meaning of *Dasein*, it is preferable
to speak in this context of a "fundamental [or foundational] ontology," seen as a preamble to the inquiry into the meaning of Being
as such. At this point, Heidegger makes the crucial move to interpretation or "hermeneutics" as the needed corollary of the being-
question: "What follows from our investigation is that the meaning of
phenomenological description as a method is interpretation (*Ausle-
gung*). The 'logos' of the phenomenology of *Dasein* has the character
of a '*hermeneuein*' (*Auslegen*) that discloses to the self-understanding
of *Dasein* the proper meaning of Being and also the basic structures
of its own existence." Differently put: "Phenomenology of *Dasein* is
hermeneutics in the primordial sense of that term." With this focus
on hermeneutics and the treatment of the being-question as hermeneutical, Heidegger inserts into Husserl's analysis an important
modification: the so-called ontic-ontological difference, or the difference between Being and beings where both terms and the difference itself are open to interpretation. "Being and its structure,"
we read, "exceed every being and every possible determination of a
being." In this sense, "Being is transcendent as such," and "every disclosure of Being is *transcendental* knowledge." However, disclosure
of Being is always intimately linked with the attempted disclosure of
the meaning of discrete, individuated beings in concrete contexts,
which requires nuanced hermeneutical interpretation. Hence, Heidegger says, "[pure] ontology and hermeneutics are not two distinct
philosophical disciplines among others"; rather, they are the core

of philosophy as such: "Philosophy is universal phenomenological ontology, starting from the hermeneutics of *Dasein*."[22]

Ereignis and "Other Beginning"

De(con)struction, as envisaged in *Being and Time*, involved basically a thorough rethinking of traditional categories and metaphysical premises in light of impending possibilities. The hermeneutical recasting of the being-question implied clearly a decisive move beyond traditional conceptions of ontology in terms of substances or fixed entities. However, how sufficient or effective was this move? Was it really possible to transgress dominant paradigms as long as the transgression was itself formulated with the help of traditional conceptual frameworks—say, the framework of "transcendental phenomenology"? In the ensuing years, Heidegger relentlessly explored pathways toward a more thorough transgression or transformation. These were difficult years, both politically and philosophically. As one may recall, they were the years of his notorious political derailment, deriving largely from self-misconstrual and misdescription. They were also the years of his intense confrontation (*Auseinandersetzung*) with Nietzsche, especially with the notions of will to power and *Machenschaft*.[23] But they were also years of major philosophical discoveries and the disclosure of new horizons—a disclosure often requiring resort to new vocabularies suitable for a new paradigmatic constellation. Among these new vocabularies, the most anticipatory terms are *Ereignis* and *other beginning*.

Although intimated in some earlier writings, the notion of *Ereignis* emerged most fully in a text of 1936 titled *Beiträge zur Philosophie (Vom Ereignis)*. Often described as Heidegger's second magnum opus (after *Being and Time*), the sprawling text offers a step-by-step guide for a philosophical-existential paradigm shift or the transgression of a given constellation toward new shores. The most difficult term signaling the new horizon is *Ereignis*—which may actually not be translatable into existing vocabularies. In English translations, the words *appropriation* and *event* are often used to capture the gist of the term, but both are highly misleading. The word *appropriation* (fastening on the connection between *proper* and *eigen*) actually points in the opposite direction because *Ereignis* is surely not something that can be appropriated. Although honoring this inability, the term *event* is likewise unhelpful because it suggests a sudden, unprecedented irruption or disruption of ordinary affairs. The term *en-owning* used by some translators is a transliteration but conveys little or no meaning.[24] What many or most translators forget is that *Ereignis* is a continuation and radical reformulation of the being-question (*Seinsfrage*)—that is, of the question of the meaning of Being and how it is encountered in its disclosure or showing forth. As Heidegger writes in the opening pages of *Beiträge,* the (sub) title *Vom Ereignis* intimates "a thoughtfully articulated belongingness of beings to Being and Being's language (*Wort des Seyns*)." The (sub)title is oriented toward "the sole question of the truth of Being as a *question.*" This inquiry into the "meaning" or else the "truth of Being" is and remains, Heidegger asserts, "*my* question and is my *only* question."[25]

What *Beiträge* thus seeks to adumbrate is the intimate belonging (*Zugehören*) or relationality of Being and beings (now no longer viewed from the sole angle of *Dasein*)—but a relationality that has been covered over or obstructed by the thick patina of traditional metaphysical conceptions. To transgress or move beyond this patina requires a "turning" (*Kehre*), not in the form of an abrupt or arbitrary reversal but in the sense of a careful journey that unsettles the boundaries of prevailing paradigms. In Heidegger's words, "The future-oriented thinking is a pathway of thought (*Gedankengang*) that traverses and renders transparent hitherto concealed realms of Being in order to reach toward its character of *Ereignis.*" During the transit between paradigms—that is, in this age of "the transition from metaphysics to the thinking of Being"—such a pathway can only be an "attempt" (*Versuch*). Against this background, *Beiträge* is said to move on a path that "opens up the transition (*Übergang*) to that 'other beginning' (*anderer Anfang*) into which Occidental thought is seeking to enter." The notion of an "other beginning" gains its meaning not from a comparison with distinct historical philosophies but from its relation to the "first" or primordial beginning of philosophical thought (during the Axial Age); transitional reflection hence is basically located between these two beginnings. What is important to remember is that access to the new cannot be the work of fabrication or willful design but requires a basic or "founding openness" (*gründende Eröffnung*).[26]

In line with the carefulness of the journey or path of thought, *Beiträge* proceeds cautiously through a sequence of steps or stages. The main stages on this reflective *camino real* are "resonance" or "initial tuning" (*Anklang*), "interplay" (*Zuspiel*), "leap" (*Sprung*), "the grounding" (*Gründung*), "the future ones" (*die Zukünftigen*), and "the last God" (*der letzte Gott*). As Heidegger insists, the sequence should not be taken as mere historiography but as a transformative-experiential encounter always pointing to the epiphany of the future. For present purposes, only the briefest indications of the path can be given. The "initial tuning" requires an abandonment of all presumed knowledge, a relinquishment of ego's claims to possession of knowledge. This step is predicated on the notion that Being presents itself first of all in the mode of withdrawal or refusal (*Verweigerung*) and thus as beyond the pale of appropriation. In accordance with this mode, any human approach has to be marked by reticence or awe, allowing for a fine-tuning of antennae in order to foster a resonance with the address of Being. In Heidegger's words, "Reticence (*Verhaltenheit*) is the strongest and at the same time the most tender readiness of *Dasein* for the happening of *Ereignis,* for its being cast into the inner cauldron of truth regarding the 'turning' occurring in *Ereignis.*" In order to ward off the conception of grounding in the sense of a substantive ontology, the text immediately cautions, "Reticence: meaning the active persistence in the un-ground (*Abgrund*)." What is particularly important to note is that *Dasein*'s readiness and reticent disposition have nothing to do with modern subjectivism or egocentrism: "Reticent awareness has left behind every 'subjectivism,' including that most insidious type hidden in the cult of 'personality.' Where personality and artistic 'genius' are celebrated, one still moves, despite denials, in the modern path of 'ego' and ego-consciousness."[27]

What Heidegger calls "interplay" (*Zuspiel*) is the placement of philosophy in the interstices between its "first beginning" as metaphysics and its "other beginning" as being-question or postmetaphysics. Thinking here finds itself in the midst of transition and bridge building—but where the bridge reaches out "to a shore as yet not determined." The "first beginning" initiated metaphysics as a theory about "beings," but without asking explicitly about the "Being" of beings. Hence, the transition reached in the interplay is oriented above all toward an "overcoming" of metaphysics. However, the latter cannot be accomplished through a simple rejection or negation but requires a renewed immersion in and transformative rethinking of metaphysics. As explained in *Beiträge*, "The transitional thinking does not display a hostility to metaphysics, but rather attempts its internal transgression." Hence, talk about the "end of metaphysics" should not lead to the impression that "philosophy is done with metaphysics"; on the contrary, precisely by showing the inner limits of metaphysics does philosophy "playfully" gain access to the "other beginning."[28] Seen against this background, the next step of the "leap" (*Sprung*) is not so much a willful or unmotivated jump but rather the embrace of another dimension nurtured by the struggle of "overcoming" and, above all, by the disposition of deep reticence and awe permeating the transitional path. Seen as the first entry into the being-question, leaping thus is not an act of self-affirmation but rather a mode of "going-under" (*Untergang*) and surrender: "Going-under is the most intimate partner of that refusal in which *Ereignis* gives itself over to human beings."[29]

Just as leaping is not a reckless jump, "grounding" (*Gründung*) is not a human fabrication or construction but rather a readiness to rely on a trustworthy ground—which is the truth of Being. From the perspective of *Dasein*, such readiness is not simply a passive endurance but an engagement: to let the ground "be" as ground. Seen from this angle, the term *Dasein* acquires a new and deeper meaning: having traversed dispossession and the shipwreck of ego consciousness, *Dasein* emerges as the emblem of belongingness (*Zugehören*) to *Ereignis*; only through this belonging are human existence and "self-becoming" (*Selbstwerdung*) possible. Differently put: being a participant in *Ereignis, Dasein* occupies a status between historical humanity and the divine ("das Zwischen zwischen den Menschen und den Göttern"). To be sure, this status is not readily available. Apparently borrowing a leaf from Nietzsche's Zarathustra and his praise of solitude, what Heidegger calls "the future or impending ones" (*die Zukünftigen*) are a small number of heralds or precursors who have traversed the path of abandonment, loss, and refusal as well as the turning and ultimate return. His text speaks here of the "strangers of even heart who are equally engaged with the gift [of Being] and the refusal." These strangers are those who are able to experience and move through the "going-under" (*Untergang*) that is the character of our time and that is "a path toward the silent preparation of the future."[30]

Heidegger's preoccupation with *Ereignis* and "other beginning" was not confined to the text of 1936. On the contrary, the war years underscored with growing urgency the need to overcome modern metaphysics (anchored in egocentrism and will to power) and to move to new horizons. The period 1941–1942 saw Heidegger immersed in the composition of two lengthy texts titled *Das Ereignis* and *Über den Anfang* (On the beginning). The first volume retraces in many ways the path discussed in *Beiträge* but now interspersed or punctuated with dramatic passages (echoing perhaps the distress of the time). The term *resonance* (*Anklang*) is used again to signal the initial inkling of an "other beginning" and of the overcoming of metaphysics—the latter seen as the interim between the two beginnings. However, metaphysics in its modern form is now the target of harsh denunciation. According to the text, late modernity is the age of "the completion of metaphysics," the age of "the abandonment by Being (*Seinsverlassenheit*) when the will to will, forgetful of Being, engineers the primacy of [certain] beings." In its completion, modernity (*Neuzeit*), particularly as developed in Europe and the West, is marked by the dominance of ideology (Weltanschauung), of technology and historicity—all underpinned by the zeal of *Machenschaft* and "will to will" (of which the "will to power" is a particularly virulent type). Exiting from this devastation cannot be the work of willful fabrication or design; rather, if it can happen at all, it can only be along the *camino real*—the path of painful loss, abandonment, and refusal.[31]

The second volume written during the same period assembles the main themes discussed so far but sometimes in particularly pithy formulations. The opening paragraphs state, "Thinking of Being as 'beginning' (*Anfang*) points forward into Being as *Ereignis*. Both terms, *Ereignis* and beginning, belong together." To obviate misunderstanding, the text adds, "Beginning is not the start of something else"; rather, "beginning is *Ereignis;* it is a self-gathering in *Ereignis*." In the same way, *Ereignis* here does not mean "a happening or event (*Vorkommnis*) that would vanish like a phase in a sequential process"; rather, it is the "fullness" in the advent of Being.

Even more than the other texts, *Über den Anfang* puts emphasis on pain, refusal, and undergoing. Taking a leaf from Meister Eckhart, the book invokes the notion of "apartness" (*Abgeschiedenheit*). Thus, we read about the apartness of Being and the beginning. One needs to ponder, Heidegger observes, "that Being (and not only beings) sometimes 'is not' and this in such a decisive way that it prevents even nothingness" (or nihilism). Like the other text, *Über den Anfang* is punctuated by semipolitical and geopolitical observations. Heidegger at this point distinguishes between Occident (*Abendland*), on the one hand, and modern Europe and the West, on the other. The Occident as "evening land" is still closely linked with the first beginning, prior to its derailment into metaphysics. By contrast, the modern West is wedded to "planetary" domination or control that is "the perversion of the beginning into the program of linear progression." In modern metaphysics, "Being operates as power, and power as *Machenschaft*."[32] To overcome this perversion, an "other beginning" is needed.

2

Letting-Be Politically

Heidegger on Freedom and Solidarity

The essence of truth is freedom.
—Martin Heidegger, "On the Essence of Truth"

Words habitually used acquire the patina of self-evidence. As previously indicated, this is one of the reasons behind Nietzsche's famous claim that the highest traditional values "devalue" themselves—once they are denuded of genuine insight and no longer enlist experiential engagement. By common agreement, the central or signature value of Western modernity is the idea of human freedom or autonomy, an idea counterposed to all forms of external determinism. The modern idea takes different shapes in different contexts. Cognitively, freedom means the scientist's ability to investigate all phenomena of nature from a superior "spectatorial" vantage point. In practical terms, freedom means the capacity to shape one's personal and social life in accordance with chosen aims or projects—or else to retreat from social life into inward solitude. Just because the accent in every case is on individual or personal autonomy, life in society constitutes a problem that needs to be resolved through a more or less artificial linkage (which in modern Western thought has taken the typical shape of a "social contract"). The revolutionary motto "liberty, equality, fraternity" juxtaposes several guiding values, but without leaving the pivotal status of the first value in doubt. Otherwise, the motto provides just a serial arrangement of ideas whose deeper meaning and mutual dependence remain opaque.

The opacity of terms, of course, in no way prevents their rhetorical or ideological employment. Thus, without any qualms, the modern West celebrates itself as the "free world" comprising the "lands of the free" while denouncing the non-West or East as a realm of despotism. Reacting to this binary portrayal, some other modern countries have valorized the ideas of community and collectivism, thus center-staging the second and third terms of the revolutionary motto. However, in doing so, they have not escaped or corrected the binary construction and certainly have not clarified the internal connection of terms. In the following, I simplify the motto by lumping together equality and fraternity under the label *solidarity*. In an attempt to clarify and "revalue" the cited categories—and thus to prevent their "devaluation" (in Nietzsche's sense)—I follow here a path that may at first glance seem unpromising and counterintuitive: I enlist the guidance of Martin Heidegger, who is frequently and even commonly accused of being far removed or distant from modern revolutionary ideas. Although agreeing to some extent with the charge, I interpret distance here as distance from the "devalued" shape of modern ideas—that is, their abuse as slogans for ideological or strategic purposes. As I try to show, far from being an enemy of freedom and autonomy, Heidegger's philosophy offers a radically new conception that can "revalue" and freshly energize the meaning of these terms. At the same time, far from being antithetical to social life, his philosophy provides a new understanding of solidarity that bypasses the binaries liberalism/socialism and individualism/collectivism. After reviewing Heidegger's treatment of the two key ideas, I by way of conclusion ponder the general significance of his thought for contemporary social life.

Freedom as Letting-Be

The counterintuitive character of my approach is particularly evident in the case of freedom or autonomy. In this domain, Heidegger's derailment in 1933—his (at least partial) involvement in the ruling "totalitarian" regime of the time—has taken a heavy toll. This is not the place to enter into a discussion of this episode, which has been done before by many commentators (including myself).[1] Yet even when the episode is bracketed, Heidegger's credentials on the topic of "freedom" are intensely contested or controversial. Interpretations of his work typically oscillate between an extreme voluntarism or "decisionism," on the one hand, and an extreme submissiveness if not "fatalism," on the other. In the first reading, freedom is seen as a form of self-creation and self-enactment where the agent both designs and implements his "projects" in the world. In the second reading, the agent is placed at the mercy of external forces or destinies that at best permit a retreat into inner solitude. Phrased in different language, freedom in the first case is a causal force producing self-willed effects, whereas in the second case causation operates in the outside world sequestering the agent in inner quietism.[2] As one can readily see, the two interpretations stand in the tradition of Cartesian dualism: the juxtaposition of thought (cogito) and object or mind and matter. On a more nuanced level, the readings reflect the Kantian dilemma of the relation between transcendental and empirical or "noumenal" and "phenomenal" domains. What needs to be remembered here most of all is that Heidegger's work, in its basic trajectory, moves beyond these modern dichotomies or binaries—a move captured already in the phrase designating human *Dasein* and agency: "being-in-the-world."

In Heidegger's work *Being and Time*, human *Dasein* is neither portrayed as a self-contained "subject" (in the Cartesian or Kantian sense) nor leveled into "extended matter" or the "phenomenal" world of things or objects. To be sure, as a "being-in-the-world," *Dasein* is also a "being" and not something extramundane, but it is also differentiated from other beings by a unique capacity or task: the capacity to "care" about the meaning or point of its being (and of the world and all beings). For this reason, Heidegger presents human *Dasein* as a hyphenated being, a midpoint between inside and outside, between immanence and transcendence. It is this hyphenated status, this ability of ordinary human *Dasein* to reach out toward the meaning of "Being" (in all its forms), that is the heart of human freedom. It is by virtue of this transcending care that human *Dasein* is neither a prisoner of itself (or its ego) nor a prisoner of outside causal forces. According to *Being and Time*, this capacity for freedom is not always actualized; it can remain dormant or enveloped in forgetfulness. But it is always there as a potential that Heidegger calls the possible "authenticity" of human life. Whenever such authenticity is achieved or approximated, the text speaks of human *Dasein* as "being-free" (*Freisein*), which is a condition where human beings properly live up to their task—namely, to care for and take care of Being. As one should note (to guard against frequent misreadings), authenticity here is not a matter of arbitrary choice or spontaneous "free will" (as if freedom could be freely chosen). Stated more sharply: free will, free choice, and free "projects" are derived from or predicated on the authentic condition of "being-free," not the other way around. Viewed as *Dasein's* basic core, "being-free" is neither imposed on it as an external fate or destiny nor arbitrarily chosen or discarded.[3]

In addition to *authenticity*, another term that has often misled readers is *resoluteness* (*Entschlossenheit*), which has tended to be equated with existential firmness or boldness (and sometimes even with a Kierkegaardian "leap of faith"). What is neglected here is that the term refers chiefly to the cultivation of the care for "Being" through which *Dasein* testifies to its authenticity as "being-free." As Heidegger states, "Resoluteness is nothing but the carefully nurtured and only through this cultivation conceivable authenticity of care." The relation to care is further underscored by the term's closeness to the notion of openness (*Erschlossenheit*), which emphasizes *Dasein's* availability to the "call of care" that is also the "call of conscience." To quote the text again: "This unique and distinctive openness witnessed in the call of conscience . . . is what we call resoluteness" (in the sense of a firm readiness to listen to and heed the call). What is most important to realize is that the "call of care"—which is also the call of freedom—does not liberate or exile *Dasein* from the world and hence does not encourage an exclusive concentration on individual preferences or personal decision making. On the contrary, precisely by heeding the call, *Dasein* becomes fully attentive to the world and all beings in it. In Heidegger's words, "The call of conscience, in summoning *Dasein* to its deeper potential, does not hold up an empty ideal, but rather calls it into its situation." Differently put: as a mode of authenticity, resolute openness "does not cut *Dasein* loose from its world, [or] reduce it to a free-floating *ego*" but rather enables it to live authentically as "being-in-the-world." Authentically grasped, freedom prompts *Dasein* to deal carefully with "things-at-hand" (*Zuhanden*) and to nurture with "solicitude" (*Fürsorge*) the co-being of others. The latter case reveals most clearly the "emancipatory" character of care. Authentic *Dasein*, we read, "sets itself free for its world." This stance enables it "to let fellow-beings 'be' in their own innermost potential and to help open up this potential in the mode of 'anticipative-liberating solicitude' (*vorspringend-befreiende Fürsorge*)."[4]

A few years later in his essay "On the Essence of Truth," Heidegger accentuated and deepened the character of freedom as "being-free." In an effort to forestall the misreading of being-free as free will or self-causation, the essay presented "disclosedness" (*Erschlossenheit*) no longer or not in the first case as the openness of human *Dasein* but as the availability of "Being" as such—that is, its readiness to show itself forth in "unconcealment" (*Unverborgenheit*) and thus in its genuine "truth" (*aletheia*). In this context, the essay takes aim at the traditional conception of truth as "correctness" or as the "correspondence" between the statements of an observer and the "facts" of the case. Heidegger at this point raises the following question: How is the correlation between statements and facts or between subject and object validated as an emblem of truth? Since the theory of correspondence is not itself grounded in such correspondence, there must be a prior enabling condition that allows the correlation to arise in the first place; this enabling condition is Being in its truth— that is, Being as seen in its "unconcealment" (*aletheia* or truth). In his words: "How can something like correctness or insertion into a correspondence happen or be rendered possible?" This can happen only "if an enabling act has already freed itself for an open region and for a disclosure happening in this region which binds every act of cognition or representation (*Vorstellung*)." However, the capacity of freeing oneself for a binding direction is possible only by *being free* for disclosure in the open region. Hence, "the inner possibility of correctness is grounded in freedom. The *essence of truth is freedom* (*das Wesen der Wahrheit ist Freiheit*)."[5]

As can be seen, Heidegger's discussion confirms and lends philosophical depth to the old adage that "the truth will set you free." As in the old adage, the disclosure or unconcealment of truth is neither purely passive-reactive nor willfully activist but rather happens in the middle voice. Truth as freedom cannot be constructed, fabricated, or engineered, nor does it befall human beings as a passively endured fate because it resonates with the inner core of *Dasein* as "being free" for care. Due to this resonance, truth also liberates *Dasein* by freeing it from the constraints of falsehood, deception, and manipulation. Finding itself liberated in this manner, *Dasein* also becomes an accomplice or participant in the reign of freedom by "letting" all beings "be" what they are without constraint or manipulation. In Heidegger's words, "Freedom for disclosure [of truth] in an open region lets beings be what they are; freedom now reveals itself as letting beings be." As he is keenly aware, the latter phrase is again open to misconstrual by being synonymous with indifference or carelessness, which would vitiate *Dasein*'s intrinsic relatedness. Hence, without in any way condoning manipulation or managerial control, the phrase stands as an expression of liberating "care": "The phrase required in this context—to let beings be—does not refer to neglect or indifference, but rather the opposite: to let be is to engage oneself with beings in a caring manner (*Seinlassen als Sicheinlassen*)." Through this engagement, other beings become also accomplices or participants of the reign of freedom; like *Dasein*, they are also "set free" by truth. "To let be," the text elaborates, "that is, to let beings be what they are, means to engage oneself with the open region into which every being comes to stand and which it carries along like an aura. This open region was conceived by Western thought in its origins as '*ta alethea*,' the unconcealed."[6]

In "On the Essence of Truth," Heidegger is particularly intent on differentiating the freedom of truth (or the truth of freedom) from prevalent Western conceptions of freedom or liberty, including the conceptions of "positive" and "negative" freedom (where the former means the pursuit of willful designs and the latter the retreat into inner solitude). To this extent, the thrust of his essay has not been fully taken into account in modern Western discussions; above all, what has not been noted is the fact that his account of "free being" (*Freisein*) blows most modern construals out of the water. As Heidegger does not tire of insisting, freedom as "being-free" or "free being" coincides neither with arbitrary choice or will power nor with external destiny. "Freedom," we read, "is not merely what common sense is content to let pass under this name: the caprice, occasionally present in our choosing, of moving in this or that direction. But freedom is not arbitrariness in what we can and cannot do. Nor, on the other hand, is it the mere submission to a requirement as fated necessity." Rather, prior to all such "positive" or "negative" construals, freedom must be seen as "being-free" and "letting-be"—that is, the free "engagement in the disclosure of beings as such." What is particularly important for Heidegger in this context is the avoidance of anthropocentrism, the linkage of freedom with human power or control. Viewed as a caring engagement (with Being and beings), freedom cannot be regarded as a human trait, faculty, or property. In Heidegger's pointed language, "Human caprice does not have freedom at its disposal. *Dasein* does not 'possess' freedom as a property; at best, the reverse holds: freedom—geared toward ek-static disclosure—possesses *Dasein*, and this so fully and originally that only it [freedom] secures for humanity that distinctive relatedness to Being as a whole which first founds all history."[7] Differently phrased: *Dasein* is neither the victim nor the causal agent of freedom and the disclosure of truth.

Roughly contemporaneously with the "Truth" essay (in the summer of 1930), Heidegger presented in Freiburg a lecture course titled "On the Essence of Human Freedom" and subtitled "Introduction to Philosophy."[8] The lecture course is important here mainly for two reasons: first, for treating the theme of freedom as a proper gateway to philosophy as such and, second, for offering a detailed analysis of Kantian philosophy and especially Immanuel Kant's conception of freedom. From Heidegger's perspective, freedom properly construed is closely related to the issue of "Being" and "beings as a whole"—which since ancient times has been viewed as *the* guiding question and opening gambit of philosophy. This view, of course, has been challenged by Kant's critical philosophy and his sidelining of "ontological" issues. Heidegger's renewal of the "question of Being" here takes on its decisive contours, especially in its relation to freedom. During the twentieth century, Kant—seen as the protagonist of Western modernity—was often attacked by thinkers critical of modern life for his center-staging of human freedom and self-determination; in lieu of this accent, these critics frequently gave pride of place to such notions as tradition, heteronomy, and authority. Heidegger's philosophy has no truck with these restorative tendencies nostalgic of premodern and precritical times. What is distinctive about his approach is his willingness to take seriously Kant's thought in its integrity and innovative élan; most importantly, he gives close and serious attention to Kant's conception of freedom and then proceeds to reformulate and rethink it in an entirely novel way. Using a cliché expression, one might say that Heidegger sublates (*aufheben*) Kant's initiative on a radically new level—something that has not been properly recognized in discussions of this topic.

As Heidegger points out, Kant's conception of freedom was located on two levels: a "cosmological" or transcendental level and a practical-moral level. On the first level, freedom signified for Kant "absolute spontaneity" or the possibility of a radically new beginning, whereas the practical meaning coincided with "autonomy of willing" or the independence of willing from external constraints. In Kant's work, the two levels were coordinated via the subordination of the practical to the cosmological dimension, such that autonomy of will functioned as a subcategory of spontaneity construed in a radical sense. Within the realm of worldly phenomena, to be sure, freedom was inserted into the nexus of "natural causality," which left no room for spontaneity; hence, the latter ultimately pointed in a transcendental or "noumenal" direction but without rupturing the idea of causality. In Heidegger's words, "The new beginning of a condition or series of events, and more specifically the absolutely new beginning is [for Kant] a grounding or causing radically different from the causality of nature or a completely distinctive mode of causality. Kant designated the latter—absolute spontaneity—as 'causality of freedom.'" What becomes evident here, for Heidegger, is the problematic relation of spontaneity and causality: "Kant basically views freedom as the capacity for a unique and distinct causation." It is on this issue—and not on the centrality of freedom per se—that Heidegger departs from Kant. As he writes, "If we force a confrontation (*Auseinandersetzung*) with Kant, our motivation is precisely to focus on the correlation of freedom and causation. The necessity of such confrontation is all the more urgent since we ourselves construe freedom as condition or grounding of the possibility of *Dasein*—which conjures up the issue of the relation between such grounding and causation." The remainder of the lectures is entirely dominated by this question whether freedom is somehow derivable from causation or the other way around: "In the latter case, where freedom provides the grounding, how must freedom itself be conceived?"[9]

For Heidegger, the limits or limitations of Kant's thought have to do with his contamination of freedom and causation, where the former is derived from the latter. Seen from this perspective, causation or causality assumes the status of a metaphysical or "cosmological" category—a category, however, that is never analyzed as a problem "on the level of a radical ontological inquiry." Once this inquiry is undertaken, causality can no longer be taken as an unquestioned self-contained presupposition but must be interrogated as to its "ontological" status—that is, as a modality of the disclosure of "Being." In Heidegger's words, "*One* ontological category among others is that of causality." However, causality as a category is not self-evident but is predicated on the deeper premise of freedom: "Thus the issue of causality belongs to the problematic of freedom and not the reverse." In a sense, this deeper premise even antidates or takes precedence over the correlation of Being and time. "The essence of freedom," we read, "comes properly into view only once we perceive it as the ground of possibility of *Dasein*, as something which precedes the nexus of Being and time." As one can see, freedom for Heidegger is a basic category of "fundamental ontology" and as such is far removed from arbitrary choice or subjective willfulness. His text at this point returns to a central claim of the "Truth" essay—namely, that freedom is not a human faculty or a quality of *Dasein*. Far from being just "one particular notion among others," he writes, freedom "underlies and permeates the totality of beings as a whole," including human beings. Seen in this light, freedom is still "more primordial than *Dasein*, which is only a guardian of freedom." In the crisp language used before, "Human freedom signifies no longer: freedom as a human property, but the reverse: humanity as a possibility of freedom."[10]

Heidegger's subsequent works modified or reformulated his conception of freedom in some details—without, however, jeopardizing its central philosophical status. The continuity can be perceived in his lecture course of 1936 titled "Schelling's Treatise 'On the Essence of Human Freedom.'" As it happened, Friedrich Schelling emerged during this period as a key figure in Heidegger's thought, and not accidentally. Broadly speaking, Schelling represented for him one of the few great philosophers after Kant, perhaps the only one who managed to push the problematic of freedom beyond the

bounds of causality in the direction of ontology (though with idealist traces). The lecture course is richly textured and touches on a
great number of issues. For present purposes, I select only two topics: first, the distinction between freedom and the traditional idea of
free will; and, second, the question of the relation between fatalism
and freedom. The first issue stands at the threshold of the course
and allows Heidegger to make a strong demarcation. "One knows
this question under the familiar label of the 'problem of free will,'"
he states, and what is debated under this rubric is "whether human
will is free or unfree and how the one or the other can be convinc-
ingly demonstrated." Freedom here is viewed "as a trait or property
of human beings; but what and who *Dasein* is, one presupposes to
know." Against this assumption, the course pits a radical counterpo-
sition: "With this question of free will—which in the end is wrongly
put and thus not even a proper question—Schelling's treatise has
nothing whatever in common. For in this treatise, freedom is not
a human property, but rather the reverse." For Schelling, freedom
is "the comprehensive and pervasive dimension of Being in whose
ambience human beings become human in the first place." This
means that "human nature is grounded in freedom." Freedom itself,
however, transcending the dimension of human willing, is "a category of authentic Being as such."[11]

The second issue of fatalism arises primarily because of Schelling's attempt to formulate a comprehensive ontological system—
which, according to some, conflicts with human self-determination.
The more immediate source of the issue is the (allegedly) "pantheistic" character of Schelling's work, his assumption that all beings are
somehow "immanent" in God or that "God is everything." In its traditional construal, however, pantheism was typically equated with
fatalism (as was done especially by F. H. Jacobi in his polemic against
Spinoza in 1785). As Schelling concedes, pantheism in most of its
traditional formulations has indeed tended to coincide with fatalism and thus a denial of freedom. What he tries to show, however, is
that this linkage is by no means necessary—more sharply put, that
pantheism is not only compatible with human freedom but actually requires such freedom as its complement and underpinning. For
Schelling, much or everything depends here on the meaning of the
copula in such formulations as "God is everything" or "everything

is (in) God"—a meaning that has traditionally been misconstrued in the sense of a static identity or sameness. A completely different understanding arises if the copula is taken in a dynamic, transitive sense such that it signifies a creative "difference in unity." If taken in this sense, the copula *is* acquires the meaning of a transitive, enabling potency—that is, of an act of "letting-be" (which does not coincide with causality). As Heidegger paraphrases Schelling's argument, "The phrase 'God is everything' or 'God is man' says: God as ground lets man and everything be as a consequence—which means: to the extent that 'man' is such a consequence, he/she must have autonomous being." Thus, God's free enabling potency is transmitted (transitively) to human beings seen as freely creative beings. Thus, far from negating freedom, the pantheistic formula "God *is* man" means that "'man' is in God as a free agent, and only free beings can properly be in God."[12]

Heidegger never abandoned his ontology of freedom—even after the so-called *Kehre* (turning) of the 1930s. What the "turning" amounted to was not so much a turning *away* from the conception of *Dasein* (outlined in his early writings) as a turning *toward* a deepened portrayal of the relational networks in which *Dasein* is always enmeshed. This turn can readily be seen in some of the major texts composed at the time—such as *Beiträge* (1936) and *Mindfulness* (*Besinnung*, 1938–1939)—which are nothing but exhortations to a creative rethinking of traditional "metaphysical" perspectives as well as a caring engagement with the new horizons opened up by historical transformations.[13] For present purposes, I want to glance briefly at some of his later writings (after 1945), mainly to correct a misunderstanding. As it happens, these writings are frequently accused of surrendering freedom entirely to a blind fatalism or ontological "mysticism." The essay "The Question Concerning Technology" (1953) shows the untenability of this charge. It is true that the essay portrays the disclosure or unconcealment of Being as a "sending," "mission," or destiny of Being. As Heidegger writes, "We shall call the commissioning that first starts *Dasein* upon the path of disclosure a sending or mission (*Ge-schick*). The essence of all history is guided by such a mission." The role played by technology in modern society also has the character of a mission. However, as the essay immediately adds, "The mission of disclosure always holds sway in history; but that mission is never a fate that compels or coerces. For *Dasein* becomes truly *free* precisely insofar as it belongs to the realm of sending and thus is one that listens (*hören*) and not simply obeys (*gehorchen*)." Differently stated (and repeating earlier formulations): freedom is not connected with will power or the causality of human willing but rather "roams in the open space of a clearing or disclosure."[14]

A similar view—together with some startling connotations—emerges in the essay "Building Dwelling Thinking" (1951). Commenting on the terminological background of "dwelling," Heidegger observes, "The Old Saxon *wuon* [and] the Gothic *wunian*, like the old word *bauen*, mean to remain, to stay in place; but the Gothic term says more distinctly how this remaining is experienced. *Wunian* means: to be contented, to be stilled, to be and remain in peace." Here, an unexpected and important linkage between freedom and peace comes into view: "The word for peace, *Friede*, means to be free(d) or what is set free, in Gothic '*frye*'; and *frye* means preserved from harm and danger and thus spared or saved. To free hence means to spare." However, sparing consists not only in not inflicting harm on what is spared. As Heidegger adds, "Real sparing is something *positive* and occurs whenever, from the beginning, we 'let something be' in its essence or return it properly into its own essence—that is, when we 'free' it in the genuine sense of the word by preserving it in peace." Thus, "to dwell, to be stilled, means to remain at peace in that open or free region which safeguards everything in its being."[15]

Co-being and Solidarity

Next to the issue of freedom, no other topic has aroused more debate or controversy regarding Heidegger's work than the status of inter-human relations. In the opinion of many critics, that work presents either no conception or only a completely inadequate or misleading conception of being with others or social solidarity. This charge was leveled early on against his writings during the "existentialist" period; it gathered momentum and even virulence during the later heyday of "postmodernism," a perspective often committed to the celebration of a radical "otherness" or an absolute or transcendental "alterity."[16] As it happens—and as can readily be shown—Heidegger was not a partisan of an individualistic or self-centered existentialism or a devotee of the absolute otherness heralded by some postmodern writers. Today, when the vogues of both existentialism and postmodernism are at an ebb, the situation seems propitious for a renewed and, we can hope, more balanced assessment of Heidegger's thought in this area. The propitiousness is enhanced by the recent publication of a number of texts or lecture courses that shed additional light on the topic. What emerges from these publications—when seen in conjunction with previously available texts—is that Heidegger's view of interhuman solidarity coincides neither with a willfully designed contractual relation nor with a collectivist communalism or communitarianism sidelining freedom.

In *Being and Time*, the issue of interhuman relations is discussed under the rubrics "being-with" (*Mitsein*) and "being-with-others" (*Miteinandersein*). What needs to be noted is that this discussion (in sections 25–27) is preceded in the text by a long chapter devoted to the elucidation of the "worldhood of the world" (*Weltlichkeit der Welt*), a chapter that in turn follows a chapter that seeks to pinpoint the "basic constitution" (*Grundverfassung*) of *Dasein* in terms of the latter's "being-in-the-world" (*In-der-Weltsein*).[17] What emerges from this sequence is that the starting point for Heidegger is by no means an isolated subject, whether construed as a Cartesian cogito or, with Kant and Husserl, as "transcendental subjectivity." Rather, the starting point is a situated *Da-sein* (literally "being-there"), which, far from being self-enclosed, is characterized by care (*Sorge*)—that is, as a being that cares or is able to care about its own being and about Being as such. This special character is what Heidegger calls "existence" (*Existenz*) and which he subsequently differentiates from other modes of being in the world, especially the modes "ready-to-hand" (*Zuhandenheit*) and "presence-at-hand" (*Vorhandenheit*). In broaching the issue of "being-with," Heidegger refers explicitly back to the preceding chapters and sections, insisting that only against this background is it possible to raise the question of the "who" of *Dasein*—the latter taken initially in its ordinary "everydayness" (*Alläglichkeit*).[18]

As Heidegger emphasizes, the question of the "who" of *Dasein* can go astray in several ways. First of all, *Dasein* may be taken not as a "who" but as a "what," allowing for substantive definitions of "human nature" (in terms of reason, soul, or the like). In that case, *Dasein* is treated not as "existence" but as a mode of presence-at-hand on a par with other things in the world. But even when this mistake is avoided, the who question may be missed through a shallow "I-talk" not amenable to further inquiry. For what seems "more indubitable than the givenness of the 'I'?" Heidegger quickly debunks this assumption, saying, "Is it really obvious that access to *Dasein* can be gained through a simple awareness of the 'I' of actions?" What if this "givenness" precisely leads us astray? It is at this point that the issue of "being-with" (*Mitsein*) enters the picture as a correction of spurious I-talk. Recapitulating earlier passages, the text states: "In clarifying being-in-the-world, we have shown that there is never given a bare subject without a world. And so, we find just as little an isolated I without others." On the level of ordinary, everyday experience, others are encountered primarily in the course of routine activities or in the use of "ready-to-hand" things. Thus, in ordinary life, others appear for *Dasein* contextually as beings in a shared world. However, to avoid misunderstanding, the text immediately differentiates other human beings from encountered nonhuman things. Being neither "present-at" nor "ready-to-hand," the status of other humans is the same as that of the encountering *Dasein*: it is that of "*Dasein* itself seen as being-in-the-world."[19]

By emphasizing the shared being of *Dasein* and others in the world, Heidegger undercuts traditional treatments of "intersubjectivity" that concentrate on the problematic passageway from self to other, from "I" to "you." As he concedes, in the talk about encountering others, the impression may arise that one is starting from a privileged and isolated "ego," from whom one then needs to "seek some passageway or bridge (*Übergang*) to the others." This impression, however, is erroneous because it misses both the character of worldhood and the caring openness of *Dasein*. The others are encountered not from the vantage point of the "primacy of one's own subject" or from a self-reference establishing "the counter-point of difference (*das Wogegen eines Unterschieds*)"; rather, they are met "from out of the world in which every caring-circumspect *Dasein* essentially dwells." On a certain level of everydayness, one *Dasein* appears to be simply "another among others." Yet care must be taken not to misconstrue *Mitsein* here in the sense of a simple fusion or bland collectivity. Like oneself, others are in "existence" and hence are marked by potential openness to Being and its possibilities. The "with" in "being-with" hence points not to an indistinct sameness but to an "equivalence of being (*Gleichheit des Seins*)" seen as circumspect coexistence. Because of this, the world is always a shared world, though one shared in different ways: "The world of *Dasein* is a with-world (*Mitwelt*); being-in (*Insein*) is a being-with (*Mitsein*) with others."[20]

If being-with involves an existential encounter or engagement (rather than a mere factual togetherness), what is the connecting link between *Dasein* and others, the bond sustaining the encounter? As indicated earlier, *Being and Time* is critical of traditional treatments of intersubjectivity that claim to find an access from self to other while presupposing the initial givenness of "subjects." One such access is contractual negotiation in which partners seek to advance their self-interest (thus not reaching the level of co-being). More sophisticated construals find the connecting link in "analogy" or else in psychic "empathy" (*Einfühlung*). For Heidegger, the accent on empathy—favored, for example, by Max Scheler—puts the cart before the horse; it ignores that being-with denotes an "ontological relation" (*Seinsverhältnis*) and not an attempt by one subject to enter the psychic realm of another. A similar mistake prevails in "analogical transference"—favored by Edmund Husserl—where the self simply "projects" itself into the other, thus making the other into an alter ego or a "duplicate of the self." The procedure shipwrecks again in the neglect of *Mitsein*, which is an "existential constituent" and not an accidental correlate of human being-in-the-world. As Heidegger acknowledges, self and other may have to make an effort to become properly acquainted and come "to know each other" (*Sich-kennenlernen*). However, this occurs on the basis of a primary being-with—and this is true even in the case of a genuine and deliberate solitude: "Even the explicit disclosure of the other in solitude grows only out of the primacy of *Mitsein*."[21]

As previously stated, on the level of everydayness (*Alltäglichkeit*), *Dasein* may appear as simply one among others. This is the basis of Heidegger's famous discussion of "*das Man*" (the They), where self and others seem to be exchangeable. This discussion has given rise to no end of misunderstandings. In the eyes of some readers, every-dayness is the central or prototypical condition of human *Dasein*—an assumption that, on closer inspection, turns out to be erroneous or at least lopsided. What is true is that Heidegger does not treat everyday life as a merely factual state of affairs from which individual selfhood needs to retreat or be emancipated. What prevents such a construal is the ontological-phenomenological character of his account according to which *Dasein*, in every one of its modalities, is a being-in-the-world enmeshed in co-being. The distinguishing factor is only that, on the everyday level, co-being is muffled and not able to rise to the level of a genuinely caring engagement. Without being unduly moralizing (or privileging antisocial individualism), Heidegger's view of everydayness has often distinctly critical over-tones. Thus, in modern daily life, he notes, there is often ruthless competition, the desire to "keep the others down (*niederhalten*)." More importantly, there is a strong tendency toward leveling and exerting collective control. As *Being and Time* states (in an almost Sartrean vein), "In the mode of everyday being-with-others, *Dasein* is held in subjection (*Botmässigkeit*) to others. It itself *is* not, because others have appropriated its being; the discretion of others disposes of *Dasein*'s possibilities of being." Heidegger at this point introduces the notion of an everyday "publicity" (*Öffentlichkeit*) in which "*das Man*" is able to wield its "real power." Under this rule (abetted by media manipulation), every excellence or distinctness is "noiselessly suppressed"; every mystery "loses its force"; in sum, all possibilities of *Dasein* are "leveled down" (*Einebnung*).[22]

How little everyday *Mitsein* exhausts the range of its possibili-ties is demonstrated by Heidegger's discussion of a more genuine kind of human relationship or solidarity that he describes with the term *solicitude* (*Fürsorge*), denoting a deliberately engaged mode of caring. Just like everyday *Mitsein* may be muffled or repressed, even deliberate solicitude may operate in recessed or defective forms. Thus, human relations on this level may take on the character of mutual neglect, aloofness, or indifference. However, according to *Being and Time*, solicitude can also assume a more positive or active shape, and it can do so mainly in two ways: in one case, solicitude through excess can overwhelm and smother the other; in the sec-ond case, it can allow or assist the other to find himself or herself

and his or her own freedom. On the one hand, solicitous engagement, we read, "can take care away from the other and substitute
itself for the other—that is, it can 'leap in' (*einspringen*) for him/her."
When this happens, the other's life is managed and becomes "dependent and subjugated." On the other hand, there is also the possibility that solicitude, rather than "leaping in," actually "leaps ahead
(*vorausspringt*) of the other" in its existential potential-for-being,
not in order to take away the other's care but "to give it back to the
other authentically as such." This second type of engagement, Heidegger emphasizes, relates to "the other's authentic care" and "helps
the other to become transparent to itself and thus become 'free for'
it." Contrary to a shallow togetherness, solicitude of this kind com-
bines "authentic bonding" (*Verbundenheit*) or solidarity with genuine human freedom.[23]

The connection between genuine solidarity and genuine freedom is explored also in other sections of *Being and Time* that
deserve brief mention here. The most relevant sections are those
dealing with "being-toward-death" and the "call of conscience"; for
Heidegger, both phenomena testify to *Dasein*'s awakening from the
slumber or muffled condition of everydayness. Regarding the "call of
conscience," the text underscores that call's importance for *Dasein*'s
authentic existence. Variously labeled "appeal" (*Anruf*) or "summons" (*Aufruf*), the call exhorts *Dasein* to shoulder its responsibility (in light of its constitutive indebtedness to others). When *Dasein*
understands and heeds the call, Heidegger speaks of its "disclosedness" (*Erschlossenheit*); and when it shoulders the call by shaping life
accordingly, he speaks of "resoluteness" (*Entschlossenheit*)—as previously mentioned. However, as needs to be noted again, shoulder-
ing the call resolutely does not "detach *Dasein* from this world," nor
does it "reduce *Dasein* to a free-floating ego"—something that cannot happen because the call actually underscores *Dasein*'s being-in-
the-world and "pushes it into solicitous *Mitsein* with others." To make
sure that the latter point is not lost, the text adds that the call enables
Dasein "to 'let' others 'be' in their potentiality-for-being" and thus
"to co-disclose this potentiality in a solicitude which 'leaps ahead'
and liberates." When this happens, resolute *Dasein* can become the
"conscience of others"; in effect, this resolute selfhood gives rise to
"authentic being-with-others (*Miteinandersein*)."[24]

Similar insights can be gleaned from Heidegger's discussion of "being-toward-death"—although this discussion too has given rise to a plethora of misunderstandings. The main source of these misunderstandings resides in the presentation of death as "nontransferable." For Heidegger, death is the cessation of *Dasein*'s "ownmost potentiality-for-being"—that is, the point marking the impossibility of any further possibility (in the world). A distinctive feature of human *Dasein* is its ability to anticipate and continuously to "be-toward-death"—an ability that, like the call of conscience, summons *Dasein* out of its absentmindedness into a more careful mode of living. By marking the end of *Dasein*'s own potentiality, death, for Heidegger, is something inevitably singular and nontransferable—which is where the confusion arises. *Being and Time* is quite explicit on the point, stating, for instance, "No one can take over the other's death. . . . Dying is something which every *Dasein* must shoulder for itself; by its very nature, death is in every case 'mine,' insofar as it 'is' at all." And according to another passage, "death is the possibility of *Dasein*'s radical impossibility. Thus death reveals itself as one's ownmost, non-relational, and unsurpassable possibility (*eigenste, unbezügliche, unüberholbare Möglichkeit*)."[25] However, care must be taken not to construe such passages as a relapse into egocentric isolation and hence as canceling *Mitsein* on a deeper (ontological) level.

As it seems to me, what the cited passages seek to guard against is only a spurious (ontic) identification of self and other, a view treating the other simply as another ego ("alter ego") or a duplicate of the self. Read in the context of *Being and Time*, being-toward-death simply testifies to the differential entwinement of being: the fact that *Dasein* and co-*Dasein* are neither identical nor separated by a radical gulf because ultimately they are held together by a shared worldhood and a shared care for being. Hence, "nonrelationality" and "unsurpassability" only undercut the chimera of a cozy, everyday togetherness; they do not undercut *Mitsein* as such. As Heidegger states in an important passage, by being free for its possibilities, *Dasein* dispels the danger that in its finitude it may "fail to recognize the surpassing existential possibilities of others or wrongly seek to appropriate them coercively. . . . As nonrelational possibility, death individualizes—but only so as to render *Dasein* as *Mitsein* open and sensitive for the potentiality-for-being of others." Contrary to frequent allegations, the singularity of death also does not mean that *Dasein* cannot show concern and solicitude for someone else's death. In exploring "the possibility of experiencing the death of others," Heidegger actually acknowledges a limited mode of sharing: "In remaining with the deceased in mournful commemoration, the survivors are indeed 'with him/her' in a mode of respectful solicitude; their relation to the dead cannot be reduced to a mere 'concerned' attentiveness." Yet survivors (relatives and others) cannot pretend that they have died the other's death or that the other's passing constitutes the ending of their own potentiality-for-being.[26]

Admittedly, the discussion of *Mitsein* and human solidarity in *Being and Time* is somewhat condensed—a fact that some interpreters have taken as evidence of Heidegger's merely passing or furtive interest in the topic. Whatever limited plausibility this claim may have had some decades ago, it can no longer be maintained in light of presently available texts, above all some lecture courses held in the immediate aftermath of the publication of *Being and Time* as well as some later writings. Most important among the former are Heidegger's lecture course on logic in Marburg (summer 1928) and the "Introduction to Philosophy" course in Freiburg (winter 1928–1929). In addition to analyzing the metaphysical premises of Leibniz's "monadology," the Marburg course offers an overview of some of the main arguments of the earlier study—an overview that, for study purposes, is summed up in a number of guiding theses (*Leitsätze*). Among the latter, one finds again the portrayal of *Dasein* as a being marked by care, a being that should by no means be conflated with "an egoistic uniqueness or an ontically isolated individual." Going somewhat beyond the earlier text, the course stresses the generic nature of *Dasein*: its "neutrality" vis-à-vis different forms of embodiment and sexuality—forms that, in a positive sense, testify to the multiplicity of modes of existence and even the "multiplicity of Being itself (*Mannigfaltigkeit gehört zum Sein selbst*)." Prominent among these forms of multiplicity is the diversity of concrete manifestations of co-being or solidarity. Moreover, as indicated earlier, *Mitsein* can happen in different modalities ranging from everydayness to authenticity. The special problem arising in authentic *Mitsein* is that *Dasein* here, despite being with others, must be genuinely free for its own potentiality. Hence, the issue is how *Dasein* as "essentially free" (for its potentiality) can exist in the freedom of solidarity—that is, "the freedom of a bonded being-with-others."[27]

The discussion of *Mitsein* in the first Freiburg lectures is vastly more extensive and detailed; for present purposes, a few comments must suffice. A central point is again the rejection of solipsism. In Heidegger's account, the modern infatuation with solipsism can be traced back to Descartes: "With the latter begins the entire malaise of modern philosophy since, in his treatment, the *ego* is so impoverished as to count hardly even as a subject: *Ego sum* in Descartes is a being without others." To be sure, being-with-others (*Miteinandersein*) does not mean a mere factual coexistence or concurrence; above all, it does not mean that "there is first an 'I' alone without the others and then, miraculously, others are added." In a section of the Freiburg course titled "Community as the Basis of Being-with-Others," Heidegger takes a stand against the entire modern "contractarian" conception of social and political life: "It is only on the basis of being-with-others that social community is possible; it is not the case that a collection of 'I's would be able to constitute this *Miteinander*." More sharply phrased: to find solidarity, "the ego does not need to break out of itself—it is already outside"; nor does it need "to break into the other" because it already exists as being-with-others. Thus, what happens when one *Dasein* meets another *Dasein* is that "it enters into the others' realm of openness, more precisely: their being-with (*Mitsein*) moves in the shared realm of openness (*Offenbarkeit*)." Another passage further underscores this noncontractual approach: "It is only because every *Dasein* is essentially *Mitsein* that something like a human community (*Gemeinschaft*) and society (*Gesellschaft*) is possible in varying degrees of authenticity and inauthenticity, stability and randomness."[28]

Relevant for present purposes among Heidegger's later writings are especially "Letter on Humanism" (1947) and the so-called Zollikon Seminars (published in 1987). As is well known, the letter takes a stand against a certain kind of "existentialism" that identifies human existence with an isolated subjectivity; against this conception (associated in part with Jean-Paul Sartre), the text marshals the openness of *Dasein* and its essential care for Being, epitomized now by the phrase "shepherd of Being." Deepening arguments in *Being and Time*, the letter denounces again the "dictatorship of publicity," meaning a shallow and spurious public opinion oriented toward the "institution and management of the openness of beings under the sway of an unconditional objectification of everything." As Heidegger significantly adds, the mere retreat from publicity into "private existence" does not yet amount to the recovery of "an essential, that is, free human self-being." Famously, the letter also polemicizes against spurious forms of collectivism, including nationalism and collective internationalism, stating: "Every nationalism is metaphysically an anthropologism, and as such subjectivism. Nationalism is not overcome through mere internationalism [globalization?] but rather [is] expanded and elevated into a global system." Differently put: being opposed to openness, every organized collectivism is Cartesian "subjectivity" writ large or totalized.[29]

In the Zollikon Seminars—seminars held between 1959 and 1969 in or near Zurich on an invitation from Medard Boss—Heidegger elaborates again on central themes in *Being and Time* (thereby implicitly rejecting interpretations of his so-called *Kehre* as a radical rupture or turning away). As he observes, a crucial theme of the earlier study was human *Dasein* construed as "a being that essentially cares about its being." In the same context, *Dasein* was also said to be marked by "an original being-with-others." This means that in caring for being "*Dasein* also cares always about the others"; hence, the portrayal of *Dasein* "has nothing whatever to do with solipsism or subjectivism." The seminars also criticize the notion of a self–other or I–Thou "relation" as misleading because it still seems to depart from a "primary isolated ego." For Heidegger, however, *Mitsein* does not arise on the basis of a "relation"; rather, the latter is the result of *Mitsein*. Putting a sharper edge to this point, the seminars observe that *Mitsein*, far from being a result or product, "means co-being, that is, a being-with-others in the mode of a shared being-in-the-world (*Miteinander-in-der-Welt-sein*)."[30]

Sharing (in) Freedom

What the preceding discussion reveals (or should reveal to a fair-minded reader) is the profound "timeliness" of Heidegger's writings, which have been shielded from view by their widespread marginal-

ization as either "untimely" or obnoxious or outlandish. This mar-
ginalization was basically the outcome of two kinds of "professional"
approaches: that of professional Heidegger experts and that of professional Heidegger "bashers." In the first case, Heidegger's work
became the province of a select academic coterie intent on preserving
their own privileged access while shielding the work from worldly
contamination; in the second case, that work was drowned in an ava-
lanche of polemical dismissals. Clearly, as long as these two types of
professionalism held sway, the real thrust of Heidegger's argument
had no chance of surfacing. It is only today—when "being-in-the-
world" reveals again its extreme fragility and vulnerability—that his
writings may reach new ears and reveal their timeliness, for, more
than ever, we are confronted today with forms of individual, sectarian, and nationalistic selfishness that threaten to throw our world
into disarray and possibly destructive chaos. More than ever, we are
facing propaganda celebrating a "freedom" identified entirely with
selfish arrogance and aggressive willfulness. Faced with this conception, critics often believe that the only remedy resides in a denial of
freedom and the resort to oppressive or nostalgic forms of collectivism. Heidegger's work shows that these options are neither attractive
nor persuasive nor exhaustive.

What is needed to grasp this point is the abandonment of the
"professional" approaches. In the case of the "bashers," this abandonment involves a thoroughgoing "deconstruction" of ossified ideological beliefs or worldviews. In large measure, the bashing has
tended to rely on a presumably superior ideological standpoint from
whose height Heidegger's views could readily be demolished but
whose cogency is by now shattered. By ensconcing themselves on
that allegedly higher platform, critics granted themselves dispensation from having to study and ponder the criticized texts. Among
the bankrupt ideological platforms is nineteenth- and twentieth-
century "liberalism" or "libertarianism" with its reliance on rugged individualism and aggressive self-assertion; whatever appeal it
may have had during a time of "cowboys and Indians," this outlook
is utterly obsolete in our closely interdependent world where some
people's rash actions can have deleterious effects on humankind as
a whole. Equally obsolete is the notion of national "sovereignty"
seen as absolute will to power—unless it serves as a defensive shield

against the strategic designs of imperial or hegemonic powers. Even on a global level, little or no support can be given to the idea of a universal political structure, except for limited peacekeeping purposes; whatever hope there may be for "universal peace" must be fostered through interactive engagement among peoples on the civil society level.[31] In all these dimensions, Heidegger's arguments against individual and collective solipsism as well as against power-hungry types of nationalism and internationalism—all based on stubborn forms of anthropocentrism and subjectivism ultimately deriving from Cartesian premises, which are no longer sustainable—prove their timely validity.

Regarding scholarly "experts," the task today is to rescue Heidegger's teachings from their entombment in ivory-tower treatises far removed from the concerns of ordinary human beings. For too long, Heideggerians have been content to talk only among themselves within carefully guarded sectarian confines. To be sure, the experts' attitude is not whimsical: it is predicated in part on normal scholarly reticence and more importantly on dangers presumably lurking beyond the ivory tower. Among these dangers, Heidegger's own political missteps certainly play a major role. However, on closer inspection and when seen in the broader context of his work, these missteps reveal themselves precisely as what Heidegger later saw them to be: forms of an "errancy" that can serve as a warning. On closer inspection again—to which these pages seek to contribute—his teachings not only are *not* compatible with but also stand in radical contrast to all the ideological tenets dear to National Socialists and fascists of any stripe—tenets such as racism, aggressive chauvinism, and totalitarian collectivism.[32] None of the ideas I have discussed in this chapter—notions such as *Mitsein* (being-with), *Sein-lassen* (letting-be), *Sicheinlassen* (mutual engagement), and *Freisein* (being-free)—fit in any shape into the customary vocabulary of fascism and chauvinism. They also do not fit readily into the vocabulary of laissez-faire liberalism, libertarianism, neoconservatism, or collectivism. Hence, anybody willing to take Heidegger's teachings seriously has to be ready to embark on open seas and to travel along uncharted paths—this means to shoulder a "new beginning."

The phrase *new beginning* is used here deliberately: Heidegger himself has frequently insisted on the need to begin anew or to venture a new start (*anderer Anfang*). To be sure, to begin anew does not mean a rupture with or simple dismissal of past ideas and events; rather, the point is to uncover and liberate the potential or promise slumbering in the past and thus to make room for untapped possibilities of life. As is well known, one of Heidegger's chief complaints about Western modernity was the sway of abstract "metaphysical" constructions that repressed or prevented any genuine "care for Being"—constructions that in due course have led to the technological "enframing" of human life. Instead of pondering the meaning of Being and of cultivating human being-in-the-world, modern metaphysics-cum-technology has unleashed the project of a total domination or subjugation of the world under geopolitical global auspices. As Heidegger wrote in 1946 in an essay devoted to some fragments of Anaximander, "Humanity is poised to pounce upon the entirety of the earth and its atmosphere, that is, to conquer the hidden pathways of nature in the form of natural forces and also to subjugate the paths of history to the plans and dictates of a global government." This strategy of conquest is a losing strategy in terms of human freedom and solicitude, for a humankind in the grip of global "security" and surveillance is no longer capable of understanding "what *is*, what the meaning of being and even of a thing is." When the totality of beings are an object of conquest and control, "the simplicity of Being is buried in utter oblivion."[33]

Awareness of this danger stirred in Heidegger an intense yearning for "another beginning." Perhaps because of the grim historical context, this yearning was most urgently expressed in some writings produced in the 1930s, especially *Beiträge* and *Besinnung*. As one should note, the new beginning is at no point presented as a "project," an agenda, a policy platform; on the contrary, it is precisely the absence of any project (realizable through will to power). As we read in *Beiträge*, "When the other beginning dawns, then it is sheltered as a great transformation—and all the more sheltered or hidden the greater the change." And a later passage adds that the "transition" or "crossing" (*Übergang*) to the new beginning occurs "and yet we do not know the direction of the crossing and when the truth of Being reveals its truth."[34] The unmanageable and unplanned character of the transition is further underscored and emphasized in *Besinnung*, where we read: "No success or failure should lure or frighten our thinking [about the crossing]; only whoever is capable of traversing again and again these reticent and prolonged pathways is fit to be an impending thinker (*künftiger Denker*). Neither calculation nor empty hope can guide the way of the crossing, but only a sustained inquiry . . . into what is 'to come' and remains open to the word of Being." A later passage there speaks of "the stillest crossing into the other beginning"—a crossing that, we are given to understand, hovers over an abyss separating two possibilities: one that unleashes humanity into the "gigantic machination" of a global will to power and one that conducts humanity into the "guardianship of the truth of Being."[35]

The notion of a thinking "to come" also brings into view the possibility of "another politics" and even of an impending democracy "to come." Although Heidegger himself did not elaborate extensively on this possibility, his work presents no obstacle to such an exploration. To some extent, Jacques Derrida sketched the contours of this vista with his idea of a "*democracie à venir*," but much more needs to be done. Clearly, a future democratic politics—seen under Heideggerian auspices—can no longer pay tribute to outmoded traditional ideologies or worldviews. As previously indicated, the legacy of self-centered liberalism, neoliberalism, and libertarianism is today completely defunct and decomposing—although in its state of decomposition it can still wreak havoc on society and the world. Equally defunct are the political agendas of totalizing collectivism and heavy-handed communitarianism. Whereas the former negates the dimensions of "being-with" and "letting-be," the latter expunges the experience of freedom connected with human openness toward the transcending quality of Being. What is missed in all prevalent ideologies is the nondomineering and nontechnological character of human being-in-the-world—a character that Heidegger in some later writings has portrayed as a "dwelling" enmeshed in the intricate web of heaven and earth, mortals and immortals. As presented in these writings, "dwelling" is not a useful instrument for commodious living but rather a distinct mode of being—in fact, a "poetic" mode of being (where "poetry" means openness to the call of Being in all its dimensions). Only by heeding this call can humankind ultimately preserve its humanity.[36]

3

The Promise of Democracy

Nonpossessive Freedom and Caring Solidarity

> Democracy is a mode of being . . . constituted by bitter experience.
> —Sheldon Wolin, "Fugitive Democracy"

I recently was invited to present a keynote address at a symposium titled "The Promise of Democracy."[1] I greatly appreciated the honor and privilege involved in this invitation. But I also felt somewhat uneasy because of the chosen theme or topic, which appears counterintuitive under contemporary circumstances. Where, one might ask, can one find today a promise of democracy or even the glimmer of a promise? Is politics—including democratic politics—not everywhere submerged in rampant power politics and the striving for parochial self-interest? Even in countries with established democratic traditions—especially Western countries—the notion of popular self-rule has been surrendered in large measure to the "iron law" of oligarchies represented by corporate and financial elites. Indeed, how can one speak of popular elections when candidates and politicians generally appear to be purchased and sustained by the highest bidders? When one turns from Europe and America to "less-developed" countries, one does occasionally find some embers of hope, but their glow can easily be extinguished by dictatorial or military fiat. Thus, for a while the world was stirred by news about an "Arab Spring" in the Near East; however, in the meantime, spring in many parts of that region has given way to the harsh winter of military intervention and factional mayhem.

Thus, even when looked at from the angle of hope, democracy appears like a fragile plant exposed to the winds of changing seasons and in desperate need of careful cultivation—which it rarely receives. Political theorist Sheldon Wolin correctly diagnosed this situation when he wrote an article on the fragile or "fugitive" character of democracy. As he remarked at that time, "Democracy is not about where the political is located but about how it is experienced. . . . [Hence] democracy needs to be reconceived as something other than a [mere] form of government: [namely] as a mode of being that is constituted by bitter experience, doomed to succeed only temporarily [and thus marked by extreme fragility]." But, he added, it is also "a recurrent possibility [or potentiality] as long as the meaning of the political survives."[2]

I want to take Wolin's comments as providing *one* of the cues (one of the *two* main cues) guiding my presentation here. That cue is the accent on the fragility—that is, on the fugitive, unfinished character of democracy, on democracy as a potentiality, as a regime constantly in the making, constantly to be renewed and reconstituted as a challenge or task. This point, I believe, is at the heart of what one means by the "promise of democracy" or democracy as a promise.[3] The second, closely related cue I borrow from such writers as John Dewey, Claude Lefort, and Mahatma Gandhi: that democracy is a *shared* task, a task that cannot be accomplished by one group or faction and that cannot be imposed unilaterally or hegemonically by one segment of the population on another. This is the meaning of the saying that "democracy cannot be owned."

Democracy as Open Potentiality

Let me elaborate somewhat on these two cues or features. I really believe that these two features are distinctive marks of modern democracy seen as a regime, marks that distinguish it from other regimes such as monarchy or aristocracy. Although, depending on the culture and traditions of a given society, democracy may come in different shapes and forms, in the absence of the mentioned marks one cannot (or should not) speak of a democratic regime. As it seems to me, the marks or features were not properly recognized by classical writers such as Plato and Aristotle or by most modern political thinkers until recently (with the possible exception of Machiavelli). One could say that with the emergence of modern democracy what happens is not just a quantitative change—from a regime ruled by one or several to a regime ruled by many or all—but a qualitative and even ontological transformation privileging potentiality over actuality, temporal flux over timeless stability, free innovation over static routines.

This is particularly evident in the first cue I mentioned. By contrast with monarchy and aristocracy, democracy is not marked by an essential stability or stable "essence." According to most classical authors, monarchy is characterized by an essential authority that ultimately is derived from or linked with divine transcendence.[4] In a similar way, one might say that aristocracy is the manifestation of a stable nobility. None of this can be said of democracy. This is also why many traditionalists (including some Christian conservatives and Islamic Salafists) regard democracy as ungodly and nihilistic. This judgment, of course, is predicated on the assumption that the divine (or noble) is by nature unchanging and transtemporal. Here it becomes obvious that the change to democracy involves a metaphysical or ontological change, which also touches on the meaning of God or the gods. Thus, in a way, the change is also theological (leading not necessarily to atheism but to Spinozism, "process theology," "negative theology," and the like).

Once the temporal (not transtemporal) character of democracy is taken into account, it becomes clear that democracy is chiefly a matter of action or praxis and not of pure theory or epistemology (or else it is theory arising out of practical experience). This, in my view, is the central contribution of John Dewey's pragmatism. From his angle, democracy is not a comfortable reclining chair in which one can rest or slumber, but an ongoing challenge requiring vigilant action. Differently put, democracy is more a *potentiality* than an actuality. As Dewey wrote in 1939 on the eve of World War II, "Belief in the 'common man' is a familiar article of the democratic creed. That belief is without basis and significance save as it means faith in the *potentialities* of human nature as that nature is exhibited in every human being. . . . This faith may be enacted in statutes, but it is only on paper unless it is put in force in the attitudes which human beings display to one another in all the incidents and relations of daily life."[5]

Looking at the issue from a slightly different angle, one might say that democracy is basically a *verb* and not a noun. Thus, we cannot *have* a democracy but only participate in the ongoing process of democratization. Dewey is famous for having stressed the priority of verbs over nouns. Take the example of the term *mind* (a derivative of the Cartesian term *cogito*). Dewey relentlessly opposed the so-called philosophy of mind, arguing that there is no mind, but only the activity of "minding" (like minding one's business). Ernesto Laclau, in a Deweyan spirit, has written about the need of "minding the gap"—although he conceived the "gap," in a non-Deweyan fashion, as a radical rupture or cleavage.[6] (I return to this point later.)

Dewey was not the only thinker privileging the verb over the noun. The same can be said, a fortiori, of Martin Heidegger. For Heidegger, *Dasein* is not a stable essence (certainly not an "animal with reason," or *zoon logon echon*), but a creature constantly searching for the meaning of Being and above all for the meaning or point of its own being and thus catapulted in the direction of its potentialities or possibilities. Heidegger is notorious for his unorthodox verbalization of concepts. Clearly, his notion of "Being" does not denote a stable essence or a logical concept, but an enabling potency constantly in need of enactment and reinterpretation. Famous are his expressions "language languages or speaks" (*die Sprache spricht*), the "world worlds" (*die Welt weltet*), and the "nothing nothings" (*das Nichts nichtet*). Closely related to these phrases is "Being beings" (*das Sein ist* or *west,* in a transitive sense). Small wonder that Heidegger placed great emphasis not only on *potentiality* but also on *praxis* (the latter seen not as an antithesis to theory or "thinking" but as a premise undergirding the theory–practice distinction). Well known are the opening lines of the "Letter on Humanism," which read: "We are still far from pondering the nature of action decisively enough." Readers familiar with the letter are bound to be also acquainted with the subsequent lines, where Heidegger states, "We know action only as something causing an effect, with the actuality of the effect being valued according to its utility." What Heidegger here targets is the predominant "action theory" according to which action is a means to accomplish an ulterior end or product—a theory blown out of the water by the following statements: "But the [real] nature of action is fulfillment (*Vollbringen*). To accomplish or fulfill means: to unfold something into the fullness of its being."[7]

Unfortunately, for many readers, these few lines—quite enigmatic in their terseness—exhaust the topic of praxis in Heidegger's thought. As it happens, however, Heidegger on other occasions has elaborated at greater length on the topic—in a manner that clarifies the letter's comments. One such occasion is a lecture course of 1928–1929 titled "Introduction to Philosophy" (mentioned in chapter 2). A crucial topic discussed there is precisely praxis or action. Relying on the teaching of Aristotle—to be sure, a very unorthodox and nonmetaphysical Aristotle—Heidegger stresses that praxis is by no means a tool or instrument for some ulterior goal or product but rather carries its value or quality in itself. In Aristotle's language, praxis is autonomous and self-fulfilling (*autarkes* and *autoteles*); it is a doing that "reaches its end or fulfillment in itself" and, in this manner, also fulfills "the being" of the agent. Heidegger, in this context, introduces the important notion of what he calls "primordial praxis" (*Urhandlung*): namely, "letting-be" (*Sein-lassen*). This letting-be, he says, "allows all beings to become manifest [or fulfilled] in their truth." Such praxis, one needs to add, occurs before or beyond the theory/practice bifurcation; it also occurs before the traditional subject/object split. "Letting-be" is not a subject-centered, goal-directed action with the agent unilaterally in the driver's seat, nor is it a purely passively endured fate. "Letting" here does not mean a coercive or paternalistic intervention, nor does it signify a retreat into solipsistic indifference. Thus, "letting-be" preserves the other's integrity, dignity, and freedom while also stressing the agent's nondomineering engagement with otherness. Shunning both the impulse of domination and the fate of being dominated, "primordial praxis" emerges as a crucial cornerstone of democracy (contradicting Heidegger's non- or antidemocratic reputation).[8]

To some extent, the difference between genuine praxis and instrumental action is preserved in Hannah Arendt's writings, especially in her distinction between "action" and "work," between *vita activa* and *homo faber*. Going beyond Heidegger, Arendt strongly insisted on the context in which political praxis occurs, a context she termed the "public realm" (a domain Heidegger tended to view mostly critically as a media-manipulated "publicity," or *Öffentlich-keit*). Unfortunately, as it seems to me, this desirable addition to Heidegger's argument is offset by some problematical aspects of Arendt's discussion of the *vita activa*, especially by a lapse into a certain existentialist and subjectivist pathos (perhaps deriving from her affinity with Karl Jaspers as well as from her general distance from Aristotle). This pathos is evident in her accent on the individual self-display or self-revealment of the agent performing in the public space. As she says, "In acting and speaking, men show who they are, reveal actively their unique personal identities and thus make their appearance in the human world." This aspect is further underscored when she describes her conception of action as "highly individualistic"—which, to me, signals an unfortunate departure from Dewey's notion of interaction and from Heidegger's view of interbeing or "co-being" (*Mitsein*). The problem is intensified when Arendt describes the essence of public action as residing not in the praxis itself (*autoteles*) but in the attainment of an extrinsic or higher goal: that of the public agent's personal "greatness" and "immortality."[9] Here, clearly, Aristotle's and Heidegger's notion of praxis is left far behind.

In a different register, Heidegger's legacy has been preserved and continued in the work of Jacques Derrida (which may have something to do with their shared roots in Husserlian phenomenology). Clearly, Derrida shares Heidegger's accent on temporal being and his privileging of potentiality or possibility over actuality. In an emphatic manner, this privileging is evident in Derrida's notion of "democracy to come" (*à venir*). This is certainly a notion that, in my view, any contemporary theory of democracy has to take seriously as an intellectual stimulus or challenge. What happens in Derrida's work, however, is that the accent on potentiality is so radicalized that the interconnection between temporalities (which both Husserl and Heidegger had always maintained) is for all practical purposes sundered, with the result that the arrival of the future appears almost like an apocalyptic event. This aspect is evident in the pervasive emphasis on "rupture" (*rupture*), disjuncture, and disruption; it is also present in the accent on *im*possibility in such phrases as "impossible possibility" or the "impossible advent" of the future. What happens in such phrases is that advent or "event" of the future is transcendentalized (or placed beyond human reach), while the aspect of human praxis or agency is minimalized or sidelined. (By the way, I would add that this construal of "event" as disruption—prevalent in much of contemporary French philosophy—nearly reverses the Heideggerian notion of *Ereignis*).[10]

On this point, I tend to agree with political theorist Romand Coles when he notes "a certain one-sidedness in many of Derrida's discussions." Although sensitive to the transcending qualities of potency, Coles finds in Derrida an "overemphasis" on rupture and discontinuity that—despite certain "strategic uses"—"courts the danger he seeks to resist, namely, that deconstruction might become an 'abstract and dogmatic eschatology in the face of the world's evil.'"[11] I also concur with my friend Stephen White when he states in *Political Theory and Postmodernism* that "an *over*emphasis on disruption and impertinence creates for postmodern thinking a momentum that threatens to enervate the sense of responsibility to otherness" (which postmodernism often seeks to foster).[12]

Democracy as a Shared Endeavor

So far I have dwelled mainly on the first distinguishing feature of modern democracy: its temporal, nonpermanent, fragile, or fugitive character that renders its promotion a constant challenge or task. I would like now to turn to its second feature: the fact that it cannot be "owned" by anyone, which renders it a "shared" task (with all the difficulties involved in sharing). To some extent, one can say that monarchy and aristocracy were owned by and embodied in an identifiable king or nobility. Louis XIV's well-known phrase comes to mind: "L'etat c'est moi" (I am the state). No one can say this in a democracy. The thinker who has articulated this feature perhaps with the greatest perspicacity is philosopher Claude Lefort (friend of the phenomenologist Maurice Merleau-Ponty). Famous is his statement that "of all the regimes we know, [modern democracy] is the only one to have represented [supreme] power in such a way as to show that power is an *empty place* and to have maintained a gap between the symbolic [or foundational/constitutive] and the real."[13] What this means is that in democracy nobody can claim to be the definitive or "essential" embodiment of the regime and that, hence, the democratic "polity" (as a regime) always exceeds the confines of actual, concretely ongoing "politics."

For me, Lefort's formulation is crucial and needs to be kept in mind. However, once again one needs to guard here against a certain "hypermodernism" (my term)—that is, a tendency to erect the distinction between *politics* and *polity* into a stark antinomy between presence and absence, reality and fiction. The term *empty space* cannot possibly mean an absolute vacuum or nonbeing. One is reminded here of the Buddhist notion of emptiness (*sunyata*), which is far from being a mere deficiency. One should also recall Heidegger's comments on nothingness (*das Nichts*) in "What Is Metaphysics?" Nothingness is "neither the annihilation of beings nor does it spring from a [mere] negation. . . . [Rather] the essence of the originally nihilating nothing lies in this, that it brings human *Dasein* for the first time before beings as such."[14] Hence, what slumbers in emptiness or nothingness is a peculiar kind of potency—an enabling kind of potency that allows human beings to "care" genuinely about Being(s). Transferring this insight to modern democracy, one might say that the relation between democratic "polity" (as a shared or holistic regime) and actual politics is not just a rupture, an abyss, or a gap, but that the former remains the (perhaps obscure) horizon or condition of possibility of the latter. In Rousseauian terminology, one might say that the *volonté générale* remains the elusive but always presupposed horizon of what the *volonté de tous* or any particular *volonté* or political faction might envisage. (In Hegel's terminology, this involves the "sublation" of particularity into *Sittlichkeit*.)

This point is at the heart of a certain disagreement I have had with Ernesto Laclau and, to a lesser extent, with political theorist Chantal Mouffe. In Laclau's writings (as mentioned earlier), the distinction pinpointed by Lefort tends to be treated as a stark dichotomy or "gap": the gap between observable politics and nonobservable emptiness or between presence and absence, activity and passivity. This view leads Laclau to the conception of democracy as exhibiting a permanent "antagonism": the struggle between dominant or "hegemonic" forces and dominated or antihegemonic forces that can never share a democratic ethos. This view is particularly articulated in the well-known book *Hegemony and Socialist Strategy* (1985), coauthored by Laclau and Mouffe. As the authors write there, antagonism or agonistic struggle means that in a democracy no faction or set of rulers can erect itself into a stable or permanent regime and that "hegemony"—even when achieved—can never be solidified into a closed, fully integrated system. As a result of the ineradicable flux or fluidity, democratic society can never attain "the status of transparency, of full presence," so that an "impossible relation" between presence and absence must be seen as "constitutive of the social [and the political] itself."[15] (Note here again the stress on "impossibility" mentioned in the case of Derrida.)

My attitude toward this perspective—often called "agonistic democracy"—is bound to be ambivalent: that is, neither purely critical nor fully supportive. What I value and endorse here is the emphasis on the impermanent and constantly shifting feature of the democratic regime, on what I have previously called its fragile or "fugitive" character. As Laclau and Mouffe correctly state, democracy does not have a finished "essence," nor can it be stably owned or possessed by a set of rulers. Although I appreciate this aspect, I depart from Laclau and Mouffe (especially from Laclau) for a number of reasons that are in part philosophical and in part practical and political in nature. On a philosophical level, I am chagrined by the exclusive emphasis on particularity or the agonistic struggle between particularities, seemingly for its own sake and without civil or ethical bonds. As Hegel and many others have shown, particularity cannot even be conceived without reference to a shared frame of reference in terms of which it is "particular." Where this framework of significance is removed, particularity lapses into a stubborn self-enclosure (an essentialism of the particular)—which, in political life, can generate a nasty and potentially aggressive kind of "identity politics" (which is in no way an improvement over a collective or nationalistic identity politics). Still philosophically speaking, the exit from a static essentialism of the whole cannot be found in a rigid antiessentialism, which only disguises an essential particularity. Using the terminology of positivity versus negativity or presence versus absence, one can say that the shared framework may not be positively present, but it is also not simply "nothing"; it is present/absent or present in its absence. (In Heideggerian vocabulary, its status is not "ontic" but "ontological.")[16]

These considerations may be somewhat distant from democratic politics as we commonly know it, so let me turn to the more practical side. I agree that democratic politics involves to a large extent a struggle or agon between competing groups and perspectives. But the question is: What kind of agon is a *democratic* struggle, and what are its limits? Are there any guideposts or civil-ethical rules of the game? As it seems to me, democratic struggle can derail mainly in *two ways,* both of them destructive of democracy (in the short or long run). The first is the decline of antagonism into "monologues," ideologically frozen and incompatible standpoints. In this case, each party speaks only to its devotees (or "preaches to the choir"). Each side or all sides denounce the idea of a common language as an illusion or a deceptive "essentialism"; the respective positions are seen as mutually "incommensurable." This is the situation—for me a deplorable one—in many societies today. It was the situation in the final stages of Yugoslavia before the breakup and eruption of civil war. It is today the situation undergirding the conflict between secularists and "religionists" in France, Turkey, and many other countries; between ethnic or linguistic factions in Belgium and Spain; between moderate Muslims and Salafists in many parts of the Middle East. To a large extent, the condition of ideological incommensurability also prevails today in the United States between progressive Democrats and antistate Tea Party extremists. In the United States, the division is reinforced by the gulf between the 1 percent and the 99 percent, between Wall Street and Main Street. What usually goes out the window in such situations is public discourse and public civility, with abusive speech and hate speech becoming increasingly prevalent and acceptable. If this situation persists or is allowed to deteriorate, we are on the verge of civil war and thus on the threshold of rampant violence outside the bonds of democracy.

This leads me to the second and most dangerous derailment of antagonism: the slide into violent confrontation. As we recall, Hitler wrote a book, *Mein Kampf,* where the term *struggle* was a synonym not for competition or a striving for excellence but for a violent assault on the regime and all competing forces in society. Hitler's seizure of power is often called a "reactionary revolution." But most revolutions tend to be violent (and monological) in large measure—including the Russian Revolution of 1917 (which left some five million dead Kulaks in its wake). Because of their descent into monologue, revolutions and violent rebellions are rarely good preparations for democracy. As mentioned earlier, a sad example in our present time is the fate of the so-called Arab Spring, which had a promising start in Tunisia and to some extent in Egypt but then plunged into (externally supported) violence in Libya and finally ended in a paroxysm of bloodshed in Syria and elsewhere. For all practical purposes, the "promise of democracy" is extinguished in many Arab lands (due in part again to foreign intervention and to the fanatical extremism and particularism of jihadism and Wahhabism).

The experiences of recent years provide valuable lessons for progressive democrats. One lesson is the need to be extremely cautious about violence (except as a *last* resort). As Hannah Arendt correctly stated, "The practice of violence, like all action, changes the world, but the most probable change is to a more violent world."[17] Basically, violence is not a good path to reach democracy, especially a pluralist democracy that demands respect for and recognition of "others." Moreover, in our time, violence is also counterproductive—apart from being often self-destructive. In a time of "terror wars," even minor disturbances or challenges—perhaps merely suspected challenges to the globally hegemonic power—may lead to extermination through assassination or drone strikes. In such a situation, progressive democrats need to be sober and try to employ what Buddhists call "skillful means"—that is, means that do not instantly invite annihilation under national "security" or "friend–enemy" auspices.

Skillful means, in this context, are means that seek to foster democracy democratically—that is, in a way that fully respects the diversity and pluralism of modern democracy (without lapsing into identity politics). In other words, skillful means are means that, although acknowledging individual and group differences, bypass the lure of "incommensurability" by remaining attentive to the "promise of democracy"—that is, the "impossible" possibility of a shared horizon or *volonté générale*. Such means are bound to be "suasive" (that is, commensurable in some sense). A well-known suasive or persuasive model in our time is "deliberative democracy," sponsored by such thinkers as John Rawls, Jürgen Habermas, and their many followers. My attitude here is again ambivalent: I find this model attractive in some contexts but quite limiting and insufficient in many respects. Obviously, in order to be suasive, democratic politics has to resort often to sound rational argumentation and deliberation. The limit emerges when—as in the case of some Habermasians—suasion is reduced to rational arguments about "validity claims." Not many people—outside secular intellectual circles—are adept at such argumentation or comfortable in expressing their views in such a manner. Many voices are liable to be excluded— for instance, religious voices and artistic voices (which encompass what Michael Oakeshott called "the voice of poetry").[18] Moreover, the insistence that argument proceeds in an established rational discourse neglects the fact that in a "fugitive" democracy the character of the language game itself is necessarily open to innovation and transformation. This means that the character of public discourse— its terminology and central concepts—is liable to constant negotiation and modification. This also means that modes of language philosophy usually shunned by discourse analysts—modes deriving from Vico, Hamann, Herder, and Heidegger—must be given broader room in democratic interactions and discussions about democracy.

Toward a Caring Solidarity

It would be a mistake to view this broadening of language as a concession or surrender to anti-intellectualism or obscurantism. Surely, reason or rather "reasoning" (as a verb) is always desirable in public deliberations. Yet the one-sided stress on rationality among discourse analysts has two main drawbacks: the sidelining of praxis or practical engagement and the sidelining of embodied feeling or affect. The kind of public life I favor—in the sense of a promised democracy—is a democracy sustained, first of all, by praxis or practical-ethical engagement. The notion of praxis invoked here— as indicated earlier—is one that stretches from Aristotle to Dewey and Heidegger as well as to Hans-Georg Gadamer. What is common to these authors is the view that ethics is first of all a matter of "doing" rather than mere "knowing."[19] The primacy of knowing is what Dewey targeted in his attack on abstract "intellectualism," an attack taken up by Heidegger in his critique of traditional metaphysics (especially the metaphysics undergirding modern technology). By center-staging practical-ethical engagement in democracy, I do not mean to support any coercive moralism or "moral majoritarianism," where a ruling elite foists its set of moral norms on the rest of society. Simply put, the ethics I have in mind is not rule centered but praxis or experience centered in the sense that "what is the right thing to do" emerges in ongoing democratic practices with a constant renegotiation of the terms of engagement.

The other deficit of rational discourse, as mentioned earlier, is the shortfall of embodied affect or motivating sensation. In this context, it is always good to remember the words of Mahatma Gandhi, the great *karmayogin,* who repeatedly stated that if one wants to reach or persuade people, the appeal should be not only to the head but also to the heart: "The appeal of reason is more to the head, but the penetration of the heart comes from suffering; it opens up the inner understanding of men."[20] As this quote indicates, the reference here is not to a shallow emotionalism but rather to a difficult cultivation or seasoning of the heart, to a humanizing pathos or passion/compassion, which is not far from the "bitter experiences" that, for Sheldon Wolin, undergird the fragile or fugitive character of democracy. Perhaps to avoid the connotations of moralism and sentimentalism, I can invoke the Heideggerian terms *care* and *solicitude.*[21] A practical-ethical democracy in my sense would be a "caring democracy," where people care or are solicitous about each other—a place where people rejoice in the joys of others and are saddened by the sufferings of others and seek to remove or at least to mitigate the sources of suffering. It would also be a "careful" setting where the praxis of "letting-be" would promote the others' freedom and integrity in an active way without resorting to unilateral management or manipulation.

Such a democracy is in no way a presently existing or actual democracy. It is a "promised" democracy, but it is by no means an empty pipedream. It is a "zetetic" or searching democracy: a democracy in search of itself, where people are in search of their better or best potential. Differently put: people there are "in search of the good life."[22] This good life (or the "common good") cannot be defined or imposed with finality because doing so would be an act of hegemonic coercion. But neither is it a pure vacuity. It is something that beckons or calls—persistently; it is the call of truth and justice. Gandhi had a word for it: *satyagraha,* the "doing of truth" ("truth" meant not epistemologically, but as a way of being). Other translations are "truth force" or "love force." This means it is a truth arising from passion, from suffering. Nietzsche says, "Weh spricht vergeh!" (Suffering says: stop, go away!).[23] In Gandhi's thought, *satyagraha* is closely linked with *ahimsa*, nonviolence. Suffering cannot be stopped through the imposition of more suffering through violence. *Ahimsa* here does not just mean "no violence," but an effort to overcome and heal suffering. Only goodness and genuine compassion can heal. The wounds of our present world cry out for healing; "Weh spricht vergeh!" This is the ultimate sense of what I call "the promise of democracy."

4

Markets and Democracy

Beyond Neoliberalism

> Democracy . . . does require that citizens share in a
> common life.
> —Michael J. Sandel, *What Money Can't Buy*

"We live at a time when almost everything can be bought and sold."
This line stands at the opening of a recent book by Harvard political philosopher Michael J. Sandel titled *What Money Can't Buy:
The Moral Limits of Markets*. The book gives examples of the staggering venality in the present world: for $82 one can upgrade one's
prison cell in California; for $6,250 one can buy the services of an
Indian surrogate mother; for $150,000 one can shoot an endan-
gered black rhino in South Africa; for varying amounts of money
one can gain admission to a prestigious university in Western
countries. These examples—which can easily be multiplied—
point for Sandel to the daunting facts that market economics has
become an "imperial" or totalizing ideology and that, despite set-
backs and financial catastrophes, the lure of "market triumphalism" continues. "The spectacular failure of financial markets [in
2008–2009]," he writes, "did little to dampen the faith in markets
generally. In fact, the financial crisis discredited governments
more than the banks." Thus, something strange and paradoxical has happened: although it threw the United States and much
of the global economy "into the worst economic downturn since
the Great Depression" and left millions of people out of work, the

crisis did not in a genuine sense prompt "a fundamental rethinking of markets" and their role in society.[1]

For Sandel, it is not sufficient to ascribe the financial crisis to the individual greed of bankers and corporate leaders—although greed certainly played a role. Rather, the issue is deeper and involves moral and even metaphysical or ontological dimensions, for what is at stake is the place of economics in society and in human life generally. As he points out, market triumphalism has two grievous consequences: the sharpening of inequality and the spread of existential corruption. "Not only has the gap between the rich and poor widened," he says, but also "the commodification of everything has sharpened the sting of inequality by making money matter more." This aspect affects the second consequence: "Some of the good things in life are corrupted or degraded if turned into commodities"; hence, we are drifting "from *having* a market economy to *being* a market society."[2] Clearly, this shift from "having" to "being" is not just a financial matter but conjures up profound existential or ontological issues—issues that professional economists are not likely to discuss.

At a closer look, the shift was not a sudden event but the culmination of a longer historical trajectory. The eminent historian of economics Karl Polanyi has described the change as "the great transformation," a process whereby market economics (more precisely, laissez-faire economics) has progressively elbowed aside all other dimensions of social life and finally established itself as total master. For Polanyi, what has happened in modernity is the steady "disembedding" of market economics from all surrounding contexts—especially social and political contexts—and the relentless transformation of real goods, such as land and labor, into "fictitious commodities"—fictitious because they were not originally produced to be sold on a market.[3] The basic victims of this disembedding commodification, he notes, are social and political life and, above all, democracy.

In this chapter, I first give a brief overview of economics from a stage of embeddedness to later stages where contexts progressively atrophied, finally leaving the market in "imperial" isolation. In a second step, I ponder some recent proposals for a reintegration of economics into a holistic perspective in order finally to turn to a discussion of what Sandel calls the "moral limits of markets" and their significance for the maintenance of democracy.

Economics: A Dismal Science?

Economics is sometimes called a "dismal" science or discipline, not without justification. It is dismal or disjointed because of the conflict of constitutive elements: deliberate or intentional human action is correlated with unintentional quasi-universal regularities. To this extent, economics shares with political science its paradoxical in-between status: between what are called the "humanities," on the one hand, and natural science and mathematics, on the other. Crudely speaking, one might say the location is between inside and outside, between the internal and the external worlds. The location was not conflicted or paradoxical as long as both worlds were still linked together in a comprehensive orientation toward "goodness" (as telos). In this scheme, economic activity still had an intelligible role to play—just as did ethics and politics (as well as metaphysics). This balanced correlation of roles still prevailed in Aristotle's philosophy—where *oikos* and *polis* were differentiated but not in a conflictual or mutually exclusive way (and both were "embedded" in a general teleology). This balanced correlation persisted in the Roman period and well into the era of the (Western) Middle Ages. According to leading scholastic thinkers, economic activity performed in the *oikos* made a necessary contribution to both the subsistence and the ethical well-being of society as well as of the religious community.[4]

This harmonious legacy came to a distinct halt with the onset of Western modernity, especially with the Cartesian split between the inner and outer worlds, between the cogito and the "extended matter" in space. At the same time, the rise of modern science— inaugurated by Francis Bacon—objectified "nature" into a target of scientific inquiry, thereby expelling it from the status of a comprehensive metaphysical matrix. To be sure, the effect of this split was not immediately felt, and its practical implications emerged only over a longer period of time. This fact is clearly evident in the birth of the modern discipline of economics during the eighteenth century. The "founder" of the discipline, Adam Smith (1723–1790), was still steeped in the older "embedded" paradigm in many ways, although he sought to make greater room for individual freedom and initiative in social life. In this respect, his outlook was representative of the so-called Scottish Enlightenment, which included among its proponents such illustrious figures as the Earl of Shaftesbury, Francis Hutcheson, Thomas Reid, and David Hume. Although acknowledging the role of self-interest in human conduct, the Scottish thinkers saw self-interest counterbalanced or circumscribed by a "moral sense" nurtured by prevailing social contexts. Smith himself was a student of Hutcheson and a friend of David Hume. With Hutcheson he studied moral philosophy at the University of Glasgow and later succeeded him in that chair. His first major work was not about economics but about ethics, titled *The Theory of Moral Sentiments* (1759), where he pinpointed the core of moral sentiment in the capacity for interhuman "sympathy."[5]

In center-staging the notion of sympathy, *The Theory of Moral Sentiments* clearly wanted to correlate or keep in balance individual purposive conduct and broader societal relations—that is, the "inner" and "outer" dimensions of human life. The book antedated by almost twenty years the publication of *The Wealth of Nations* (1776), through which Adam Smith gained worldwide fame. Although mostly identified with the later work, the author himself apparently regarded the ethical text as in many ways superior.[6] Whatever the relation between the two works may have been, it seems hardly justifiable to view them as divided by a stark contrast. What is true is that following the ethical work Smith undertook extensive travels in Europe, especially in France, where he encountered the so-called Physiocratic School (led by François Quesnay), which placed a major emphasis on large-scale economic processes. One of the main teachings of the Physiocrats was that, quite independently of individual (moral or immoral) conduct, large-scale processes turn out for the best, as if guided by a "hidden hand' (their motto was "*Laissez faire, laissez passer; le monde va de lui-même*"). The encounter with these teachings quite likely triggered a certain shift in Smith's interest from the individual ("micro") to the societal ("macro") level of analysis—but never to the point of a complete divorce. Although occasionally adopting the notion of the "hidden hand," Smith never wavered in locating the real "wealth of nations" not in mysterious processes but in productive human labor—a point in which he basically agreed with John Locke (as well as the much later teachings of Karl Marx).

As is well known, Smith's work has become a highly contested legacy and, in fact, has spawned ambitious, even totalizing ideologies. Basically, the contest is between those who view the work as offering a balance between the microlevel and the macrolevel anchored in human labor and those who center-stage macroprocesses and the effects of the "hidden hand." In the latter case, economic growth is attributed not to labor but to capital and capital accumulation; seen in this light, Smith emerges as the iconic defender of "pure"—that is, decontextualized and unregulated—capitalism. The high point of the latter trajectory was reached in "neoclassical" economics as represented first by the so-called Austrian School and later by members of the Chicago School. In terms of the character of economics as a discipline, the same trajectory led to a progressive removal of economics from the ambit of the humanities and moral theory and its merger with mathematics and natural-science methodology. What defenders of "neoclassical" (or neoliberal) economics conveniently forget are Smith's critique of monopolies and the collusive nature of business interests as well as statements in *The Wealth of Nations* such as "Wherever there is great property, there is great inequality" and "Every tax is to the person who pays it, a badge not of slavery but of liberty."[7] Against the overblown claims of neoliberal triumphalism, it is good to remember these lines by linguistic philosopher Noam Chomsky: "Smith was 'pre-capitalist,' a figure of the [Scottish] Enlightenment. . . . Everybody reads the first paragraph of *The Wealth of Nations* where he talks about how wonderful the division of labor is. But not many people get to the point hundreds of pages later, where he says that division of labor will destroy human beings and turn people into creatures as stupid and ignorant as it is possible for a human being to be."[8]

The downhill slide of modern economics from the height of the Scottish Enlightenment to the celebration of profit seeking and capital accumulation was started by offshoots of the Physiocratic School and later continued by "doctrinaire" French liberals in the nineteenth century. In the works of doctrinaire thinkers (such as François Guizot), individual profit seeking—identified with economic "freedom"—was increasingly separated from social and political domains as well as from historical and cultural underpinnings. According to the dominant liberal conception of the "night watchman state"—"the state that governs least governs best"—politics and political institutions were reduced to a marginal and negligible appendix of private-property relations. To be sure, the slide into economic triumphalism was not unopposed during the nineteenth century. Resistance arose in many quarters—from the anticapitalist ideas of socialism and Marxism to the more nuanced pleas in defense of historical and cultural institutions. What united the diverse strands of resistance was the conviction of the dehumanizing and ultimately socially destructive effects of "laissez-faire" liberalism (or libertarianism). Although politically influential in some quarters, none of the resistance movements managed to stop the seemingly inexorable drift of economics as a discipline into amoral self-containment (and ultimately "econometrics"). This drift was greatly accelerated and exacerbated in the twentieth century by the rise of the Austrian School of economics, led by such luminaries as Ludwig von Mises (1881–1979) and Friedrich Hayek (1899–1992).

Angus Sibley has admirably dissected the character of the Austrian School in his book *The "Poisoned Spring" of Economic Libertarianism* (2011). A native of Scotland and trained in the Scottish tradition, Sibley rightly points out that Adam Smith was "in the first place a moral philosopher" and that his ethical and economic writings ultimately aimed to constitute "a greater, very ambitious synthesis" (which was never completed).[9] In Sibley's view, the attempted synthesis later fell apart into its "*disjecta membra*," pitting "private" against "public," individual against society, selfish interest against the common good. A crucial pacemaker in this direction—though not the only or last one—was the Austrian School, initially inaugurated by Carl Menger (1840–1921) in the so-called dispute over method (*Methodenstreit*) whereby economics as a discipline was purged of historical and cultural connotations and founded solely on rational self-interest. For Menger, the value of a good is by no means determined by the labor cost involved in its production but rather by the buyer of the good, whose "best price" is the lowest or whose price is formed at the "margin" (a view that gave rise to the "marginal theory of value"). As can be seen, this approach was entirely slanted in the direction of buyers or people with economic means, while the well-being of workers or producers was slighted or treated as negligible. In Menger's own words, "Neither the means of subsistence nor the minimum subsistence of a laborer can be the direct cause or determining principle of the price of labor services."[10]

Ludwig von Mises vigorously continued and reinforced this pro-capital or pro-business slant. Following in Menger's footsteps, Mises strove to purge economics of any historical, cultural, or ethical traces. In line with the Cartesian inside/outside split, he insisted that economic theory has to be an a priori science proceeding by way of deduction from basic axioms or principles; to this extent, economics was like logic or mathematics—although the kinship was tempered by the reliance of economics on human purposive activity, that is, activity geared toward maximum utility at minimal cost. For Mises, to achieve this maximum utility the economic activity has to be designed and engineered by the autonomous agent (or ego) completely unhampered by external cultural, ethical, or political contexts. As he stated in *Human Action,* in days long past "social problems were considered ethical problems"; the development of modern economics "overthrew this opinion." The kind of "values" he was willing to consider are purely instrumental values designed to facilitate private goals; otherwise, economics is neutral or "value free." The same neutrality was also said to extend to the consequences of economic activity, such as social inequality and the spreading of poverty (immiseration): "The inequality of incomes and wealth is an inherent characteristic of the market economy. Its elimination would totally destroy the market economy." On this point, Mises did not hesitate to wax fervent as champion of the (market) faith, declaring that socialism or any form of "*Gemeinwirtschaft*" is "the spoiler of what thousands of years of civilization have created."[11]

In this fervor for market liberalism, Mises was ably seconded and even outdone by Friedrich Hayek, his foremost economic student in Vienna. Following the lead of Isaiah Berlin, Hayek defined economic freedom entirely as "negative liberty"—that is, the absence of external constraints on one's conduct. As he writes in *The Constitution of Liberty,* economic freedom means "the state in which a man is not subject to arbitrary coercion by the will of another or others" (although he may be subject to his own arbitrary will). Like all neoclassical economists, Hayek recognized, of course, that "free" economic activity is always exercised in the context of the "market"—that is, in a network of interlocking activities. However, as long as this network operates in an autonomous, quasi-mechanical fashion—in accordance with the motto "*laissez-faire, laissez-passer*"— economic liberty is not jeopardized (something that could happen only in case of human, especially political, intervention). In line with Mises, Hayek insisted that the market, operating autonomously, is neutral or indifferent vis-à-vis substantive ethical or political goals. In modern economics, he writes, "common concrete ends are replaced by common abstract rules. Government is needed only to enforce these abstract rules [especially private property], and thereby to protect the individual against coercion, or invasion of his free space, by others." For Hayek, where this basic principle is ignored or sidestepped, society is on "the road to serfdom" (never mind the fact that governments may try to lift people from the serfdom of poverty). Going even beyond Mises, Hayek launched an all-out assault on "the mirage of social justice," denouncing the latter as "an empty phrase with no determinable meaning."[12]

In his review of neoliberal (or libertarian) ideas, Angus Sibley has little difficulty in pointing out some gross misconceptions and intellectual fallacies. One of the most obvious defects of neoliberal economics is the complete absence of balance: "Too often it calls for utmost freedom for the entrepreneur, best possible value for the consumer [or buyer], maximum return for the investor, keenest possible competition, minimum public spending," while totally neglecting the effects on other parts of society. Central to the theory is the lopsided and impoverished conception of human freedom. By contrast to older conceptions viewing freedom as "a positive quality" achieved through the pursuit of goodness, justice, and the respect for sound public laws, neoliberalism deprives freedom of any ethical moorings, construing it as a purely "negative quality"—namely, the "absence of constraints imposed by other people" (though not constraints imposed by the market). Closely connected with this construal is the accent on an "exaggerated individualism" depicting individuals as "self-sufficient" agents completely severed from bonds of interdependence and solidarity. If these features are connected with such ancillary ideas as the conception of human labor as "disutility" and the value neutrality of injustice, one arrives at the overarching doctrine that has dominated economics in recent times—and that has rightly been described as "market triumphalism" or the "idolatry of the market." It is this doctrine, Sibley concludes, that provides "the basis for the financial deregulation that has allowed greedy, reckless, overcompetitive bankers to ruin their banks and their customers, and even to gravely damage the whole world economy."[13]

Prominent Economic Antidotes

The antisocial edge of the Austrian School was continued and even sharpened by economists teaching in Chicago, London, and many other places in the world.[14] As indicated earlier, neoliberal ideals were not confined to theoretical-academic exercises but produced profound practical or real-life consequences: in 2008–2009, the "poisoned spring" of capitalist economics yielded the bitter harvest of financial meltdown, banking fiascos, and large-scale impoverishment of masses of people. Apart from its devastating social results, the financial debacle had the effect of triggering spirited reactions from distinguished intellectuals and economists. One broad salvo was fired at the debacle by the well-known journalist and social analyst Robert Scheer in his book *The Great American Stickup* (2010). As Scheer points out, the meltdown was not the result of a "hidden hand" but can be traced to concrete machinations "that served the richest of the rich and left the rest of us holding the bag." The major blame, in his view, can be attributed to people who "developed and implemented a policy of radical financial deregulation," above all economists and bankers "who inflated a giant real estate bubble by purposely not regulating the derivative markets, resulting in oceans of money that was poured into bad loans sold as safe investments."[15] An equally strong indictment was issued by economist and Nobel Laureate Paul Krugman in *The Return of Depression Economics and the Crisis of 2008* (2009). In his account, economic triumphalism (read: neoliberalism) had led America and the world into a downward spiral: "By a number of measures, the world has experienced a slump every bit as severe as the first year of the Great Depression." Only a full analysis of "the logic of depression economics"—its background and flawed premises—can offer a "defense against economic disaster."[16]

Probably the most nuanced and well-argued response to the debacle was written by economist and Nobel Laureate Joseph Stiglitz in his book *Freefall: America, Free Markets, and the Sinking of the World Economy* (of 2010). Already a decade earlier (in 2001), Stiglitz had taken up the basic arguments of Polanyi's book *The Great Transformation* and eloquently restated their broader significance. As he noted in a foreword to that book—in the teeth of a fashionable neoliberal triumphalism—among Polanyi's central theses "are the ideas that self-regulating markets never work; their deficiencies, not only in their internal workings but also in their consequences, are so great that government intervention becomes necessary; and that the pace of change is of central importance in determining these consequences." The foreword also denounced popular doctrines such as "trickle-down economics" as a sham, not backed up by adequate historical support. For Stiglitz, Polanyi's work had stripped of "respectable intellectual support" the proposition "that markets, by themselves, lead to efficient, let alone equitable outcomes." Basically, "whenever information is imperfect or markets are incomplete— that is, essentially always—interventions exist that *in principle* could improve the efficiency of resource allocation." To be sure, for Stiglitz, the remedy to the "myth" of free markets cannot be found in a state-run economy: "Only diehards would argue for the self-regulating economy, at the one extreme, or for a government-run economy, at the other." The main insight that Polanyi had articulated (in Stiglitz's view) was the close relationship between economy and society, between economic, social, and political interactions (something nowadays called "social capital"): "Polanyi saw the market as part of the broader economy, and the broader economy as part of a still broader society. He saw the market economy not as an end in itself, but as a means to more fundamental ends" (such as social well-being).[17]

Polanyi's insights were fully borne out in the debacle of 2008–2009. In *Freefall*, Stiglitz minces no words about the character of the debacle and its underlying roots. "The only surprise about the economic crisis of 2008," he writes, "was that it came as a surprise to so many." At a closer look, it was a "textbook case" that was not only predictable but also predicted: "A deregulated market awash in liquidity and low interest rates, a global real estate bubble, and skyrocketing subprime lending were a toxic combination." In combination, these factors revealed "fundamental flaws in the capitalist system, or at least the peculiar version of capitalism that emerged in the latter part of the twentieth century in the United States"—a version predicated on radical neoliberal or libertarian premises. For Stiglitz, these premises have been shown to be deeply flawed or simply wrong. In his analysis, the Nobel Laureate does not shield his own profession of economics from blame. Many of the leading "economic gurus" during recent decades, he states, had provided "the intellectual armor that policy-makers invoked in the movement toward deregulation"; as an academic profession, economics was awash with the praise of "self-regulating markets"—even though serious research had shown the "limited conditions" under which this theory operates. Misguided theories combined with irresponsible practices, Stiglitz states, conspired in guiding the economy of America and the world inexorably to the precipice: "In October 2008 America's economy was in freefall, poised to take down much of the world economy with it." But in this general "falling apart" of things, there was a common source: "the reckless lending of the financial sector which had fed the housing bubble, which eventually burst."[18]

The magnitude of the crisis and its implications are certainly staggering; one of its victims is the "American Dream." According to *Freefall*, the crisis like a lightning bolt revealed a stark landscape: "a society marked by increasing inequality; a country where . . . the statistical chances of a poor American making it to the top are lower than in 'Old Europe.'" One would assume that such economic realities would have put "market fundamentalism" or triumphalism finally to rest. But this is not as widely the case as one would expect or hope. The forces of resistance to change are rooted in habit and lethargy—but also in prevailing structures of privilege and power. Against this background, Stiglitz's book is a wake-up call for economists and people at large: a call for a rethinking of the premises of economics and social life. As he writes, "The marketplace for ideas is no more perfect than the marketplace for products, capital, and labor." But there is good news: although the "nonsense of perfect markets" may have held sway in the past, some scholars have been trying to understand "how markets actually work," and their ideas can be used by those "who wish to construct a more stable, prosperous, and equitable economy." Stiglitz's own work is exemplary in this effort to restore a greater balance to the relation between politics and economy, between public and private domains (or between polis and *oikos*). Here is a poignant statement: "I believe that markets lie at the heart of every successful economy, but that markets do not work well on their own. In this sense, I am in the tradition of the celebrated British economist John Maynard Keynes, whose influence towers over the study of modern economics. Governments need to play a role, and not just in rescuing the economy when markets fail. . . . Economies need a balance between the role of markets and the role of government. . . . In the last twenty-five years, America lost that balance."[19]

Nobel Laureates' opinions are certainly weighty and deserve careful attention, yet by themselves they may not provide sufficient motivation for a broader reorientation in the field. Fortunately, during the past decade a number of initiatives have been launched both in America and in the rest of the world that aim at a serious rethinking of the character of economics and its role in society. One prominent inspiration for such a rethinking comes from the New Economics Institute located in Massachusetts and New York. Among the activities sponsored by the institute are the organization of conferences attended by leading economists; the publication of a series of books, pamphlets, and journal articles; and the encouragement of grassroots discussions about economics on the local level. Among the founding members of the institute's board of directors is economist Gar Alperovitz, well known for a string of innovative texts, articles, and conference lectures. In 2005, well before the financial crisis, Alperovitz published a book that was widely discussed and articulated some of the institute's guiding aspirations: *America beyond Capitalism: Reclaiming Our Wealth, Our Liberty, and Our Democracy.* Reflecting the intent of what Alperovitz calls "evolutionary reconstruction," the book was not content with merely modifying or fine-tuning existing structures of neoliberal capitalism, nor did it seek to abolish or curtail economic markets, which would also curtail if not abolish freedom and democracy. As Alperovitz states in the opening pages, "This book argues that the only way for the United States to once again honor its great historic values—above all equality, liberty, and meaningful democracy—is to build forward to achieve what amounts to systematic [economic] change." Although critical of neoliberal ideas or ideologies, he acknowledges firmly that "serious ideas count. Moreover, people understand and respect serious ideas."[20]

The ideas that his book presents for serious attention are not reducible to grand ideological formulas or summary prescriptions. Rather, the path it recommends is one of tentative, progressive experimentation—a path well suited to an age that has been imprisoned for too long in binary oppositions or dichotomies: collectivism versus radical individualism, state planning versus unrestrained free enterprise, public versus private domains. The activities of the New Economics Institute were intensified and expanded after the financial debacle. In the period following the crisis, the institute organized a series of workshops, meetings, and conferences that explored the possibility of a genuine "paradigm shift" in the operation of the American as well as the global economy: a shift from laissez-faire to market governance in the public interest; from shareholder primacy to stakeholder primacy in corporations; from mindless consumerism to sufficiency and mindful consumption; and, above all, from plutocracy and "corporatocracy" to genuine democracy.[21] From June 8 to June 10, 2012, the institute convened a major conference at Bard College in New York on "strategies for a new economy." On that occasion, Alperovitz presented a plenary address. There he ably summarized the vision that inspired the institute and its many collaborators and sympathizers in America and the world. As he pointed out, a "turning point" has been reached in the way economics is conceived and practiced. The old economic paradigms of neoliberalism and state-run collectivism have failed; long-standing assumptions about banking and the financial system, about the nature of corporations and ownership, and about the imperatives of growth have been effectively challenged. The time has come to explore the prospects of a fair and sustainable economy anchored in a democratic political context.[22]

Moral and Political Limits of Markets

Leading economists' objections to market fundamentalism are significant especially because of their expert training and competence in the discipline of economics. To a considerable extent, the objections amount to an economic indictment: on strictly economic grounds, the maxims of unfettered capitalism are untenable and unsustainable. However, mixed in with the economic indictment there is also a deeper ethical and philosophical claim: economics cannot exit or abscond—or can abscond only at an intolerable cost—from considerations of social justice and equity, considerations that are constitutive of human life in society, especially life in a democracy. In *America beyond Capitalism,* Alperovitz is clearly aware of the cited cost. "A society committed to enhancing equality, liberty, and democracy," he writes there, "that is unable [or unwilling] to achieve such values in practice . . . is committed to a morally incoherent politics." If such a politics continues over time, he adds, "ever greater cynicism must develop" and with it "an ever deepening sense that American society has lost its moral compass, that government policies are merely the result of power plays and brokering between interested parties that do not and cannot claim any deeper democratic or moral legitimacy."[23]

With these comments we are back at the subtitle of Sandel's book mentioned at the beginning of this chapter: *The Moral Limits of Markets.* The notion that there are such moral limits has been acknowledged not only by some economists but also emphasized by many social and political thinkers as well as theologians and church leaders. In *The "Poisoned Spring,"* Angus Sibley refers extensively to Catholic social teachings, especially the encyclicals *Laborem exercens* (1961), *Centesimus annus* (1991), *Deus caritas est* (2006), and *Caritas in veritate* (2009). Among many other passages, he quotes approvingly the statement by John Paul II in *Centesimus annus* that church doctrine is "not directed against the market, but demands that the market be appropriately controlled by the forces of society and the state, so as to guarantee that the basic needs of the whole society are satisfied." Similar approval is given to Benedict XVI's statement in *Deus caritas est* that "the pursuit of justice must be a fundamental norm of the state. . . . The aim of a just social order is to guarantee to each person . . . his/her share of the community's goods." Based on these and other documents, Sibley concludes that in Catholic doctrine there is "no viable alternative" to the quest for good government as defined by the church. Although eloquently formulated and exuding the spirit of religious generosity, the invoked teachings, in my view, unfortunately have two drawbacks. First, penned mainly by theologians and church leaders, the teachings are not readily persuasive (or even intelligible) to trained economists, especially market economists. Second, the teachings are addressed chiefly to practicing Catholics, and even on that level they are rejected by "Catholic libertarians" or Catholic devotees of the "health and wealth gospel" (as Sibley reluctantly recognizes).[24]

Perhaps to be more broadly persuasive, arguments in favor of the "moral limits of the market" should best be advanced on the basis of interdisciplinary teamwork through which economists will have the benefit of learning from philosophers, humanists, and theologians—and vice versa. A prominent example of such teamwork was the collaboration between the economist Herman Daly and the theologian John Cobb Jr., a collaboration that—long before the 2008–2009 financial crisis—resulted in the publication of the book *For the Common Good: Redirecting the Economy toward Community, the Environment, and a Sustainable Future.* The bulk of the study was directed toward laying the groundwork for a new economics, an innovative paradigm bypassing the defects of both neoliberalism and socialist collectivism. As the authors emphasized (in the spirit of Adam Smith), their animus was not directed against the market per se. Modern economics, they readily admitted, "contributed to freeing individuals from hierarchical authority, as well as to providing more abundant goods and services"—achievements of such importance that for a long time "people of good will" have tended to ignore possible negative effects. However, in the wake of the Industrial Revolution and the rise of finance capitalism, benign neglect is no longer possible. The time has come to forge a new path between and beyond laissez-faire and state control. "Our position," the authors state, "is that centralized economic planning is inefficient, that allocations are better effected in the market than by bureaucratic planning." The role of the government is simply "to set fair conditions within which the market can operate." However, "the market is not the end of society and not the right instrument through which the ends of society should be set." Turning to these wider "ends of society," the study ventures into theological and cosmological speculation by proposing a moral and religious vision—which the authors term a "biospheric vision"—designed to protect and enhance all forms of life in the world: "The well-being and flourishing of human *and* nonhuman life on earth have value in themselves . . . [and are] independent of the usefulness of the non-human world for human purposes."[25]

The benefits of teamwork can sometimes be garnered by broad-gauged scholars who in their careers have been able to cross the narrow boundaries of disciplines. A good example in this respect is Michael Sandel, a scholar well educated in many areas. In his numerous writings, Sandel has established himself as a competent and well-informed participant in the fields of political philosophy, ethics, economics, and even religious studies. With regard to the "moral limits of the market," he has gained broad recognition through his discussion of ethical or moral theory in his book *Justice: What's the Right Thing to Do?* (2009). This discussion remains important because the meaning of ethics or moral theory is by no means settled and allows for multiple readings or interpretations. In this book, Sandel distinguishes between three main versions or construals of moral theory: utilitarianism, "deontology" or theory of moral obligations, and virtue ethics. Whereas the first, utilitarianism, concentrates on the nexus of pleasure and pain and links morality with the maximization of pleasure (for the greatest number of people), the second, deontology, ascends to a normative level (beyond desire) and finds morality in the acceptance of universal maxims by autonomous agents. Overcoming the desire/duty split, virtue ethics, finally, sees moral goodness as the intrinsic telos embedded in human strivings. *Justice* is generally critical of the utilitarian pleasure principle, which the book closely associates with libertarianism and neoliberal economics. Although respectful of deontology (especially in its Kantian version), the book finds rational maxims too abstract and the postulated "autonomy" too individualistic—which, in the end, leads Sandel to endorse a (moderate, interactive) form of Aristotelian virtue ethics: "A just society cannot be achieved simply by maximizing utility or by securing [individual] freedom of choice. To achieve a just society we have to reason together about the meaning of the good life, and to create a public culture hospitable to the disagreements that will inevitably arise."[26]

Sandel's excursus into moral and ethical theory serves him well in his later book, *What Money Can't Buy*, lending added credibility and competence to his critique of market fundamentalism. Such a critique, he notes there, has become rare—to the detriment of both economics and democratic politics. "Our reluctance to engage in moral and spiritual argument," he writes, "has exacted a heavy price: it has drained public discourse of moral and civic energy, and contributed to the technocratic, managerial politics that afflicts many societies today." What is needed to energize this discourse again is the willingness to reflect upon and engage with "competing conceptions of the good life"—a terrain that today is left vacant or abandoned to the whims of markets. "Our only hope of keeping markets in their place," Sandel adds, "is to deliberate openly and publicly about the meaning of the goods and social practices we prize." This hope has to be nurtured not so much for the sake of economic utility but for the sake of both human flourishing and revival of democracy, which today is in danger of being "commodified" and asphyxiated under the weight of plutocratic and managerial commodification. "Democracy," he concludes, "does not require perfect equality, but it does require that citizens share in a common life."[27] This conclusion agrees with the basic vision of Michael Polanyi, as one of Polanyi's leading students states: what emerges from the experiences of state control and market triumphalism is the possibility "that ordinary people in nations around the globe engage in a common effort to subordinate the economy to democratic politics and rebuild the global economy on the basis of international cooperation."[28]

5

Rights and Right(ness)

Humanity at the Crossroads

> The fact that something is desired only raises the *question*
> of its desirability; it does not settle it.
> —John Dewey, *Democracy and Education*

The notion of human rights is a pivotal conception of modern thought, especially of modern democracy. And clearly, given the experiences of autocracy, despotism, and totalitarianism, the importance of human rights is beyond doubt. Yet, despite the obvious significance of the conception, its meaning and range of application are not easily determined, which has to do in large part with the elusive character of its terms. The rights in question are called "human," which has a certain intuitive appeal. But what is "human"? Does the term denote a compact entity, with fixed or clearly defined boundaries? Sometimes (or rather most of the time) the rights are called "individual rights" in conformity with the modern penchant to identify "human" and "individual." But again: Does the latter term designate a compact entity with fixed and unalterable contours? And when we turn to the composite expression *human rights,* are rights here somehow humanized (which would yield something like "humane rights")? Or is it not rather the common assumption that rights are attached to the "human" (whose fixity is presupposed) and attached to it like a rightful possession or property? Which means that, in addition to other belongings, human beings also "own" rights. And when it comes to the notion of rights, can we assume that their exercise is always rightful or "right"? Hence, what is the rightness of rights?

97

The preceding questions only scratch the surface of the cauldron of issues connected with the conception of human rights. What is clear is that the conception stirs up difficult questions about human nature, justice, and the good life; hence, its discussion can hardly proceed without attention to such fields of inquiry as anthropology, philosophy, and even cosmology. It is commonly acknowledged that the phrase *human rights* arose basically in Western modernity and hence forms part and parcel of a complex constellation of ideas that circumscribes the meaning of "modernity." This constellation differs significantly from the premodern nexus of ideas and life-forms prevailing in (Western) antiquity and the Middle Ages; it also differs profoundly from many non-Western constellations of thought and conduct. In addition, as preceding chapters have tried to suggest, our contemporary period is marked by a transition between paradigms, bringing into view new horizons of life—including new horizons for the understanding of "human rights." Hence, the notion (to the extent it is transferrable) occupies a different place in different constellations and cannot simply be transposed intact. All one can do is to look for "equivalences" (provided the differences are not ignored).

Moreover, different cultural contexts are not available for neutral inspection; they are not reified pieces in a cultural museum. If paradigms, especially linguistic paradigms, are also "forms of life" (as Wittgenstein said), then any move beyond a given paradigm involves an existential agony, a wrenching experience challenging ingrained assumptions and habitual modes of conduct. In this chapter, I want to explore some of the "wrenching" induced by cross-paradigmatic comparison. In a first step, I review Raimon Panikkar's arguments about human rights and his comparison of the modern Western conception with traditional Indian views. Next, I extend the comparisons to the East Asian (Confucian) and West Asian (Islamic) regions. By way of conclusion, I explore what character "human rights" might assume in the dawning postmodern and post-Western era.

Is "Human Rights" a Western Concept?

Probably the most troubling and frequently debated issue about human rights is whether they are culture specific or at least potentially universal. The Spanish Indian philosopher Raimon Panikkar discussed this issue in an illuminating way some three decades ago in an essay titled "Is the Notion of Human Rights a Western Concept?" He answered the question ultimately with "yes" and "no," but only after having subjected the notion to close cross-historical and cross-cultural scrutiny. Broadly speaking, one might say that the concept of human rights is one way in which human beings generally articulate the desire for a just social order. "Human rights," Panikkar states, "are *one* window through which one particular culture envisages a just human order for individuals." But, of course, there are other possible approaches, and those who live in a given culture "do not see the window" (or do not see it as a window). Other cultures or historical contexts may use different formulations that are what Panikkar calls "homeomorphic equivalents" to though not identical with human rights. Yet this very broad and irenic way of looking at things is not how the concept is predominantly used today. In distinct contemporary usage, the notion of human rights glances definitely through a particular window—that is, modern Western culture—and bears the earmarks of the genesis and unfolding of Western modernity.[1]

To grasp this modern character, historical comparison is helpful. The modern age (so called) emerged through rupture from a preceding and very different paradigm: a premodern paradigm in which human beings and all particular entities were subordinated to and integrated into a broader social and cosmological fabric. In Panikkar's words, Western societies have been involved in "a process of transition from more or less mythical *Gemeinschaften* (feudal principalities, self-governing cities, guilds, local communities . . .) to a 'rationally' and 'contractually' organized 'modernity' as known to the Western industrialized world." Differently phrased, life in the West passes "from a corporate belonging in a community based on practically accepted custom and theoretically acknowledged authority, to a society based on impersonal law and ideally free contract, to the modern state," a passage accompanied by the steady "growth of individualism." Nowhere is the drama of the passage more evident than in the work of Thomas Hobbes (whom Panikkar does not mention). In a radical move, Hobbes brushed aside Aristotle's holistic teleology and cosmology and proceeded to disaggregate social wholes into an array of isolated particular individuals struggling for survival in the "state of nature." To human beings in this condition he assigned basic human rights—in effect a "right to everything" (*ius ad omnia*) necessary for their survival. Here the paradigmatic reversal is clear: whereas previously the "whole" (*omnia*) embraced particulars, the latter were now entitled to appropriate the whole as a proprietary right. This proprietary character came to overshadow and mark the subsequent course of Western "liberalism"—as is manifest in John Locke's formula "life, liberty, and property" (where the first two are likewise natural possessions).[2]

Panikkar's essay lucidly distills the basic "assumptions and implications" of the modern Western paradigm. Focusing on the Universal Declaration of Human Rights of 1948, he notes the "liberal Protestant roots" of that document. Among the declaration's guiding ideas, he singles out chiefly these features: the assumption of a "universal human nature common to all people" that is knowable through the exercise of reason and that is "essentially different from the rest of [nonhuman] reality"; further, the assumption of the basic "dignity of the individual" irrespective of rank, race, or religion, coupled with the autonomy of that individual vis-à-vis society, nature, and the cosmos; and finally the assumption of an (actual or possible) "democratic social order" where all individuals are equal in rights and where society is the aggregate of individual wills and interests. Summing up these various assumptions, Panikkar finds underlying the declaration the premise (not always consciously embraced by the framers) of "a certain philosophical anthropology or individualist humanism" (often called anthropocentrism and egocentrism). As he acknowledges, this general premise is contested even within modern Western culture. Thus, we find religious dissenters (who challenge the "naive optimism" regarding human goodness and autonomy); cultural dissenters (who challenge the cogency of the paradigm based on the rise of multiculturalism); and economic, especially Marxist, dissenters (who treat human rights as a camouflage for class rights and economic privilege). But even in their critical remonstrations, dissenting voices often share basic features of the contested paradigm.[3]

To illustrate the contours of the modern conception of rights, Panikkar turns to the Indian philosophical and religious tradition as recorded in the *Dharmashastras*, the *Bhagavad Gita*, and the great epics. As he points out, the term *dharma* is perhaps "the most fundamental word" in the entire Indian tradition and could conceivably serve as a "homeomorphic equivalent" to the term *human rights*. However, the equivalence is undercut or rendered doubtful by the multivalent character of the word *dharma*, which can mean, in different contexts, "law, norm of conduct, right, truth, justice, righteousness," and even religion and cosmic order. To find the common core of these notions, one has to uncover the "root metaphor" of all these meanings, which reveals that the term basically refers to "what maintains, gives cohesion and thus strength to any given thing, to reality, and ultimately to the 'three worlds' (*triloka*)," or the cosmos. In every case, the emphasis is on keeping together, keeping intact, maintaining order. Thus, dharma in its various shadings is "not concerned with finding the 'right' of one individual against another or of the individual vis-à-vis society." In Panikkar's words, "The starting point here is not the individual, but the whole concatenation of the Real." Differently phrased, dharma is "the order of the entire reality, that which keeps the world whole or together." To be sure, to maintain this order, individuals and all particular elements have to play their part. Thus, the individual's duty is indeed "to maintain his 'rights,'" but the latter here signifies the task "to find one's place in relation to society, to the cosmos, and to the transcendent world."[4]

At this point, one needs to guard against holistic extremism. The Indian tradition also has the notion of *svadharma*—that is, a dharma that is appropriate for the "self" or one's own life. However, even here the equivalence is limited because the notion cannot be abstracted from the holistic order. In confrontation with the Western model, Panikkar notes, the Indian tradition would critically stress "that human rights should not be absolutized"; it would contest "that one can speak of human rights as 'objective' entities standing on their own in isolation from the rest of the Real." Proceeding on this critical plane, the essay highlights a number of important distinctions. First of all, from the Indian vantage, human rights are "not *individual* rights only" because, in that tradition, the individual is seen only as a "knot" embedded in a "net" of relationships that form the fabric of reality. Hence, individuality is not a "substantial category." Basically, the cosmic structure is "hierarchical"—although this does not mean that "higher echelons have the right to trample upon the rights of lower ones." Second, rights are "not *human* rights only." They mesh with "the entire cosmic display of the universe." Thus, animals, all sentient beings, and even supposedly inanimate beings are involved in the interaction or correlation of "dharmic" rights. Finally, human rights are "not *rights* only" because they are also duties, and both are interdependent. Thus, taking the core right in the Western model—that of survival or self-preservation—one can say that human beings, in the Indian vision, have the right to survive only insofar as they also perform "the duty of maintaining the world" (*lokasamgraha*). As Panikkar states, "Our right is only a participation in the entire metabolic function of the universe." From this angle, the Universal Declaration of Human Rights of 1948 would need to be amended as or renamed the "Declaration of Universal Rights and Duties in which the whole of Reality is encompassed."[5]

Panikkar does not claim or pretend that the traditional Indian model can be preserved or reaffirmed intact in our time. He is fully aware of the blemishes and defects of traditional culture as it developed through the centuries, especially the blemishes of untouchability and an increasingly rigid caste structure—defects against which Mahatma Gandhi, B. R. Ambedkar, and many others have struggled so valiantly in recent times. Moreover, he realizes that Western modernity has penetrated Indian culture and society on all levels, bringing with it such changes as urbanization, a market economy, and an increasing focus on the rights of individuals and particular groups. As he states clearly, the notion "that the rights of individuals be conditioned by [or dependent on] their position in the net of Reality can no longer be admitted by the contemporary mentality."[6] There is also a further consideration: under present-day conditions, clinging to old-style holism can be misleading and even dangerous. In a context steadily marked by Western-style individualism and anthropocentrism, holism is in danger of being perverted into an ideological project manipulated by demogagous or extremist political leaders. The example of Hindutva (India for Hindus only) and the excesses associated with the Hindu–Muslim dispute over Ayodhya are vivid reminders of this possible decay. This does not mean that concern for the "whole" or the "common good" must be completely abandoned, but it does mean that such terms have to be used with utmost caution as denoting something in the distant horizon and always with full awareness of prevailing differences of perspectives that are precisely not "common."

What emerges from these considerations is the desirability of a midway position, of a simultaneous affirmation and critique of the Western model. Panikkar is emphatic regarding the needed affirmation, especially in view of the immense dangers to human dignity posed by the rise of modern megapowers, such as megastates and megacorporations. In his words, "For authentic human life to be possible within the *megamachine* of the modern technological world, human rights are imperative. . . . A technological civilization without human rights amounts to the most inhuman situation possible." At the same time, the Western model should not be unduly glorified, for it seems excessive to claim that "the rights of individuals [or groups] be so absolute as not to depend at all on the particular situation or context." To make such a claim conjures up the noted perils of anthropocentrism and egocentrism. For Panikkar, the sensible position involves negotiation, more specifically a mutual learning process between cultural paradigms or constellations: "A mutual fecundation of cultures is a human imperative of our times." To make such fecundation possible, an "intermediary space" needs to be found that allows for mutual learning, criticism, and transformation. This intermediary space is that of dialogue—what he also calls a "diatopical dialogue" because it involves a movement between different places or contexts (*topoi*). "No culture, tradition, ideology or religion," we read, "can today speak for the whole of humankind, let alone solve its problems. Dialogue and intercourse leading to a mutual fecundation are necessary." To be fruitful, such dialogue has to rely on mutual interpretation and hence on the resources of a "diatopical hermeneutics," which makes it possible "from the *topos* of one culture to understand the constructs of another."[7]

Panikkar's essay is most helpful and promising for future developments when he turns from a simple opposition of models to some fruits of intercultural fecundation. One such fruit concerns the bearer of human rights. Moving beyond the absolutism of separate individuals (marking the Western model) and the collectivist holism (of tradition), he introduces the notion of the "person" seen as an ensemble of relations. "The person," he writes, "should be distinguished from the individual." Whereas the latter is an abstraction, the former, "my person," calls forth all my correlates: "my parents, children, friends, foes, ancestors and successors"—none of whom can be called my property or accessory. Thus, an individual is an "isolated knot," but a person is "the entire fabric around that knot, woven from the total fabric of the Real." An equally important fruit has to do with a reformulation of the philosophical character of rights, a reformulation intimating a new correlation of "knot" and "net" or fabric. On the one hand, Panikkar writes, "traditional cultures have stressed the net (the role of each part in relation to the whole), so that often the knot has been suffocated and not allowed sufficient free space." On the other hand, "modernity stresses the knots (individual free will to choose any option), so that often the knot has been lost in loneliness, or else wounded or killed in competition with other more powerful knots." Traditional culture may be termed "cosmocentric" and the modern Western model "anthropocentric," but maybe the time has come for a "cosmotheandric vision of reality," where "the divine, the human, and the cosmic" are given their due, functioning in harmonious cooperation and allowing for "the performance of our truly human rights."[8]

Human Rights in East and West Asia

The question of the possible universality of human rights is not confined to the Indian cultural context but applies to all Asian cultures from the Near East to the Far East (the former sometimes called "West Asia"). In the East Asian context, Confucianism is to a large extent the predominant cultural and philosophical paradigm. Its strengths or virtues are as evident as those of the Indian classical tradition, but so are its historical shortcomings or drawbacks. Confucian ethics is often and rightly described as a "relational" ethics, with the focus placed on the so-called five relationships (*wu-lun*) between husband and wife, parent and child, older and younger sibling, ruler and minister, and friend and friend. This is an excellent ethical model, comparable to some degree with the classical Indian fabric of dharma. However, like the Indian paradigm, the Confucian model has traditionally been marred by a rigid hierarchical rank order, evident particularly in the unequal character of the cited relationships. Typically, the husband was supposed to exercise firm authority or control over the wife, the parents over their children, older siblings over younger siblings, and—of course—imperial ruler over all court officials and subjects. The only relationship exhibiting a degree of equality was friendship, but this relation was considered purely private. There was no equivalent—not even a "homeomorphic equivalent"—to citizenship and the idea of citizens' equal rights. So as one can see, traditional Confucianism exhibited a strong preponderance of "higher" over "lower" or, in Panikkar's language, of the "net" over the "knots."[9]

In the course of the steadily intensifying encounters between China and the modern West, the imperial structure was increasingly challenged and the traditional hierarchy called into question. In a sequence of innovative moves (from the constitutional efforts at the turn of the century to the May 4 movement and beyond), China underwent a series of profound structural changes until finally the turmoil of World War II and its aftermath ushered in the Communist regime. The dramatic force of these changes—it goes without saying—had a profound impact also on Chinese culture and intellectual life. One of the areas where this impact can readily be gauged is the field of human rights. Adopting a broad (perhaps excessively broad) perspective, one can say that Chinese attitudes to human rights today can be divided into three main types: a liberal, a Marxist, and a Confucian approach.[10] Whereas traditional Marxists still tend to view such rights as "bourgeois" class rights, liberals on the whole endorse the modern Western model with the focus on individualism, free enterprise, and the profit motive. The situation regarding Confucianism is highly complex, spanning the spectrum from absolute negation to affirmation. Whereas many Chinese—still in the grip of the Cultural Revolution (1965–1976)—consider Confucianism a feudal relic of the past, some others embrace it virtually in its traditional, premodern form. In my view, the most innovative approach is engaged in the rethinking and recharting of the Confucian legacy in light of contemporary needs, thus encouraging a paradigm shift. Probably the leading "rethinker" in this sense is the philosopher and Confucian expert Tu Weiming.

In several of his writings, Tu Weiming has charted a thoughtful and promising path between nostalgic traditionalism and the Western model. Although deeply attached to Confucian teachings, he is fully aware how easily the latter accommodated themselves to a hierarchical and often oppressive context. "We cannot ignore the historical fact," he writes, "that [imperial] Confucian China was unquestionably a male-dominated society." Throughout the centuries, "the education of the son received much more attention than the education of the daughter; the husband was far more influential than the wife, and the father's authority significantly surpassed that of the mother." Generally speaking, the status of women was deplorable in all stages of their development: in their dependency on the father in youth, on the husband in marriage, and on the son in old age. But not only women were kept in subjection: in relation to the imperial ruler, all Chinese were in a state of complete submission. Hence, there is definitely a danger of Confucian "values" to serve as "a cover for authoritarian practices"—a situation that persisted for many centuries. Yet, for Tu Weiming, the answer lies not in an abandonment of the tradition but in a rethinking and reformulation of it designed "to retrieve the deep meaning of its [potentially] universal humanistic teachings." Thus, just as for Panikkar, cultural tradition for Tu is not a fixed abode sheltered from change but rather a dynamic resource available for creative reassessment in light of ongoing experiences. The "authentic approach," he writes, is "neither passive submission to structural limitations [of the past] nor a Faustian activation of [Western-style] procedural freedom, but a conscientious effort to make the dynamic interaction between them a fruitful dialectic for self-realization."[11]

Tu Weiming wants to revitalize the Confucian tradition by highlighting or prioritizing certain features that in the past were not always given their proper due. One such feature is the Confucian notion of *jen,* usually translated as "humaneness" or "goodness," a notion undergirding all human efforts and hence capable of undercutting or at least softening traditional inequalities. Following the Chinese scholar Wing-tsit Chang, who designated *jen* as "the source of all specific virtues," Tu upholds the notion as a "living metaphor"— that is, a metaphor for an ethical and properly humanized way of life applicable to all people. Although, in accord with the Asian notion of *tao,* ways of life are not uniform or standardized, a way inspired by *jen* is neither an arbitrarily chosen "project" nor a collective fate but rather an interactive path or—in Tu's words—"a continuous process of symbolic exchange through the sharing of communally cherished values with other selves." This comment carries over into another feature Tu highlights: the Confucian notion of selfhood or "self." To the extent that Confucian texts recognize the notion, he writes, this self is not an atom or isolated individual—a knot without a net—or the mere occupant of a functional role—a net devoid of knots—but rather a relational self, a center or resonance chamber of relationships. In this respect, too, one can find a parallel with Panikkar's account because the idea of a relational self is very close to the latter's view of person or personhood. Seen as a center of relationships, the self or human being is endowed with inner richness and diversity and at the same time opens up to or resonates with the call of others and the world. In the effort to foster *jen,* says Tu, the self must both cultivate itself and "transgress its self-centered character." Differently put, the maturation of the self involves "a dynamic interplay between contextualization and decontextualization."[12]

Perhaps the major parallel that emerges concerns the broader philosophical paradigm: the emphasis on cross-cultural learning or "fecundation" on a global scale. The inclusion of Confucian teachings in the human rights discourse has, for Tu, the double benefit of softening the harsh individualistic edges of the Western model while also transforming hierarchical Asian "values" in the direction of a fuller recognition of general human rights. The revived Confucian teachings, he writes, are no longer a "fundamentalist representation" of ancient doctrines; rather, they are by and large "transvalued traditional values rendered compatible and commensurate with the main thrust" of the modern rights discourse. To this extent, the incorporation of Confucian values provides us with "an opportunity to develop a truly ecumenical agenda allowing the human rights discourse to become a continuously evolving and edifying conversation." One additional bonus of this ecumenical agenda is the overcoming of the rigid divide between secularism and religious faith, including the divide between anthropocentrism and theocratic fundamentalism. It is here that the basic openness of the rights-bearing "person" reveals its full scope. In line with Asian religious sensibilities, the transgression of the (narrowly construed) Western model implies, for Tu, a move toward "the unity of Heaven and humanity"—a unity that "transcends secular humanism, a blatant form of anthropocentrism characteristic of the intellectual ethos of the modern West." For the new model, he uses the term *anthropocosmic* to capture the relationality "between self and community, between human species and nature, and between humanity and Heaven." The resonance of this term with Panikkar's notion of a "cosmotheandric" vision is manifest.[13]

In the Islamic context in West Asia, the picture is much more complex and tension ridden. Traditional Islam is basically "theocentric" and hence leaves little or no room for human rights. Accordingly, any rapprochement between traditional Islam and the modern rights discourse is arduous—and often bluntly denounced as un- or anti-Islamic. In the words of Near East scholar Ann Elizabeth Mayer, traditional Islamic culture "lacks features that in the West contributed to the development of human rights." In that culture, she notes, there is no equivalent to the paradigm shift in Western history— "the abandonment of premodern doctrines of human duties and the adoption of the view that the '*rights* of man' should be central in political theory." As Mayer recognizes, Islamic tradition is not compact and uniform but also exhibits tendencies or perspectives that might support the idea of human rights. However, the late-modern ascendancy of an orthodoxy hostile to humanism and rationalism has stifled this possibility. As a result, the strictly orthodox view (among both Sunni and Shia Muslims) is that "Muslims should unquestioningly defer to the wisdom of God as expressed in Islamic doctrines representing instructions from the Qur'an and the example of the Prophet." Thus, the stress here is "not on the rights of human beings but rather on their duties to obey God's perfect law."[14] Former Pakistani minister of law and religious affairs A. K. Brohi clearly articulated this outlook in an article in 1983:

> The Western man's perspective may by and large be called anthropocentric in the sense that there "Man" is regarded as constituting the measure of everything since he is seen as the starting point of all thinking and action. The perspective of Islam, on the other hand, is theocentric, that is, God-consciousness, the Absolute is here paramount; man is only to serve His Maker. . . . Thus, there is a sense in which Man has no rights within a theocentric perspective; he has only

duties to His Maker—although these duties, in turn, give rise to all his rights.[15]

After September 11, 2001, and as a corollary of the US "war on terror," opposition to Western-style humanism and human rights was intensified in many parts of the Muslim world. In Mayer's words, "Proponents of 'Islamization' call for the extirpation of Western cultural influences and a return to [orthodox] Islamic models in the areas of government, law, social organization, and culture"; for such proponents, it is "an article of faith" that Islam is a "comprehensive ideology and scheme of life" that cannot tolerate any Western intrusion.[16] To be sure, in making this claim, radical Islamists vastly overstate their case. Despite the undeniable preponderance of orthodoxy, traditional Islam also embraced a variety of deviant strands—which, although marginalized in the past, can be retrieved today for innovative initiatives more hospitable to human rights. One such strand is the current of rationalism propounded in the early days by the so-called Mu'tazilites, whose influence peaked in the ninth century but was afterward repressed. For adherents of this current, a proper understanding of Islam required a rational interpretation of Islamic sources, including the Qur'an; it also required a resolute engagement on behalf of justice and popular freedom in political and social domains. Next to this group, there is the current of Islamic philosophy represented by eminent thinkers such as al-Farabi, Ibn Sina, and Ibn Rushd (Averroes), who managed to create a symbiosis between Greek philosophy and Islamic faith—to the chagrin of orthodox clerics, who succeeded in suppressing or sidelining philosophy for several centuries. Despite clerical opposition, some facets of this philosophical tradition were revived in the nineteenth century (by Muhammad 'Abduh and others), but with limited success. In recent times, however, there has been a veritable eruption or renaissance of Islamic philosophy carried forward by many (often expatriate) thinkers from both Sunni and Shia Muslim countries.[17]

In part as a result of this internal renaissance and in part due to Western prodding, a fledgling human rights discourse can today be found in many parts of the Islamic world. Although responsive in many ways to Western influence, this discourse exhibits an ambivalent but also promising and innovative character: unwilling to embrace a Western-style individualism or anthropocentrism, it also resolutely distances itself from the antihumanist "theocentrism" sponsored by orthodox elites. A good example is the Malaysian thinker and political activist Chandra Muzaffar. In his writings, Muzaffar has persistently critiqued the Western model for its addiction to a selfish and irresponsible individualism (cum anthropocentrism), an irresponsibility shared by many Western political leaders, but he has equally criticized Islamic governments or elites engaged in unjust practices and the suppression of legitimate human rights. In Muzaffar's view, the Western rights model, despite its inspiring universalist vision, is tarnished by its collusion with imperialism and neocolonialism as well as its dismissive treatment of non-Western people's rights—a treatment resulting in a "skeptical and critical" attitude among the latter toward "the West's posturing on human rights." In turn, some non-Western, including Islamic, governments use such skepsis as an alibi to reject human rights altogether in favor of abusive practices. Some Asian governments, Muzaffar writes, "have chosen to focus solely upon the adverse consequences of crass individualism upon the moral fabric of Western societies." But although justified in part, this focus is not sufficient, for "it is not just the moral crisis of Western society that we need to lament; we are [or should be] no less sensitive to the moral decadence within our own societies—especially within our elite strata." Thus, if we are advised to adhere to "a universal spiritual and moral ethic," then we should not hesitate "to condemn the suppression of human rights and the oppression of dissident groups that occur from time to time in a number of our [Muslim] countries."[18]

Thus, in accord with other progressive thinkers, Chandra Muzaffar is inclined neither to embalm orthodox Islamic traditions nor to throw religious and ethical teachings to the wind. This outlook leads him to appreciate the need for a creative rethinking and reinterpretation of traditions in order to render them "timely." As he observes in another context, "It goes without saying that . . . Muslims will continue to be inspired by the illustrious accomplishments of the past," but precisely for the sake of this continuity "they will have to reinterpret anew the values in the Qur'an in order to reconstruct alternative models" of social life. Hence, like Hindus and Buddhists and adherents of other religions in East and Southeast Asia, "they will have to draw out those universal values found in their respective traditions, reinterpret them afresh in the new circumstances confronting them" in our time.[19] In this stress on creative reinterpretation, Muzaffar is ably seconded by Abdullahi An-Na'im, the Sudanese American expert on Islamic law and philosophy. Although acknowledging the value of cross-cultural fertilization, An-Na'im places particular emphasis on the creative rethinking of indigenous resources or traditions. The point is that proponents of critical or innovative views are more likely to achieve acceptance "by showing the authenticity and legitimacy of their interpretation within the framework of their own culture." Ultimately, of course, internal and cross-cultural resources need to cooperate to yield the most fruitful result. Paralleling Panikkar's and Tu Weiming's arguments, An-Na'im finds that contemporary human rights discourse cannot achieve universality unless it is conducted "within the widest range of cultural traditions"; only by enlisting both intra- and cross-cultural sensibilities can a way be found for "enhancing the universal legitimacy of human rights."[20]

Rights and Right(ness)

The preceding discussion attests to an impending paradigm shift in the area of human rights: a shift from the exclusive focus on the Western model to a more global and ecumenical model of rights. In their basic thrust, the reviewed arguments (from Panikkar's and Tu Weiming's to Muzaffar's and An-Na'im's) seek to modify or at least supplement the Western focus on individual self-interest and anthropocentrism with a greater attentiveness to ethical and religious considerations. However, although valuable, this ethical-religious correction by itself may not be sufficient to satisfy universal aspirations. There are other impediments to the universal functioning of human rights. These obstacles have to do mainly with geopolitical, economic, and technological asymmetries. Here, the question raised by Theodor Adorno becomes relevant: How is ethics supposed to function in the general context of a "damaged life"— that is, a context where rights and ethical concerns are systematically marginalized?[21] What emerges here is the realization that the question of human rights presupposes the cultivation of a broad context of "rightness" reaching from political to economic and social domains. This context might be called the "rightness" frame of rights.

As it happens, contemporary human rights discourse is aware of this need for a broader frame. It is customary in this discourse to distinguish between three "generations" of rights: first, civil and political rights (anchored in modern Western individualism); next, social and economic rights (sponsored chiefly by socialist or socially progressive movements); and finally, cultural and collective rights (championed mainly by non-Western and indigenous peoples). The three generations are by no means in harmony or easily reconciled. In fact, the dominant Western rights discourse grants almost exclusive preference to the first generation while sidelining and even accepting the infringement on second- and third-generation rights. For this reason, the East Asia expert Henry Rosemont Jr. calls the dominant human rights discourse a "bill of worries" that conceals or papers over underlying conflicts and inequities. Chandra Muzaffar has eloquently highlighted these inequities in his comments on the three generations: "By equating human rights [solely] with civil and political rights, the rich and powerful people in the North hope to avoid coming to grips with those economic, social and cultural challenges which could well threaten their privileged position in the existing world order. What the rich and powerful do not want, above all, is a struggle for economic transformation presented as a human rights struggle, a struggle for human dignity." Indian social theorists Smitu Kothari and Harsh Sethi ably second these comments in their book *Rethinking Human Rights* when they charge the Western model with hiding from view the plight of the vast majority of humankind, including the majority of people in their native India.[22]

What these critical voices challenge is not so much the importance of civil and political rights per se as these rights' presumed ability to operate in a vacuum separated from social, economic, and cultural aspirations. Viewed from this angle, what the contemporary "Axial Age" brings into view is a new and integrated human rights paradigm where the "generations" of rights would be reconciled on a global level. According to Kothari and Sethi, what is demanded in our time is a human rights praxis that is also a "humane" rights praxis inspired by "rightness"—that is, "a social praxis, rooted in the need of the most oppressed communities, that aims to create shared norms of civilized existence for all."[23] As it seems to me, this kind of social praxis was at the heart of the American civil rights struggle led by Martin Luther King Jr., a struggle that aimed not only at securing for African Americans political rights in a narrow sense but also at fostering their economic, social, and cultural freedom and dignity. It was a similar comprehensive vision that guided Mahatma Gandhi in his struggle for Indian independence, where the ouster of British rule was meant only as a preamble to the cultivation of India's flourishing in the political, economic, and cultural domains.

To this extent, King, Gandhi, Nelson Mandela, and others have been pioneers in rekindling in our time the integral sense of humaneness (*jen*), rightness (dharma), and justice as guiding motifs for the conduct of human and public life. The point today is not to erect monuments to these pioneers, thus reducing them to museum pieces. Rather, the task is to follow their lead by practicing "rights" not in a unilateral manner but rather in an interactive and ethically responsible manner oriented toward the "cosmotheandric" or "anthropocosmic" flourishing of humankind.

6

"Man against the State"

Community and Dissent

Let your life be a counter-friction to stop the machine.
—Henry David Thoreau, *Essay on Civil Disobedience*

The opening part of *Thus Spoke Zarathustra* contains these stark lines: "State is the name of the coldest of all cold monsters. Coldly it tells lies too; and this lie crawls out of its mouth: I, the state, am the people."[1] These lines resonate strongly with contemporary ears, not only in totalitarian autocracies but also in (so-called) democracies as well. Everywhere people are confronted with mammoth corruption and vile deceptions perpetrated by states. Nietzsche calls the state the coldest monster because it is devoid of human sensibility and, in fact, has turned into a huge technical artifact or machine. In Western thought, Thomas Hobbes was the first to call the state an "artificial body," but in his era this artifact was still embodied in a human sovereign. In the meantime, the sovereign has been replaced or supplemented by an immense bureaucratic apparatus inhabited by "specialists without spirit" and wedded solely to digital calculation and electronic surveillance. More importantly, under the aegis of this apparatus, life and death are increasingly mechanized, with military valor being replaced by automated killing machines. "Indeed," Zarathustra exclaims, "a hellish artifice was invented here, a horse of death, clattering in the finery of divine honors." If these developments continue, the prospects for human life and freedom are dismal: "Verily, this sign [of the state] signifies the will to death. It beckons to the preachers of death."[2]

The state castigated in Nietzsche's text is far removed from the older conception of a political community or polis, a shared public life sustained by ethical bonds and by what Aristotle called a "watery kind of friendship." Nietzsche is not dismissive of this older notion. In fact, he puts into Zarathustra's mouth these memorable lines: "It was creators who created peoples and hung a faith and a love over them: thus they served life." And with creative life comes freedom: "A free life is still free for great souls. . . . Only where the 'state' ends, there begins the human being who is not superfluous." As one should note here, a "free life" is not intrinsically opposed to a freely shared solidarity—that is, to a life shared with friends in whom (as Nietzsche says) "the world stands completed, a bowl of goodness."[3] The aim of this chapter is to show the compatibility between a properly conceived freedom and a properly conceived solidarity or, more precisely, between an unselfish or self-transcending freedom and an uncoercive, future-oriented public community. It must be recognized, however, that this relationship is always tensional and fraught with profound hazards—hazards that can arise from either side or from both, leading to a rupture of the ethical social bond. Despotism and totalizing autocracy provoke a rupture "from above," while radical individualism and violent rebellion tear the social fabric "from below."

In modern Western thought, the antithetical formula "man versus the state" is associated chiefly with a certain type of liberalism or "libertarianism" promoted by Herbert Spencer and his followers. In a first step here, I discuss this formula, sometimes called "social Darwinism," which has exerted great influence in the West in recent times. In a second step, I turn to more nuanced and ethically sensitive formulations of the "freedom–solidarity" conundrum advanced by Henry David Thoreau, Mahatma Gandhi, and Albert Camus. By way of conclusion, I offer some additional examples of the freedom-solidarity nexus by turning to the trial of Socrates and the ethically inspired resistance movement against the Nazi regime in Germany.

Herbert Spencer and Social Darwinism

Tensions and internal conflicts are endemic to most societies and political regimes. As history teaches, societies East and West have always been periodically in the throes of domestic upheavals and

rebellions. However, in the past such rebellions have typically originated in perceived social and political ills and motivated by the goal
of establishing a more just or acceptable regime (from the angle
of the insurgents). One of the strikingly novel features in Western modernity is that domestic challenges are sometimes directed
against regimes as such—that is, against the very notion of a shared
public order. In large measure, this feature is associated with modern liberalism (sometimes shading over into anarchism), a doctrine
anchored in the primacy of individual self-interest. Still, even in the
context of modern liberalism, a radical antisocial or "antistate" animus developed only slowly. Thus, although assuming a radically individualistic and asocial "state of nature," Hobbes maintained firmly
that reason and internalized moral codes would eventually lead people to construct a stable regime. Likewise, although departing from
a similar (though more peaceful) state of nature, John Locke's liberal
public order inserted individual rights squarely into the framework
of an established social community (whose unraveling was treated
as a rare exception). It was only in the nineteenth century, under the
impact of positivism and evolutionism, that the liberal creed became
virulent in the sense of normalizing the Hobbesian state of nature.

Basically, the nineteenth century witnessed a confluence of intellectual tendencies, many of which conspired to drive the notion of
a shared normative order underground. One was the emergence of
the discipline of "sociology," inaugurated by Auguste Comte, with
its focus on empirical description in opposition to the "metaphysical" assumptions of the earlier age of Enlightenment. Another feature, located in the ethical domain, was the rise to prominence of
"utilitarianism," a quasi-psychological doctrine initiated by Jeremy
Bentham that located normative standards not in abstract "laws of
nature" but in the empirical calculus of pleasure and pain. A third
trend gathering momentum throughout the century was biological
evolutionism, which reached its most mature expression in the work
of Charles Darwin. In an instructive and exemplary fashion, the
three cited trends converged and reached an (unstable) synthesis in
the writings of Herbert Spencer (1820–1903), a prominent sociologist and social philosopher deeply influenced by Comtean positivism, utilitarian teachings, and, later in his life, Darwin's work *On the
Origin of Species* (first published in 1859). Because of this intellec-

tual indebtedness, Spencer is sometimes regarded as a purely derivative thinker, which is not entirely fair. One of his aims was clearly
to "synthesize" teachings (and even to produce a "synthetic philosophy"), but this aim still left room for intellectual independence
and sometimes for formulations more sensible or balanced than
those of his mentors. Thus, although honoring Comte, he did not
embrace his historical "stage theory" and favored a more flexible
evolutionism. With regard to utilitarianism, he sought to improve
the dominant rigid empiricism by preferring a more "rational" or
enlightened version (which even made room for "natural rights"
dismissed by Bentham). His relation to Darwin was complex and
by no means reducible to a simple transfer of ideas from biology to
sociology.[4]

During his lifetime, Spencer's writings were received widely
and mostly favorably; however, none of his other texts could match
the impact, both then and later, achieved by the book published in
1884 under the title *The Man versus the State*. The book is a collection of essays dealing with a variety of topics; however, its central thrust is a virulent polemical attack on what Spencer called the
"new Toryism"—a code word for the shift of British liberalism in the
direction of an interventionist and paternalistic "statism" (typical of
old-style Tory conservatism). In eloquent and stirring language, the
book pits against each other a military and "militant" regime associated with Toryism/conservatism and a commercial or "industrial"
social order promoted by genuine liberalism; whereas in the former
social bonds are hierarchical and compulsory, in the latter they are
voluntary and minimal (in accordance with laissez-faire principles
of individual freedom and private property). Contemporary readers
of the text, confronted with the "monstrosity" of state bureaucracies,
are likely to appreciate Spencer's polemic—especially when the latter is extended to a scathing critique of state-sponsored colonial or
imperial expansions across the globe. As it happens, however, this
appreciation is bound to diminish or be muted by Spencer's political naïveté, his inability or unwillingness to ponder the effects of
the ongoing replacement of "industrialism" by new capitalist hierar-
chies whose leaders were eager to step into the vacated place of public institutions. The disaffection is deepened by Spencer's relentless
attacks on public education, unionism, and social welfare legisla-

tion that seek to provide a buffer against the new forms of economic domination.

In many ways, *Man versus the State* follows the lead of earlier liberal thinkers—but with a significant twist. Like Hobbes and Locke, Spencer starts from the assumption of individual liberty in a pristine "natural" condition: "There are no phenomena which a society presents but what have their origins in the phenomena of individual life, which again have their roots in vital phenomena at large." In contrast with his predecessors, however, Spencer does not find original social life beset with sufficient inconveniences so as to prompt members to leave that condition in favor of a mutual engagement leading to the formation of a public regime. As if guided by natural instinct, participants in society—on Spencer's account—pursue their individual self-interest while respecting definite limits and, as good merchants or businessmen, abide by commercial contracts negotiated for their mutual benefit. "Though mere love of companionship prompts primitive men to live in groups, yet the chief prompter is experience of the advantages to be derived from cooperation." On what condition, he asks, can such cooperation arise? "Evidently only on condition that those who join their efforts severally gain by doing so." If this expectation is frustrated or if mutuality is disrupted, there will be "a reversion to that rudest condition in which each man makes everything for himself. Hence, the possibility of cooperation depends on the fulfillment of [commercial] contract, tacit or overt." Drawing the conclusion from these comments, the text insists that only industry and, in fact, a "vast elaborate industrial organization" can ensure social progress: "For in proportion as contracts are unhindered and the performance of them certain, the growth is great and the social life active."[5]

As one should note, the maintenance of commercial engagements is entrusted here entirely to the "natural" disposition of individuals, quite outside the functioning of public institutions and outside any civic education (nurturing moral and civic habits among individuals and groups). It is in this sense that "man" (in "man versus the state") is originally in possession of "natural rights," including the right of individual liberty and the secure enjoyment of private property. If Bentham's disciples had taken this stark opposition more seriously, Spencer argues, they might have been led "to treat less cavalierly the doctrine of natural rights." For Spencer, rights, far from having anything to do with public institutions or rules, originate simply in the spontaneous "mutual limitation of activities" among people, as demonstrated by "the few peaceful tribes which have either nominal governments or none at all." Having been established "more or less clearly before government arises," rights "become obscured as government develops." Spencer, to be sure, is not unaware that commercial agreements are vulnerable to breach and need to be somehow maintained or guaranteed. Hence, the central maxim of his text is "that contracts shall be free and fulfillment of them enforced." However, enforcement takes the form chiefly of spontaneous self-limitation (reducing the role of government to that of a "night watchman" of property). "There must be, in the first place," he writes, "few restrictions on man's liberties to make agreements with one another, and there must be, in the second place, an enforcement of the agreements which they do make." But, preferably, these checks are "those only which result from mutual limitation," and consequently "there can be no resulting check to the contracts they voluntarily make."[6]

In addition to Comtean and utilitarian leanings, Spencer was also greatly attracted to Darwin's work and to biological evolutionism more generally. This attraction has prompted many critics to present him as a proponent of "social Darwinism" (a label meaning the transfer of the principle of natural-biological selection to social relations).[7] Used as a summary verdict, this portrayal seems exaggerated, especially given Spencer's preference for "synthesizing" many views (including the utilitarian maxim of "the greatest good for the greatest number"). Nevertheless, it is hard to deny certain "social Darwinist" features in his work. Thus, after having read *On the Origin of Species*, he is reported to have coined the phrase "survival of the fittest," an expression that soon became a catchphrase in discussions of both biological and social evolution. That Spencer himself was ready to transfer aspects of the "survival" motto to the social and political domain is evident from *Man versus the State*. As we read there, the "vital principle" of individual and social life—indeed, the vital principle of "social progress"—is maintained if each individual is "left secure in person and possessions to satisfy his wants with its proceeds." Despite this principle's broad generality, its concrete application quickly reveals stark social differences, deriving from the diversity of individual aptitudes and energies. The principle, Spencer adds, is a guarantee of progress "inasmuch as, under given conditions, the individuals of most worth will prosper and multiply more than those of less worth." Seen in this light, the idea of "utility," properly understood, enjoins "the maintenance of individual rights" despite different outcomes. Any attempt to interfere with this principle—especially by "meddling legislation"—is "a proposal to improve life by breaking down the fundamental conditions to life."[8]

Whatever Spencer's own leanings may have been, reception of his work soon inspired (rightly or wrongly) a broad movement of "social Darwinism" throughout the world. In America, the undisputed leader of the movement was William Graham Sumner (1840–1910), a sociologist and social theorist who combined Spencer's teachings with neoclassical ideas of free enterprise, a combination made plausible by the rapid rise of unfettered capitalism in America at that time. In a highly influential pamphlet published in 1883 under the title *What Social Classes Owe to Each Other*, Sumner insisted that social classes owe each other precisely nothing, relying for this conclusion on a version of the "survival of the fittest" motto. In a stark swipe at any form of socialism, Sumner excoriated all attempts to alleviate or uplift the lot of disadvantaged people or classes as an assault on social progress and advancement; given their essential role as social pioneers, businesspeople and economic enterprises were to be left as free as possible from taxes and public regulations.[9] From England and America, Spencerian and social Darwinist ideas migrated to many other places, with their initial emphases often being greatly revised or modified (sometimes becoming fused with doctrines of racial eugenics). The strongest and most lasting impact of *Man versus the State,* however, was exerted on the field of neoclassical economics, especially the so-called Austrian School of economics wedded to the celebration of the untrammeled pursuit of private and corporate profit. As formulated by one of the school's leaders, the basic principle of capitalism is public nonintervention in the market (laissez-faire), especially noninterference in status differences: "The inequality of incomes and wealth is an inherent characteristic of the market economy. Its elimination would totally destroy the [capitalist] market economy."[10]

Civil Disobedience and Dissent

Strictly construed, Spencer's formula "man versus the state" erects a gulf between individuals and governments; in a slight modification, social Darwinism places the gulf between individual advancement and social or public arrangements that hamper the pursuit of self-interest. In each case, the guiding assumption is that of a "zero-sum" game—a radical antithesis of interests where neither side owes anything to the other. What is (at least tendentially) expunged in this game is the notion of shared social bonds or a civic community circumscribing naked self-interest. To be sure, bonds of this kind do not by themselves eliminate the possibility of profound tensions and even conflicts in society. The cause of such conflicts is typically some agents' failure to live up to the ethical obligations implicit in social life. On the part of individuals (or groups of individuals), remonstrations or uprisings typically take the character of "civil disobedience" or conscientious "resistance" to perceived public corruption or repression. What is important to note here is the stark difference between social Darwinism and conscientious disobedience: whereas in the former case antipublic conduct is rooted in the pursuit of private self-interest, in the latter case the motive is to enhance or restore public well-being and justice in society. A particularly inspiring text along these lines was penned by the New England writer Henry David Thoreau in his essay *Resistance to Civil Government* (1849), later renamed *Essay on Civil Disobedience*.

The opening lines of the essay seem to place Thoreau squarely on the side of Spencer and other laissez-faire liberals of the time. "I heartily accept the motto," he states, "that 'government is best which governs least'; and I should like to see it acted up to more rapidly and systematically." Government, he adds, is "at best but an expedient, but most governments are usually, and all governments are sometimes, inexpedient." Even in democracies, where people presumably choose their leaders, government is "equally liable to be abused and perverted before the people can act through it." Take the example of the US government, an institution that has a venerable tradition but that "each instant is losing some of its integrity." Although formally democratic, it has turned into a vast bureaucracy, a "complicated machinery" imposing itself on the people; it is "a sort of wooden gun to the people themselves." Echoing some of Spencer's more captivat-

ing lines, Thoreau exclaims: "This government never of itself fur-
thered any enterprise. . . . It does not keep the country free. It does
not settle the West. It does not educate. The character inherent in
the American people has done all that has been accomplished." The
upshot of these comments is that government is more a burden to
than a benefactor of the people or an engine of progress: "Government is an expedient by which men would fain succeed in letting
one another alone; and . . . when it is most expedient, the governed
are most let alone by it."[11]

Although seemingly toeing a radical libertarian line, Thoreau's
essay at this point adds a twist in a completely different direction.
"But to speak practically and as a citizen," he states, "unlike those
who call themselves no-government men, I ask for, not at once no
government, but *at once* a better government. Let every man make
known what kind of government would command his respect, and
that will be one step toward obtaining it." With these words, Thoreau
introduces an ethical standard that Spencer and radical liberals side-
step: the standard of social justice discerned by human conscience.
"Can there not be a government," he asks, "in which majorities do
not virtually decide right and wrong [relying on their power alone]
but conscience?" A government where majorities decide or determine "only those questions to which the rule of expediency [not
rightness] is applicable"? This question leads to the role of citizens
in a public regime. Should citizens simply "resign their conscience"
to the government? But, then, "why has every man a conscience?"
"I think," Thoreau insists, "that we should be men [human beings]
first, and subjects afterwards." This principle also applies to business enterprises: "It is truly enough said that a corporation has no
conscience; but a corporation of conscientious men is a corporation
with a conscience." In every instance, the guiding yardstick must be
that "it is not desirable to cultivate a respect of the [positive] law so
much as for the right" or just law. When this rule is reversed, human
beings become lackeys of government and possibly "agents of injustice." In that case, Thoreau adds with some sarcasm, "you may
see a file of soldiers, colonel, captain, corporal, privates, powder-
monkeys and all, marching in admirable order over hill and dale
to the wars, against their wills, ay, against their common sense and
consciences."[12]

In eloquent language, Thoreau's essay anticipates and condemns the steady transformation of governments into soulless machines, grotesque bureaucratic apparatuses of control. People who follow such governments in blind obedience, he asks, "what are they?" Are they "men at all, or rather small movable forts and magazines, at the service of some unscrupulous man in power?" Unfortunately, even in democracies, such blind submission is widespread: "The mass of men serve the state thus, not as men mainly, but as machines, with their bodies. They are the standing army, and the militia, jailers, constables, *posse comitatus.*" In such circumstances, there is in most cases "no free exercise whatever of judgment or of the moral sense" because "they put themselves on a level with wood and earth and stones—and perhaps wooden men [or automata] can be manufactured that will serve the purpose as well." According to Thoreau, even people who are "commonly esteemed good citizens" often prefer to act in conformity with mechanical rules rather than raise their voice in alarm or opposition. In most societies, exceptions to this conduct are rare—and they are usually made to pay for their nonconformism. In Thoreau's words, "A very few—as heroes, patriots, martyrs, reformers in the great sense, and *men*—serve the state with their consciences also, and so resist it for the most part." But, he adds (in a warning to all conscientious objectors, civil resisters, and whistleblowers), "they are commonly treated as enemies by it."[13]

Thoreau not only wrote about the consequences of resistance but also took some upon himself. For some six years he refused to pay a poll tax, and he was put into prison for a while. But he did not seek to evade the penalty. As he states in his essay, "Under a government which imprisons any unjustly, the true place for a just man is also a prison." His refusal to pay the tax was meant as a protest against slavery and against the Mexican-American War, both of which he considered profoundly unjust. (One can safely guess what he would have done at the time of the Vietnam and Iraq Wars.) The important point to consider is that his act of resistance was prompted not by any desire for personal gain, profit, or influence, but for ethical reasons that sometimes require suffering or sacrifice. If an injustice is of such a nature, he writes, "that it requires you to be the agent of injustice to another, then, I say, break the law. Let your life be a counter-friction to stop the machine." His sentiments toward his own government prior to the abolition of slavery were radical, and they still upset some American readers. "How does it become a man to behave toward this American government today?" he asks. "I answer, that he cannot without disgrace be associated with it. I cannot for an instant recognize that political organization as *my* government which is the *slave's* government also" (or which enslaves other people). He adds, again somewhat provocatively, "Action from principle, the perception and performance of right, changes things and relations; it is essentially revolutionary and does not consist wholly with anything which was." What remains crucial here is that change is not pursued for its own sake but for the sake of social and public improvement: "I please myself with imagining a state at last which can afford to be just to all men, and to treat the individual with respect as a neighbor."[14]

Thoreau's text was favorably received by many audiences in both Western and non-Western countries. The most important non-Western reader was Mohandas Gandhi, who considered the text a welcome supportive inspiration for his own endeavors. To be sure, although a lifelong admirer of Thoreau (as well as of John Ruskin and Leo Tolstoy), Gandhi modified Thoreau's approach in many ways, mainly by shifting the accent from individual or solitary initiatives to the collective concerns of broader social movements (without neglecting, of course, the role of individual conscience). As is well known, the idea of civil and social resistance first preoccupied Gandhi during his struggle against apartheid in South Africa from 1893 to 1914, a struggle that later morphed into the movement for national independence from British rule in India. Despite the vastly changed location of resistance—from Walden Pond ultimately to India—the spirit or guiding animus of the struggle remained largely the same: the pursuit of justice and social-political improvement. At no time in his life was Gandhi motivated by the desire for wealth, influence, or public power; even when independence was within reach, he refused to seek a governmental position. Upon initiating the resistance in South Africa, Gandhi tellingly gave to his movement the name *satyagraha,* which literally means "truth doing"— that is, active pursuit of truth and justice. It has also been translated as "truth force," "soul force," or "love force." As Erik Erikson has pointed out in his famous study *Gandhi's Truth* (1993), it was precisely the ethical and spiritual motivation that gave to Gandhi's independence struggle its special quality, distinguishing it from purely political rebellions. If the stress is placed only on struggle for power, he said, one misses "the spiritual origin of nonviolent courage in Gandhi's truth."[15]

Erikson's comment points to an important aspect of Gandhian truth performance or justice seeking: its reliance on nonviolence. There can be little doubt that for Gandhi the guiding principle of social struggle and resistance was nonviolent action (*ahimsa*) and that, in his view, *satyagraha* and *ahimsa* were intimately linked. As he states in one of his writings on the topic, "In the application of *satyagraha*, I discovered in the earliest stages that pursuit of truth did not admit of violence being inflicted on one's opponent, but that he must be weaned from error by patience and sympathy."[16] The main point here is that for Gandhi—as for Socrates and Jesus before him—it is better to suffer injustice than to impose injustice on others. In Erikson's interpretation, Gandhian truth performance was governed by "the readiness to get hurt and yet not to hurt"; if there was a guiding "dogma" in this approach, it was the maxim that "the only test of truth or justice is action based on the refusal to do harm." This maxim—importantly—not only was a cognitive or theoretical formula but achieved its cogency by being "put to work" in concrete circumstances. Gandhi's enactment of the maxim was evident throughout his life in his willingness to accept suffering in the form of fasting, imprisonment, abuse, and ultimately death—a willingness guided by the desire to appeal to his opponents' conscience and better ethical qualities. Here is another quotation from Gandhi's work: "Suffering is the law of human beings, war is the law of the jungle. But suffering is infinitely more powerful than the law of the jungle for converting the opponent and opening his ears, which are otherwise shut to the voice of reason."[17]

Despite these and similar forthright statements, some interpreters have raised questions about the role of *ahimsa*—questions that (mistakenly) seem to place on an equal footing violence and nonviolence, justice and injustice. Admittedly, Gandhi was not an "absolutist" in this field and made room for some departures from *ahimsa*. However, as in the case of the "law of peoples," the departures were narrowly circumscribed and basically limited to acts of self-defense against an imminent violent attack or acts performed as a last resort and with due regard for proportionality. Performed outside these limits, acts of violence are, for Gandhi, illegitimate because they negate the very spirit and goal of *satyagraha*. As Gandhi persistently insisted, the means of struggle have to accord with the goal of struggle—that is, their relation is not purely instrumental but ethical. This is the gist of his well-known statement (not far from biblical teachings) that "the means may be likened to a seed, the end to a tree; and there is just the same inviolable connection between the means and the end as there is between the seed and the tree. . . . We reap exactly as we sow." Commenting on this passage, Gandhian scholar Anthony Parel finds that it reflects both biblical and Hindu spiritual teachings and is "based in the supposition that there is an inviolable connection between ends (*sadhya*) and means (*sadhan*)."[18]

In recent times, this connection highlighted by Gandhi has come to be widely sidelined or entirely thrown to the winds—with predictable results. Totally neglecting both Thoreau's and Gandhi's teachings, some recent so-called rebellions have preferred to indulge in orgies of violence and unspeakable acts of barbarism, always eagerly employing mayhem not as a last resort but as the first. But the consequences cannot be in doubt, for how can a rebellion pursued with brutal and destructive means lead to anything other than a brutal and destructive regime? How can a movement willing to repress and slaughter all opponents lead to anything other than a repressive machine slaughtering dissenters? Against the engines of violence spiraling out of control, it is important and timely to invoke the teachings not only of Thoreau and Gandhi but also of the French writer Albert Camus, whose famous book *The Rebel* (1951) is a celebration of life and an antidote to the cult of death and destruction.

Camus's book takes its point of departure from the late-modern condition of nihilism, the progressive retreat and ultimate self-devaluation of traditional values. In the face of this situation—that is, the perceived lack of a preordained meaning of things—the nihilist concludes that everything is permitted, including killing and murder. *The Rebel* is in the first instance a rebellion against this conclusion. As Camus shows, the encounter of the nihilist and the perceived meaninglessness of the world—what he calls the "absurdist" encounter—is based on an act of judgment that presupposes the self-affirmation of the judging agent and hence an affirmation of life. "It is obvious," he argues, "that absurdism [the absurdist encounter] hereby admits that human life is the only necessary good since it is precisely life that makes this encounter possible. . . . To say [as the nihilist does] that life is absurd, the conscience must be alive." However, the affirmation of life cannot stop at the banishing of suicide or self-annihilation but carries a broader significance. "From the moment," the text continues, "that life is recognized as good, it becomes good for all men. Murder cannot be made coherent when suicide is not considered coherent." For Camus, proceeding on the premise of nihilism, there can be no half-measures: "Absurdist reasoning cannot defend the continued existence of the spokesman and, simultaneously, accept the sacrifice of others' lives. The moment we recognize the impossibility of absolute negation—and merely to be alive is to recognize this—the very first thing that cannot be denied is the right of others to live."[19]

As can be seen, rebellion in Camus's treatment is not a purely individualistic or self-centered venture but has broader social implications: the freedom of the rebel relies on a solidarity with other human beings and, in fact, with humanity. "Rebellion, contrary to current opinion, questions the very idea of the [isolated] individual. If the individual, in fact, accepts death and happens to die as a consequence of his act of rebellion, he demonstrates by doing so that he is willing to sacrifice himself for the sake of a common good which he considers more important than his own destiny." In going beyond his own self-interest or selfish desires, the rebel affirms and upholds an ethical order of rightness and justice that reveals a deeper human bond. In resisting an unjust order, he signals that the order "has infringed on something in him which does not belong to him alone, but which is common ground where all men—even the one who insults or represses him—have a 'natural' community." Thus, in contrast to Spencerian libertarians, rebellion for Camus is not "an egoistic act," but a conduct gaining its sense or significance from its insertion into a social community. Basically, even in challenging existing rules, the rebel does so in order to improve them, bending them in the direction of social justice. As Camus adds in a stark modification of the traditional Cartesian formula, "In our daily trials, rebellion plays the same role as does the '*cogito*' in the realm of thought: it is the first piece of evidence. But this evidence lures the individual from his solitude. It founds its first value on the whole human race: I rebel—therefore we are."[20]

Long before the terms became common currency, Camus's book spoke of violent "state terrorism" and the equally violent counterterrorism—either irrational or ideologically sophisticated—unleashed by insurgents. For him, the two sides of terror feed and have always fed on each other. "All modern [violent] revolutions," *The Rebel* states, "have ended in a reinforcement of the power of the state"—from Napoleon to Stalin and Hitler. In Nietzschean language, the text speaks of "the growing omnipotence of the state" and of "the strange and terrifying growth of the modern state" seeking to impose total domination on populations. In the case of German fascism, the book denounces the striving for "a technological world empire," for a "religion of anti-Christian technology"—a striving that did not come to an end in 1945.[21] However, violent revolutionaries—today called "terrorists"—only replicate the striving for total control and the elimination of dissent. Camus carefully distinguishes genuine rebellion from violent revolution. "The revolutionary," he writes, "is simultaneously a rebel or he is not a [genuine] revolutionary but a policeman and a bureaucrat who turns against rebellion. But if he is a rebel, he ends by taking sides against revolution" (operating as terrorism). A genuine rebel refuses to be treated as an "object," a cog in a totalizing machine, or to be reduced to part of an engine of history. An act of rebellion, for Camus, introduces a breach in the totalizing apparatus of power; it testifies to the unique dignity of human beings and to something "common to all men which eludes the world of power." Ultimately, rebellion involves both a rejection or negation and an affirmation: it rejects the dominant nihilism and all forms of complicity in violent destruction and mayhem; at the same time, it upholds and cherishes life, fully aware of human limits: "The affirmation of a limit, a dignity, and a beauty common to all men entails the necessity of extending this value to embrace everything and everyone."[22]

These comments lead Camus to the most inspiring part of his book: "Thought at the Meridian." As he observes, rebellion assigns a limit to oppression and totalizing power; in doing so, it acknowledges the dignity common to all human beings. It places in the center of its frame of reference "an obvious complicity among men, a common texture, the solidarity of chains, a communication between human being and human being which makes men similar and united" (in their differences). By contrast, murder or mayhem "cuts the world in two"; it sacrifices commonality by "consecrating difference in blood." What motivates the rebel is an ethical impulse, a desire for concrete interhuman justice. "If injustice is bad for the rebel," we read, "it is not because it contradicts an eternal idea of justice, but because it perpetuates the silent hostility that separates the oppressor from the oppressed. It kills the small part of existence that can be realized on this earth through the mutual understanding of men." Murder and mayhem are not only acts of physical violence but also destroyers of shared meanings. All totalitarian regimes and all totalizing forms of terrorism proceed by way of monologue "preached from the top of lonely mountains," but "on the stage as in reality, monologue precedes death." In rebellion, thus, freedom and solidarity necessarily cohere. To be sure, extreme or limitless freedom—the freedom to kill others—is not compatible with rebellion. But the rebel requires the freedom to act against injustice, which excludes "the right to destroy the existence and freedom of others." Camus sums up his argument in these lines: "It is then possible to say that rebellion, when it develops into destruction, is illogical. Claiming the unity of the human condition, it is a force of life, not of death. Its most profound logic is . . . the logic of creation."[23]

Dissent in Community

The preceding discussion has sought to highlight the difference between two main forms of dissent or critical resistance: on the one hand libertarian social Darwinism and on the other ethically motivated conscientious resistance. In the former case, resistance aims to further the pursuit of particular, more or less self-centered interests; in the latter case, it serves to advance in some fashion the public interest or the "common good." The first type is enacted for the sake of a particular private benefit; the second involves an appeal from a corrupted or oppressive public life to a reformed and more legitimate public regime. Differently phrased: resistance is directed in one instance against community as such, whereas in the other instance it involves dissent within (or in the bounds of) community. As I should add, what matters here is not whether resistance is the work of a solitary individual or a group of like-minded individuals. The issue concerns the purpose of action, not the number of agents.

My presentation, I trust, leaves no doubt about my own preferences in this matter: I find social Darwinism and selfish libertarianism deeply flawed, and my sympathy is with public-spirited resistance as exemplified in the life work of Thoreau and Gandhi and in Camus's rebel. To lend added support to this preference, I want to mention—by way of conclusion—two other examples: one taken from the dawn of Western civilization and the other from its dusk (or the time of its derailment). The first example involves Socrates and his conflict with the collective opinion of his city, Athens. As is well known, Socrates was accused of impiety (of not honoring the gods of the city) and of corrupting young people by disturbing reigning beliefs. The story is reported in both *The Apology* and *Criton*, and both texts reveal the central issue: the clash between an upright critical mind and a lethargic or manipulated public opinion. In *The Apology*, Socrates drives home this issue by asking whether the multitude or public opinion is always right in questions of ethics or justice, as his accusers claim. But how can this be if the multitude never bothers to inquire into these questions, whereas he, Socrates, has made such inquiry his all-consuming business? Regarding the issue of impiety, he has always followed an inner spiritual guidance—as even his accusers acknowledge—and how could this practice entail a rejection of the divine? In the end, Socrates reluctantly acknowledges a near-insoluble conflict between the public and critical dissent. "The fact is that no man in the world will come off safe who honestly opposes either you or any other multitude, and tries to hinder the many unjust and illegal doings in a state."[24]

Recounting the final hours before Socrates's death, *Criton* is a paean to the dignity of the human spirit in confrontation with collective prejudice and meanness. As is clear from *The Apology*, the charges brought by his accusers against him were unjust, and so was the final verdict of death handed down by the court. The basic issue here was the relation between the city—or the opinion of the multitude in a city—and the rule of justice. Was it the case that, due to the injustice inflicted on Socrates, the rule of justice and the bond linking Socrates and the city had been broken and that he was now free to escape the verdict by seeking refuge elsewhere—as his friend Criton suggests? But, by seeking to escape the verdict, Socrates himself would commit an injustice and thus descend to the level of the ignorant and vindictive multitude. This Socrates refuses to do, arguing, "We must not do wrong in return, or do evil to anyone in the world, however we may be treated by them." With this refusal, Socrates seals his fate, but he also maintains the idea and the bond of justice linking him to the city (which he had never left throughout his life). With his final action, Socrates strongly affirms his freedom—a freedom from injustice though not from the city and its ethical bond of solidarity. In dissenting from the multitude, he aims not to destroy the city but to lift it up to the rule of justice, without which a city cannot endure.[25]

The second example is taken from the time of modern civilization's derailment, when the modern state in Germany decayed into Nazi totalitarianism. Although there were pockets of dissent acting sporadically from the beginning of the regime, more organized forms of resistance surfaced before and during the course of World War II, mainly within the military establishment. Even prior to the outbreak of the war, a group of officers sought to avert the looming disaster through political means, but the fast pace of events nullified this effort. Once the war was under way, repeated acts of resistance—in the form of assassination plots or suicide-bombing attempts—were planned or carried out by members of the higher officer corps, but unforeseen circumstances always foiled these moves. In evaluating the attempts, one has to take into account the extreme complexity of the situation: the fact that military officers are bound by an oath of loyalty to their country—an oath weighing especially heavily during wartime (and even more so when the war was turning against Germany). One can be certain that many or most officers involved in the resistance felt deeply this burden of loyalty, while also being profoundly troubled by the growing barbarism and criminality of the country's leaders. Thus, like Antigone long ago, they were starkly conflicted between two loyalties: one to their "city" or political regime and the other to the higher "rule of justice" and the "better angels" of their country. This may account for some of their prevarications and periods of indecision. The resistance movement against Hitler came to a head in 1943 with Operation Valkyrie. One of the members of the plot was a young staff officer, Graf von Stauffenberg (who was also troubled by religious scruples in addition to his scruples as an officer). The plot to kill Hitler was enacted on July 20 but failed in its main goal; Stauffenberg and fellow resisters were executed.[26]

As one should add, anti-Nazi resistance was not exclusively in the hands of military officers but also had civilian support in some quarters. One instance was the antiwar campaign White Rose, launched and carried forward by some students and teachers at the University of Munich in early 1943—a campaign that was quickly crushed and its leaders executed. Another important civilian figure in the resistance movement was Dietrich Bonhoeffer (1906–1945), a Lutheran pastor, theologian, and lifelong antifascist. Bonhoeffer had studied theology in Berlin, where he discovered the neo-orthodox "dialectical theology" of Karl Barth. He subsequently spent a year at Union Theological Seminary in New York under the guidance of Reinhold Niebuhr. After returning to Germany, he immediately launched an attack against Hitler, publicly calling the führer a *Verführer* (seducer or pied-piper). In early 1934 at a gathering of Lutheran clergy, he endorsed the so-called Barmen Declaration (drafted by Barth), which insisted that Christ and not a political despot was the head of the church. At the same time, he was instrumental in founding the Confessing Church in opposition to Protestant clergy co-opted by the regime. The regime was quick to retaliate by harassing Bonhoeffer in his clerical and academic activities. In 1936, a teaching position he held in Berlin was revoked, forcing him into the role of an itinerant clergyman. At the beginning of the war, he became acquainted with members of a resistance movement located in the heart of German military intelligence (the so-called Abwehr), a linkage that made him familiar with assassination plots. As in the case of Stauffenberg, Bonhoeffer's scruples were deeply nurtured by his faith and the divine commandment against killing. As he wrote in *Ethics*, "When a man takes guilt upon himself in responsibility, he imputes his guilt to himself and no one else.... Before himself he is acquitted by his conscience, but before God he hopes only for grace."[27] Arrested in April 1943, he spent a year and a half in military prison. In February 1945, he was moved to Buchenwald, where he was hanged on April 9, just two weeks before the camp was liberated.

Many decades have passed since the Great War, and it is argued that in the meantime totalitarianism has disappeared. But has it really? Or has it returned in different guises? One should probably not underestimate the ingenuity and resourcefulness of the modern state—that "cold monster" and "horse of death" bemoaned by Nietzsche. Quite likely, the great Leviathan has not been caught or tamed; even when outwardly assuming innocuous airs, it may still seethe inside with fires of destruction. Moreover, since the totalitarianism of the previous century, Leviathan has acquired new and unheard-of methods: unprecedented technological powers of mayhem, unlimited capabilities of surveillance, and uncanny forms of brainwashing and "double-speak." Camus's *The Rebel* contains some dark lines that one needs to ponder: "The sources of life and creation seem exhausted. Fear paralyzes a Europe peopled with phantoms and machines."[28] What is the meaning of the politics of fear recently gripping the West? What should one make of the cult of violence and death evident in movies, in video games, and often in real life? What does the cult presage? Here, by way of conclusion, a line from Nietzsche's *The Wanderer and His Shadow*: "Rather perish than hate and fear. And twice rather perish than make oneself hated and feared—this must someday become the highest maxim for every single commonwealth too."[29]

7

Faith and Communicative Freedom

A Tribute to Wolfgang Huber

Where the Spirit of the Lord is, there is freedom.
—2 Corinthians 3:17

On March 23, 2012, in his inaugural speech before the German Parliament, incoming federal president Joachim Gauck addressed crucial issues of contemporary public life. His address stood under the motto "Let's not succumb to fear but promote courage." Given the somber context of the time—the financial meltdown of the preceding years, the perceived "crisis" of European integration, and the widespread upsurge of chauvinism—his comments were themselves courageous and meant to be uplifting as an antidote to fear and despair. The courage displayed in the address was particularly noteworthy when profiled against the dark episodes of German history in the twentieth century: the Nazi regime and the ensuing division of Germany after the war. Without in any way neglecting or belittling these episodes, Gauck pleaded for a balanced historical perspective as a shield against defeatism. Despite the dark shadows of guilt and failure, he said, one should not forget also "that other part of our history": the part involving "the foundation of a new political culture of freedom, of lived responsibility, and of the capacity for peace and solidarity among people."[1]

In extolling the idea of a "political culture of freedom," Gauck

seemed to reiterate language familiar from the Cold War with its
opposition between Western freedom and Eastern totalitarianism.
In reality, however, his speech entirely transcended Cold War rhetoric. As he made clear, freedom for him was by no means synonymous with egotism or the rampant pursuit of self-interest but was
closely linked with moral responsibility and the quest for justice and
solidarity. In his eloquent formulation, "Freedom is a necessary condition of justice. For what justice, including social justice, means and
what we have to do in order to approximate it cannot be decreed
in paternalistic fashion but can only be found through intensive
democratic discussion." Conversely, "the striving for justice is indis-
pensible for the preservation of freedom."[2] As one should note, the
relation between freedom and justice for Gauck was (and is) not
a preestablished harmony but rather a tensional correlation, an
unsteady equilibrium/disequilibrium requiring constant renegotiation. This understanding is in accord with his basic view of democracy as an ongoing experiment, a system continuously capable of
learning (*lernfähig*)—a conception not far removed from Martin
Luther's view of Christian churches as institutions requiring permanent reformation (*ecclesia semper reformanda*).[3]

This parallel between democratic and ecclesial reformism provides me with a welcome opening wedge for this chapter's main
theme: the review of Wolfgang Huber's work (on the occasion of
his seventieth birthday). Despite certain differences of life trajectories—which have placed Gauck in the public square and Huber
more in ecclesial contexts—the affinities between the two individuals are striking. Both were trained as theologians (the former in East
Germany, the latter in West Germany); both have been ministers in
evangelical or Lutheran churches (with Huber serving as president
of the German Evangelical Church from 2003 to 2009); but both
have also tried to bridge the divide between public and religious life,
between state and church (Huber was even nominated as candidate
for the federal presidency in 2010). Above all, for both there is an
urgent need for freedom and creative innovation in public as well as
in ecclesial contexts—although freedom (in opposition to license)
remains for them embedded in shared or constantly renegotiated
meaning structures (what Huber calls "communicative freedom").
In this chapter, I want to concentrate on the correlation of freedom

and solidarity in Huber's thought, using some prominent texts as my guide. I hope my comments will shed light on the compatibility (though not identity) between democratic politics and faith.

Consequences of Christian Freedom

Born in 1942, Wolfgang Huber was not a direct witness of the Nazi regime. His outlook has been decisively shaped by the experiences of fascist (and Communist) totalitarianism. More broadly, his outlook must be seen as a reaction to some of the profound dilemmas or bifurcations characterizing Western liberal modernity, such as the dualisms public reason/private faith and external structures/internal conscience (dualisms that gain a measure of support from the neo-Protestant theory of "two worlds" stipulating a gulf between immanence and transcendence). Faced with these modern antagonisms, religious faith seemed to be left with only two options: either to be co-opted by the "secular" world and merge into prevailing power structures or else to withdraw from this world into a realm of inner self-cultivation. Employing a different vocabulary (which I have used in other places), one might call these options the temptations or derailments of "politicization" and "privatization"—both of which deprive faith of its capacity to serve as the "salt of the earth."[4] Against these dangers or derailments, Huber has followed a critical path that seeks to overcome the "two worlds" thesis by insisting on their differential entwinement (or their unity in difference). In charting this path, he followed to some extent in the footsteps of Karl Barth's "dialectical theology" as well as of Dietrich Bonhoeffer's critical or "professing" (*bekennend*) Protestantism. These and other lines of influence are clearly articulated in one of Huber's earlier studies, *Folgen christlicher Freiheit* (Consequences of Christian freedom), which I take as my initial text.

As the book's subtitle indicates, its argument is developed "in the horizon of the Theological Declaration of Barmen." The reference here is to a declaration adopted by a gathering of evangelical theologians on May 31, 1934, under the leadership of Karl Barth. In essence, the Barmen Declaration constituted a rebellion against the Nazi regime's radical attempt to co-opt and politicize Christian churches for the regime's benefit. In opposition to this attempt, the assembled theologians reaffirmed the basic integrity and independence of religious faith vis-à-vis all political ideologies and power structures—an independence they found "most seriously threatened" at the time. As the declaration's preamble pointedly stated, when co-opted by political regimes, "the church ceases to be a church." The basic relation between faith and public life was pinpointed in a series of theses, the first of which was particularly adamant in "rejecting the false doctrine" that, next to God's word, the church could or should recognize "other powers, figures, and doctrines" as equally valid. This point was forcefully reiterated in the fifth thesis, which wholeheartedly rebuked totalizing claims that the state can provide "the sole and total order of human life"—or else that the church (beyond its religious mission) can "arrogate to itself state functions and state-like dignity," thus becoming an "established" church. As one should note, however, the rejection of totalitarian ambitions did not lead the theologians to endorse the retreat of faith into a purely inward or private domain. According to the second thesis, such a retreat was impossible because God's word lays claim not only to our inwardness but to "our whole life," thus enabling us to be socially engaged while "joyously liberated" from ungodly constraints.[5]

In his comments on the Barmen Declaration, Huber concentrates especially on the critical and liberating (or emancipating) quality of Christian faith vis-à-vis totalitarian power and all kinds of political co-optation. Among the egregious falsehoods debunked in the declaration, he notes, are the doctrine that the state can serve as "total order" of human life (subjugating religious institutions) and that religion (especially Christian religion) can be "instrumentalized in the service of political panaceas." As he correctly adds, once the modern state is elevated to the level of a "sole and total human order," the central meaning of politics and of public life is corrupted and falsified; hence, it belongs to the proper task of churches to remind the state and political leaders of the purpose and intrinsic limits of their calling. What is particularly noteworthy in Huber's comments, however, is their attention not only to negative delimitations but also to the positive role of religion in public life. From his angle, the so-called doctrine of the "two realms" (*Zwei-Reiche-Lehre*)—that is, the distinction between the realm of God and the temporal realm—cannot or should not be construed as a radical separation (just as it should not be fused in a totalized order). "Both in its negative and in its affirmative statements," says Huber, "the Barmen Declaration addressed certain dilemmas or 'deficits' in the life of churches." Thus, it constitutes a deficit or failing if the church allows itself to be sequestered in the "domain of privacy or inwardness," thereby losing the capacity to proclaim the Gospel in its relevance to life as a whole. Similarly, it is a deficit if the church insists on its separateness and, out of concern for structural self-identity, "loses the courage to speak critically on public issues" (that is, to speak truth to power).[6]

For Huber, the correlation between the critical-delimiting and the positive functions of the church—or, in Isaiah Berlin's terms, the correlation between "negative" and "positive" liberty—was illustrated at the time especially by two Christian pastors and theologians: Dietrich Bonhoeffer and Martin Niemöller. Bonhoeffer's pastoral work is memorable both for his resolute opposition to the state's totalizing claims and for his reaffirmation and creative reinterpretation of Gospel teachings. In his death at the hands of the Nazi regime, the liberating/emancipatory and the "confessing" (bekennend) sides of Christian faith were fused in exemplary fashion. The spirit of Bonhoeffer's example was continued by several pastors, but especially by Martin Niemöller, whose work was crucial during the German reconstruction after the war. In contrast to a tendency toward privatization and ecclesial self-contentment, Niemöller at that time energetically defended the church's public relevance (Öffentlichkeitsanspruch), as articulated in the declaration's second thesis. As he stated in an important speech he gave in August 1945 criticizing the rigid bifurcation of state and Christian faith, "It is not sufficient or helpful to treat the state as a pagan institution and confront it with sacred commandments. . . . If the Christian church is to have a place and to be listened to in this world, then we have as church an interest and an obligation to provide people with justice and freedom also in the public life of the state. . . . After all, democracy is more congenial to Christianity than any kind of authoritarian regime that deprives individuals of their right and freedom."[7]

Apart from citing the testimony of important pastors, Huber's commentary also refers to crucial theological debates revolving around the doctrine of the "two realms," debates whose high points

can be found in the works of Karl Barth and ultimately Martin
Luther. Surprisingly, in view of his reputation (among some theologians) as a rigid dualist, Huber finds an ally of his views in Barth's
"dialectical theology." That theology, he writes, "which is reputed to
have proclaimed the divorce between the modern world and Christian faith . . . [,] triggered a process of reflection in which the relevance of Christian faith in social contexts and hence the question of
the political responsibility of the church were strongly underscored."
This view of the "differential correlation" of the two realms was not
a new discovery of the Barmen Declaration but can be traced to earlier formulations in 1922. Already at that time, Barth—in critical
confrontation with other theologians—corrected the static dualism of realms through the injection of a temporal or eschatological dimension. He interpreted the "paradoxical doctrine of the two
realms," states Huber, in the sense of an "eschatological difference
between God's realm and the world," whereby the former acquires
the quality of a pervasive leaven or ferment (or "salt of the earth").
By contrast, a static dualism of realms—especially when construed
as the dualism of inside and outside—cancels this dialectical, eschatological ferment. In that case, the realm of inwardness is religiously
valorized, whereas the world is spiritually denuded. What is left is
a "psychological implementation" of God's will, and its social and
political implementation is resolutely rejected.[8]

In Huber's view, a similar "differential correlation" can also be
found in Martin Luther's theology of the two realms—again despite
its frequent misconstrual as a rigid dichotomy. As Huber concedes,
Luther's teachings in this respect do not form a "fully developed or
systematic doctrine"—something that had to do with the turbu-
lent and fluid historical context of his work. Nevertheless, despite
varying formulations, it is possible—for Huber—to detect a "basic
structure" (Grundform) of theological thought that involves "the
unity of difference and coordination (Einheit von Unterscheiden und
Zuordnen)." Although the difference between God and humans is
the "basic distinction," theology cannot stop here and in the very
next step has to correlate the difference by thematizing God's turning toward humans and the turning of humanity to God. For Huber,
whenever addressing the issue of the two realms, Luther always took
these two steps, distinguishing and correlating, thereby display-

ing the "basic structure" of theological thought in exemplary fashion. As Huber adds, this structure was Luther's leitmotif not only in the question of "realms" but also in the domain of ecclesial functions and offices. In opposition to the privileging of solitary God-encounters, Luther always stressed the role of mediating ecclesial (or communicative) relationships. In Huber's words, Luther repeatedly insisted "that God wishes to save humans via humans, that salvation is humanly mediated. God's incarnation has as a consequence that nobody can claim to have 'direct access' to God while exiting from the human community."[9]

As it happened, the genuine point of Luther's teachings was often missed in post-Reformation times—a fact that can be attributed to worldly or "secular" developments but also to the attitude of Christian churches at the time. On the secular side, Western modernity unleashed an immense array of economic, industrial, and technological innovations tending to dwarf or marginalize religious faith; in reaction, Christian churches often retreated into self-maintenance. Modernity, says Huber, stands under the aegis of "the expansion of human domination over nature"; as a result of this expansion, "a gulf opened up between the faith in divine rule of the world and the conviction of the complete human dominion of the earth. . . . The notion that the world is ruled by a benevolent God could not or only with great difficulty be reconciled with the reality of the growing human domination of the earth." Faced with these developments, Christian churches have often curtailed their active mission, thereby surrendering themselves to the dictates of an advancing "secularity." This was especially the case in the field of economics. What tended to remain immune from critique, Huber notes, were especially the guiding principles of economic life. In fact, "all these guiding ideas of industrial expansionism"—the "quasi-religious halo" surrounding unlimited economic growth and the unrestricted disposition over private property, together with the steadily growing human control of nature and the reduction of life's meaning to material conditions of production—"were, if at all, only to a very limited extent targets of religious ideological critique."[10]

Returning to the Barmen Declaration, Huber provides a detailed narrative of its aftermath—what Hans-Georg Gadamer would have called its "effective history" (*Wirkungsgeschichte*). As Huber points out, the period after the war was characterized by a tendency to accentuate some of the declaration's theses while deemphasizing or bracketing others. Thus, some interpreters placed the entire stress on the negative-delimiting phrases of Thesis 1—coupled with a focus on ecclesial self-regulation in Thesis 5—whereas others valorized the emancipatory language of Thesis 2 with its call to "a life of religious freedom and responsible service." On the whole, however, developments in postwar Germany—in Huber's view—tended to privilege the first while maginalizing the second, more socially and politically engaged interpretation. This means that the central concern was with the delimitation of religion from totalitarian (fascist or Communist) derailments, a delimitation that had as a corollary the focus on the cultivation of private faith accompanied by attention to ecclesial self-management and self-contentment. This tendential shift of focus brings back into view the previously mentioned "deficits" of religious life, especially the deficit resulting from the willingness of Christian churches to be sequestered in the "domains of privacy and inwardness" while abandoning or neglecting the relevance of the Gospels for the "wholeness of human life."[11]

As Huber's study shows, the sketched trends took their toll. He writes pointedly that the development of evangelical churches in postwar Germany signaled in important respects "a regress behind the text of the Barmen Declaration"—a regress attributable to the "forces of restauration" that gained steady ascendancy not only in social and political contexts but also in the life of churches. What is particularly deplorable is the fact that these restorative trends were aided and abetted by the "neo-Protestant" accent on individual inwardness and privacy, a stress totally obscuring the role of social, political, and ecclesial communities. From this angle, the idea that "Christian political action is a service making possible a life of freedom," just as the idea that "Christian ecclesial communities provide the venue for properly understanding this service"—these and similar ideas were pushed into the background and not even mentioned as "collateral considerations" (Begleitgedanken). At this point, it becomes clear that freedom for Huber is not a private faculty, not an ego-centered property or a power-legitimating control. For Christians, he notes, freedom is always a "promise" (Verheissung), a gift or grant of which we are the beneficiaries and not the authors. As he writes in a chapter of *Consequences of Christian Freedom* titled "Freedom and Institution," "Freedom is realized when one experiences the other as enrichment and as task of one's own life. Hence, it surges forth only in community and mutual dialogue, in *communio* and *communicatio;* hence it may be called 'communicative freedom.'"[12]

In the Spirit of Freedom

In many ways, Huber's study of 1983 laid the foundation for an impressive intellectual development expressed in a long string of publications, lectures, and sermons in subsequent years. Despite variations of accent and a steady growth of insights, the trajectory displays a remarkable continuity of arguments clustered around the notion of "communicative freedom." For present purposes, to show the continuous unfolding of horizons I want to focus briefly on a study published some fifteen years later: the book titled *Im Geist der Freiheit: Für eine Ökumene der Profile* (In the spirit of freedom: For an ecumenism of profiles, 2007). Basically, the book shows Wolfgang Huber wrestling with some of the most prominent features of the time: trends such as multiculturalism and globalization as well as their repercussions on "ecumenism" (defined as the relation between Christian confessions) and on broader interfaith relations. In this context, the study develops a notion that is crucial for a well-understood social and religious "pluralism": interconfessional contacts must acknowledge both the communalities and the differences between religious partners and thus be oriented toward "unity in diversity." As Huber points out, for many people "ecumenical progress" means that confessional distinctions are steadily erased, making room for an undifferentiated amalgam. This, however, is a non sequitur. In his view (which I take to be correct), ecumenism means that churches are open to and willing to learn from each other without merging into a bland fusion. This is the significance of his phrase "ecumenism of profiles."[13]

What this phrase implies is that ecumenical discussions, however polite and friendly, must reflect both the "unity in spirit" (as recommended in Ephesians 4:3–7) and the confessional distinctness deriving from historical and religious contexts. As Huber notes, it is in such discussions that the "special evangelical accent on freedom" comes to the fore. His willingness to profile this accent is evident in numerous passages, especially in some exchanges or encounters with Pope Benedict XVI. In August 2005, Huber addressed the newly elected pope in a speech that for the first time used the notion of profiles. Referring to the Peace of Augsburg concluded 450 years earlier (in 1555), Huber reminded his interlocutor of "the long and arduous path toward the peaceful coexistence of confessions in our land." Along this path, he stated, our churches have learned that every spiritual disagreement presupposes "the search for truth in the shared commitment to peace"; they have also learned at long last "how to distinguish between state and church, between citizenship and confession, between human dignity and religious faith." Turning to the specific confessional distinction at hand, the speech stated that the acknowledgment of commonalities and the desirable removal of mutual prejudices cannot cancel the existence of "clear differences" in many areas. Becoming even more specific, it stressed the need for "thoroughgoing theological work" if we genuinely want to converse "about the meaning of pastoral office and Eucharist, of apostolic succession and the role of women in the church."[14]

The speech is not the only encounter between Huber and the pope discussed in the book. Another example of confessional "profiling" can be found in a fascinating section titled "Glaube und Vernunft" (Faith and reason). The section takes its departure from the Protestant accent on *sola fide* and the frequent allegation that by privileging faith Protestantism is hostile to reason. As it happens, Benedict XVI leveled a similar accusation against Islam or Islamic culture in his Regensburg speech of September 2006. In that speech, the pope exhorted Muslims to embrace Greek philosophy as a viable ally of faith (apparently forgetting the role of Alfarabi and Ibn Rushd in Islamic history). Whatever the value of that exhortation to Muslims may have been, the pope on other occasions implicated Protestantism in the sidelining or divorcing of reason from faith. A prominent exemplar of this divorce is Immanuel Kant, who, according to Benedict, had "to put reason and thought aside in order to make room for faith." As Huber correctly points out, this charge depends on the character or meaning of reason—of which there are many. In the instant case, it seems to rely on a precritical rational metaphysics that Kant indeed put aside, but he had his own conception of rationality and his own way of correlating reason and faith. According to Huber, Kant's work did not banish God outside the confines of rational thought; rather, he "liberated the idea of God" from the grip of an overarching dogmatic metaphysics. A similar point can be made regarding Protestant thought from Luther to Kant and beyond. For Huber, that thought does not disdain the rational side of faith, but the connection here "has necessarily something to do with critical judgment, with scholarly dialogue, and with responsibility in the forum of public reason." To this extent, one can say that Protestantism—like any genuine religious outlook—"would dissolve itself when abandoning the connection of reason and faith."[15]

The confessional "profiling" is continued in a section dealing with the magisterium or the church's authority in matters not only of faith but of reason. In his encyclical *Deus caritas est* of 2006, Pope Benedict addressed the relation between church and state, between ecclesial and public functions. In this context, he affirmed in modified form the medieval legacy of the church's "indirect power" (*potestas indirecta*) in the public domain. The need for such an indirect influence was predicated in the encyclical on the weakness of human thought, on the tendency of unguided reason to go astray in the world. To counter this tendency, the pope at the time introduced the idea of a needed "purification of reason" (*Reinigung der Vernunft*), a purification to be effected preferably by church leaders through the magisterium. Faced with this potential blending of secular and religious authority, Huber in response returns to the tenets of the Barmen Declaration of 1934—that is, the differentiated coordination of "two realms." Although he acknowledges that reason can go astray and hence needs to be purified in some way, in his view the remedy cannot be found in an ecclesiastic monopoly in matters of thought. The ground for this argument is that thinking necessarily involves questioning, which cannot proceed without freedom—a freedom that in modern times has given rise to a pluralism of perspectives (which cannot be synthesized without coercion). "If rationality itself has a multi-perspectival and hence plural character, the rationality contained in Catholic social teachings cannot be universal" and has to allow for contestation. More broadly stated: "From an evangelical angle, the claim that the church alone is responsible for the purification of reason needs to be critically called into question, for such purification (if one wishes to retain the term) has to be viewed rather as a dialogical process in which the church needs not only to teach but also to learn."[16]

In Huber's text, the profiling effort is not limited just to ecumenical relations (in the narrow sense) but extends more broadly to interfaith relations (between world religions). Despite an emphasis on openness and respectful tolerance, the difference between religions—for Huber—should not be papered over in a fictitious synthesis; precisely under the aegis of goodwill, it should be possible to voice critical reservations without arrogant polemics. A case in point is the status of politics or the public realm in many or most Muslim countries. In his view, the separation of church and state—a "basic presupposition of equal human rights"—is "not yet guaranteed in the Islamic world" (or at least large parts of it). Rather, "the state functions as organized religion," which means that "law is religious law and the sources of law reside in religion." In this respect, a mutual learning process is needed, especially in Europe. Europeans should learn about the uplifting aspects of Islamic faith, but Muslims also need to learn important lessons about human rights and about the foundations of a free democratic order that also guarantees freedom of religion. In the latter respect, Huber's text contains forceful statements that deserve to be lifted up and pondered. "Freedom of religion," we read, "constitutes the crucial test [Nagelprobe] for the attitude of the state toward human freedom." The "free exercise of religion" (to use the American formula) must be granted to religious communities as well as to individuals to the greatest possible extent—but not without limits; these limits are reached whenever the free exercise shades over into monopolistic domination of the public domain. Here, a basic acquisition of modernity comes into play: "Only the religiously neutral [or not religiously co-opted] state can guarantee religious liberty in the full sense. By contrast, a religiously 'bound' state tied to a particular religion runs the risk of privileging one faith over other faiths."[17]

In Huber's text, one finds many similar pithy formulations and political-theoretical insights, but of course not all can be discussed here. Remarkable in their clarity are his comments on different types of "secularization" and on the possibly misleading connotations of the term postsecularity; equally impressive are his elaborations on the meaning of the terms *church* and *ecclesial office* (*Amt*).[18] For present purposes, I want to draw attention briefly to two additional themes: globalization and "evangelical virtues." As Huber clearly states, globalization is a complex phenomenon "with many faces." Under its auspices, it is possible to spread national, ethnic, or religious hatreds quickly across the world, but it is also possible to organize within a short span of time rescue actions for victims of tsunamis or nuclear disasters. Under the same auspices, it is possible to bring a measure of economic prosperity to disadvantaged people, but there is also the prospect that economic power is wielded selfishly, thus derailing economic justice. It is precisely these economic abuses that trigger—or should trigger—Christian evangelical protest. As Huber writes, amplifying comments in his earlier study, we live in a time when—silhouetted against pockets of immense wealth—"a stark inhuman poverty prevails among millions of people," yet in many parts of the world economic and social inequality is not tamed but grows by leaps and bounds. Here is Huber's unequivocal response to these inequities: "In questions of economic justice, Christian faith cannot be neutral; it does not submit to the omnipotence of economics." Instead of surrendering itself to so-called economic laws, Christian faith finds its yardstick in the Gospels: "Human dignity, human rights, and social justice are the basic standards for judging economic behavior."[19]

In order to combat social and economic injustice, strong efforts are required on the part of churches as well as of engaged citizens. It is in this context that the notion of "evangelical virtues" plays an important role. The invocation of virtues is surprising and somewhat puzzling given the traditional Protestant emphasis on faith and grace alone (*sola fide, sola gratia*), which serves to sideline human effort. As Huber admits, in the Christian and especially the Protestant tradition, virtues are not seen as human accomplishments or achievements but as gifts of divine grace. Hence, the notion of evangelical virtues is by no means "self-evident." This is particularly true of the so-called theological virtues (faith, hope, and love), for, clearly, faith here is not anchored in human virtue, but virtue in faith. Hence, from an evangelical angle, questions of virtues and vices are essentially predicated on "the human relation with God." For Huber, the same holds true also for the classical "cardinal" virtues (courage, temperance, wisdom, justice), which likewise are grounded in faith.[20] What may be neglected here is that in the Aristotelian formulation virtue requires not only an opening toward goodness but also human work and continuous practice, a practice sometimes amounting to strenuous labor. Perhaps from an evangelical perspective this labor is overshadowed too much by spiritual inwardness. There is a further consideration that applies especially to a modern democratic life. Precisely in modern pluralistic democracies that embrace many types of believers and nonbelievers, the conduct of members cannot be guided uniformly by Christian or evangelical virtues; precisely in view of the separation of church and state, public ethics has to be nurtured by many religious and secular resources. Differently put, what is needed is the robust cultivation of civic or public virtues without which democracy cannot flourish. But I have a feeling that Bishop Huber probably would agree with me on this point.

Communicative Freedom

Far from being finished, Huber's opus is very much a work in progress. In preparation for his seventieth birthday celebration in 2012, a new book was published with the title *Von der Freiheit: Perspektiven für eine solidarische Welt* (On freedom: Perspectives for a world of solidarity). Ranging over many important themes, the far-flung book constitutes a kind of summa of Huber's teachings (at least for the time being). It reached me so recently that I cannot fully explore here the richness of its insights. For present purposes, I want to reflect only on the issue of communicative freedom, which in many ways is Huber's core idea and serves as leitmotif of his new study. In fact, the opening prelude is dedicated to its meaning. As he acknowledges, freedom is something precious, but its meaning is hard to define. It seems easier to define it negatively—namely, as the absence of external obstacles hindering or obstructing the pursuit of one's goals. In this connection, freedom is often seen as a legal right, a claim one can marshal against the interference in one's interest by others or by the state. Basically, freedom is seen here as an individual prerogative allowing the drawing of clear boundaries around oneself. For Huber, this construal is deeply flawed or defective; it neglects the character of freedom as an engaged mode of being that is instantiated in daily practices. As soon as such instantiation takes places, freedom cannot be individually sequestered but enters into an "indissoluble relation with social justice." Seen from this angle, freedom is no longer a private property but is realized in a "shared order that grants to all access to freedom." Thus, communication and solidarity are not limits but "genuine expressions of freedom."[21]

The meaning of this constellation is further elucidated in a subsequent section of the book devoted to "responsible freedom." In this section, Huber takes his departure (again) from the predominant modern conception of freedom as individual or private autonomy. To some extent, this conception was epitomized in Kantian and neo-Protestant ethical teachings. By locating the criterion of ethics strictly in internal "goodwill," Kantian ethics abstracted from concrete human conduct and especially from the societal and institutional contexts of action. Instead of forming part and parcel of morality, such contexts were assigned to the external domain of legality. To some degree, this one-sidedness was overcome in Hegel's idea of *Sittlichkeit* (ethical life), where goodwill was able to reach concrete manifestation. For Huber, it is important to recognize that individual moral action is always embedded in societal contexts and especially in the institutions of human interaction. Seen from this perspective, Christian theology cannot (or should not) blithely ignore teachings of interactive sociology and social psychology. What is evident in many of these teachings is that human life is not a solitary venture and that social interaction cannot be reduced to a Hobbesian "war of all against all"; rather, a properly conducted human life achieves fullness precisely in "reciprocal openness and transparency." Borrowing a page from social (transactional) philosophy, the text concludes that freedom does not consist in isolation or mutual delimitation but in an engagement where "one experiences the other as enrichment and as task of one's own life." For this reason, freedom requires community and communication, which again justifies the label *communicative freedom*.[22]

By way of conclusion in this chapter, I want to profile briefly what I consider to be the general significance of Huber's work. I think this work marks a crucial step beyond the narrowly individualistic and privatizing character of liberal "neo-Protestantism." As Huber says in *In the Spirit of Freedom*, "At a time when the modern individualistic conception of freedom has undeniably reached a dead end, it is a distinctive task of evangelical churches to exemplify concretely a way of life where freedom and responsibility, self-determination and reliability are connected."[23] In opposition to a widespread celebration of solitary inwardness, his work leads us back to a renewed appreciation of community life and the ethical role of institutions. To this extent, it links up with certain "communitarian" tendencies in recent Protestant theology worldwide and especially in the United States. Thus, the writings of theologians such as Stanley Hauerwas and John B. Cobb Jr. are unintelligible except as a critique of the predominance of self-contained Protestant individualism.[24] To be sure, in Huber's case, the appreciation of community life does not lead to the endorsement of a heavy-handed, authoritarian "communitarianism"—an outlook that Charles Taylor at one point characterized as "paleo-Durkheimian dispensation" hostile to the emancipatory qualities of modern life.[25] Rather, the issue is precisely the reconciliation of freedom and community, of individual and social responsibility, bringing back into view the notions of *ecclesia semper reformanda* and *societas semper reformanda*. As Huber states, "The dynamic tension between tradition and innovation is constitutive for evangelical churches. Protestants know that a critical engagement with the past is necessary precisely for religious renewal." To this extent, evangelical churches address their message to mature (*mündig*) Christians, and their notion of community is that of a "church of freedom," more specifically of "communicative freedom."[26]

To grasp the sense of the latter phrase more clearly, some attention to its intellectual provenance may be helpful. As Huber indicates, the notion was first suggested to him by Michael Theunissen, the philosopher famous for his studies on self–other relations and for his interpretation of Hegel's notion of *Logic* as the interactive unfolding of the divine (or absolute) "spirit." What impressed him in this notion, Huber says, is its ability to convey the essence of Christian faith where "freedom and love of fellow beings are closely linked."[27] Other tributaries to the notion come from post-Kantian "critical" philosophy as formulated by Karl-Otto Apel and Jürgen Habermas as well as from aspects of Charles Taylor's "liberal" communitarianism. Following the "linguistic turn" in twentieth-century philosophy, both Apel and Habermas have recast the Kantian focus on transcendental consciousness in the direction of a "communicative" or "interpretive" community or else the gathering of participants in a normative "discourse." Although appreciating some of the insights of critical theory, Huber distances himself from it mainly along two lines. First, the communicative community postulated by that theory still seems to be composed of self-interested individuals and thus to reflect the premises of social contractarianism. The other, more important difference resides in the fact that post-Kantian discourse is predicated on procedural and "deontological" assumptions and thus reflects the Kantian bifurcation between "is" and "ought," empirical conduct and normative standards.[28] To correct these limitations, Huber seems willing, at least in part, to replace deontology with teleology and thus, in line with Taylor and Franklin Gamwell, to orient social and public life in the direction of "goodness" or the "good life." To the extent that this might be the case, one wonders whether evangelical ethics might eventually find more common ground with virtue ethics.[29]

What is most important to remember is that, for Huber, the message of the Gospels cannot be confined to inwardness or be sequestered in the walls of churches. As he emphasizes in all his writings—especially in his text from 2007—evangelical work cannot be entirely nonpolitical or nonpublic. Rather, the message of the Gospels imposes on all "the responsibility for justice and peace, for the dignity of human life and the integrity of nature." When one speaks of the "public role" (*Öffentlichkeit*) of Christianity, what is involved is not only the relation between church and state but also "the significance of faith for civil society." As Huber stresses in eloquent language, the evangelical church in the twenty-first century has to be a "socially engaged and vigilant church"; it cannot be self-contained but has to be a church for the world and "for others" (*Kirche für andere*). Basically, it has to keep alive "the hope in the coming kingdom of God"—a kingdom where (according to Psalm 85:11) "peace and justice kiss each other."[30] Read in this way, Huber's work is not far removed from Gauck's inaugural speech, which I mentioned at the beginning of this chapter and which, despite the dark shadows of the present, invoked the idea of a "political culture of freedom" and the vision of "peace and solidarity among people." Addressing himself to the younger generation—the generation of his children and grandchildren—President Gauck at that time sought to delineate the character of the country to which that young generation might willingly refer as "our country" or "our homeland." "Our land," he said, "must clearly be a country that unites both: freedom as condition of justice and justice as the precondition for the lived experience of freedom and human well-being."[31] I think these lines could also have been written by Wolfgang Huber.

8

Between Holism and Totalitarianism

Remembering Dimitry Likhachev

> The kingdom of God is freedom and the absence of
> power of man over man.
> —Nikolai Berdyaev, *Freedom and the Spirit*

In May 2013, I was honored with an invitation (which I accepted) to participate in the International Likhachev Conference in St. Petersburg.[1] I am not an expert on Russian history or culture, but I consider myself a humanist, a devotee of the so-called humanities, and when reading Dimitry Likhachev's works (those available to me in English), I am struck by his deep and unwavering humanity. He suffered a great deal during the Soviet era: he spent some four years in a gulag (in Solovki), but he never allowed his mind to be poisoned by the spirit of hatred, vengeance, or vindictive animosity. Historian Miklós Kun, in introducing Likhachev's memoir, speaks of his "gentle perseverance" in the midst of great deprivation and suffering. He also praises his "refined wisdom" and his "total, resolute honesty." But perhaps the greatest praise is contained in the statement that by virtue of his personality and perseverance he left behind him "ideals such as the Russian soul will have insatiable need in a totally different historical situation. He took the helm of the ship of Russian culture and steered it to a hopefully better world."[2]

Kun bestows on Likhachev another title: one of "the last of the

Russian intelligentsia." In doing so, he puts him in the company of an august generation of thinkers and writers including Nikolai Berdyaev, Sergei Bulgakov, Mikhail Bakhtin, Pitirim Sorokin, and Boris Pasternak (one of Likhachev's favorite authors). This was an incredibly talented generation of thinkers whose ideas found resonance in many foreign countries (including Europe and America) but were largely shunned or purged at home. Their worst punishment, says Kun, was that—"contrary to the traditions of Russian culture"—their works were never allowed really "to strike root in the blood-soaked Russian soil."[3] What I want to do here, in all brevity, is first to comment on Likhachev's memoir, next to turn to his celebrated reflections on Old Russian literature, and finally to draw attention to some of his initiatives following the demise of the Soviet Union. What should emerge from my discussion is his exemplary ability to balance modern freedom and solidarity.

A Memoir

The English translation of Likhachev's memoir is titled *Reflections on the Russian Soul* (the original Russian title was *Vospominaniya*). Here we learn that Dimitry Sergeyevich (1906–1999) came from a long-established, well-to-do merchant family in St. Petersburg, the city where he also grew up. Although belonging by birth to a middle-class (perhaps upper-middle-class) family, Dimitry in his attitude and conduct never displayed any class-based arrogance or snobbery; on the contrary, he was and always remained close to the ordinary people, whose aspirations for a decently good life he shared. According to Kun, what motivated him was never "any sympathy with victorious political parties" but rather "empathy with the people, always defeated and persecuted."[4] Likhachev's memoir is full of detailed recollections of childhood in his beloved St. Petersburg, a multicultural and multiethnic city (long before these terms became fashionable). Despite the charm of these recollections, however, Dimitry also seemed aware of some dark shadows hovering over or penetrating into the old czarist regime. As he writes tellingly at one point, "The beauty of Petersburg was not only tragic but also hidden (in the palaces and behind the signs). The Winter Palace was absolutely dark at night, as the

Emperor and his family lived in the Aleksandr Palace in Tsar-skoye Selo. . . . Over the river from the palace the fortress-prison loomed out of the darkness with its towering cathedral spire, a weather-vane-cum-sword poised menacingly above."[5]

Until his arrest in 1928, Dimitry's childhood and early adult-hood, including university studies, were spent in St. Petersburg, renamed Leningrad after the revolution. Given the dark hor-ror that was to follow, it seems desirable to lift up some of the city's more joyful or wistful memories. "Nowhere," Likhachev writes fondly, "is there a city so proudly beautiful as Peters-burg in spring, especially when the parks abound with luxuriant lilac blossoms." After the heat of summer, the beauty returns in fall: "The air is transparent on the windless, sunlit days of early autumn, and every contour of the Neva can be seen. The riverside palaces look like appliqué work, cut out of paper and glued onto the blue cardboard of the sky." In winter, snow comes in many different shapes: "Sometimes it falls softly, sometimes it whirls about or is driven into a blizzard; sometimes it falls as wet flakes, sometimes as dry powder." As a good humanist and psycholo-gist, Likhachev knows the effect of seasons on human disposi-tions. "Weather," he says, "always has a relationship with man. It influences him and determines his mood. Petersburg is like a vast theatrical set, a spectacular arena for the greatest historical trag-edies, and sometimes for comic improvisation too."[6]

In the memoir, these passages read like the lull before the storm. As Likhachev observes, it is often assumed that the harsh-est repression during the Soviet era began in 1936–1937 at the time of the great show trials, but this assumption is mistaken. Sta-tistics can show, he says, that "waves of arrests, imprisonments, and deportations" began as early as 1918, even before the Red Terror (which was formally unleashed on September 5, 1918). As early as 1918–1919, the Likhachev family—watching from the windows of their flat in Laktinskaya Street—could hear "bursts of machine-gun fire" from the direction of the Peter and Paul For-tress. The persecution had clearly begun, but it had not yet fully penetrated into public consciousness. During the 1920s and early 1930s, when officers, professors, and clergy as well as Russian, Ukrainian, and White Russian peasants were being arrested and killed by the thousands, it all seemed somehow "natural" or like a passing misfortune. But what came then was what Likhachev calls the "self-devouring aspect of power," when the revolution steadily devoured its children. And with this spreading mayhem came fear, dissembling, and corruption of the spirit. In his early youth, the author reports, he had come into contact with people of "the 'Silver Age' of Russian culture," and he had sensed "their strength, their courage and their ability to oppose all the processes of disruption in society." But the purges steadily undermined the legacy of the Silver Age: "With every passing year . . . I sensed an encroaching spirit of corruption which sapped the amazing, life-giving strength that came from the older generation of the Russian intelligentsia."[7]

What particularly grieved Likhachev during these years was the ongoing destruction of the Russian Church. In Kun's portrayal, Likhachev was always "profoundly religious, of unquestionable probity," but at no time a bigot or religious reactionary opposed to all social change.[8] The account offered in his memoir is gripping. "One always remembers one's youth as a happy time," he writes. "I, however, and my contemporaries in school, university and intellectual circles have something painful to recall, something which stings my memory and which was the hardest of all to bear in my young days. This was the destruction of Russia and the Russian Church which took place with murderous savagery before our very eyes." This persecution, he adds, "began almost contemporaneously with the October cataclysm" and was accompanied by many other acts of hostility, such as the confiscation of church land and treasures. In the process, the memoir notes, the Soviet regime became "theomachist." The result for Likhachev and many other intellectuals was a sense of loss and deep sadness. "Many are convinced," he states, "that loving the Motherland means being proud of her. No! I was brought up to another sort of love tinged with pity" and sorrow. As the persecution of the church became more widespread and executions more numerous, Likhachev and his friends felt "an ever keener grief for the Russia that was dying. Our love for the Motherland resembled least of all pride in her, her victories and conquests. . . . We didn't sing patriotic songs—we wept and prayed."[9]

In 1923, in the midst of these developments, Likhachev began his university studies in Leningrad in the field of Old Russian literature and art. I comment later on this choice of subject matter and here offer just a few words on his ongoing "life of the mind." His memoir contains a section titled "The Making of a Philosophy," and he insists that he means "philosophy, *not* ideology." With this insistence, he clearly distances himself from the co-optation of thought by party-political agendas, from the instrumental abuse of ideas in a totalitarian context. What emerges in this section is that Likhachev—in addition to being religious—also had a genuinely philosophical outlook, a disposition to question the world and himself. "Since before my schooldays," he writes, "the world has always seemed to me something of a riddle," which is just a rephrasing of the Platonic *thaumazein* (wondering). Already during his senior year at Lentovskaya High School, he was surrounded by inquiring, philosophically searching friends. His closest friend was attracted to Nietzsche, but instead of embracing a doctrinaire formula (such as "will to power"), he favored a "kindly Nietzscheanism." His Jewish friend Misha Shapiro liked Oscar Wilde and dreamed of an "intellectual aristocracy" after the fashion of the Venetian Republic. In the company of these and other friends, his mind was able to grow and mature. Likhachev speaks of a "moral environment" and offers this description: "The contents of these moral surroundings comprised a collective [shared] psychology that presupposed freedom of the person, a collective [shared] morality, a collective [shared] super-philosophy that brought together the intelligent people of the world, collective [shared] intellectual interests, even freely changing vogues for deep philosophical currents." In such a moral environment, we are told, philosophy becomes "natural behavior" in the wide sense of the term.[10]

During his student years in Leningrad, Likhachev participated in a number of philosophical circles that provided a kind of moral environment and at the same time served as a buffer against the dismal events of the time. The names of some of these circles—"Brotherhood of St. Serafim of Sarov" and "Cosmic Academy of Sciences"—already signal their distance from the official totalitarian ideology. Likhachev's own thinking during this time—qualifying not quite as a "philosophical system"—bore the earmarks of a spiritual existentialism revolving around the great issues of time and eternity, God and humanity. Although he recognized the distinctness or difference of these terms, his thinking also stressed their interrelation and even interpenetration. "The prototype of eternity is present also in time. The simplest example is music. . . . The partial fusion in music of past, present, and future is a faint reflection of that eternity into which all that exists has been absorbed." Moreover, it was important to think of eternity not just as an infinite duration but as "an infinitely great essence, momentary and all-embracing." The nexus of eternity and time carries over into the relation between divine omniscience or omnipotence and human free will. In this respect, Likhachev perceived a grand "synergy," a kind of "union of divine omnipotence and human freedom." From this angle, the human "soul" emerges as a crossroads, a manifest mystery and "greatest secret." All these speculations and their moral environments were eventually swept aside by the purges. In Likhachev's words, "The monotone culture of the 'proletarian dictatorship' ousted the polyphony of intellectual democracy. . . . The country subsided into silence—there were only monotones of praise, a unison, a deathly boredom—and 'deathly' is the word, because unanimity and unison were equivalent of a death sentence for culture and cultured people." In early February 1928, he was arrested.[11]

Old Rus

I shall not pursue further the story related in his memoir, which is full of grim episodes: his imprisonment in the gulag of Solovki, his release some four years later, the repressions of the 1930s, the German invasion and siege of Leningrad, his exile to Kazan later in the war, his appointment as professor in Leningrad in 1950, his later acceptance into the Academy of Sciences, and his final public recognition. All of these events, especially the wartime episodes, make for dramatic reading. I want to turn to his studies of Old Russian literature and art, however, because it is on his work in this field that his scholarly reputation is in large measure founded. His motivation for studying Old Russian culture is not in doubt. As he writes plainly, "I wanted to sustain Russia in my memory as the children sitting round her bed want to retain the image of a dying mother and gather up representations of her to show them to their friends and tell of the greatness of her tormented life." At this point, Likhachev adds a sentence that can serve as passkey to his entire work: "My books are, in essence, memorial notes offered for the repose of Russia's soul: You can't remember everything when you are writing a book—you jot down the dearest names, and for me such names are associated with Ancient Rus."[12]

Likhachev wrote many books or rather "memorial notes" in this field. I select here one work that is perhaps most representative: *The Great Heritage: The Classical Literature of Old Rus.* The book deals with the first seven hundred years of Russian literature, covering a period that compares roughly with the European Middle Ages. In its opening chapter, the author raises immediately the central question: "What was Russian literature like during the first 700 years?" The issue at this point is not so much the content of specific texts (which are discussed later in the body of the book), but rather the general spirit pervading these texts, their paradigmatic character. Here it emerges that Old Russian literature was not particularistic or individualized but rather like a big tapestry, a holistic fabric in which everything is connected with everything. It was, Likhachev writes, "closer to folklore than to the individualized creation of writers in our own time." The literature of the period was basically "not a literature created by individual writers"; rather, "like folk art, it was supra-individualistic . . . created by collective experience . . . a body of work written by nameless authors." In this sense, Old Russian literature was a coherent cosmos, rising above seven centuries "as a single whole." Differently put: "Old Russian writers did not build free-standing buildings, but were urban planners working on one, unified, magnificent ensemble."[13]

What was the glue or, rather, the spirit that held this ensemble together? "Every literature," Likhachev says, "creates its own world embodying the world of ideas held by contemporary society." Hence, "let us try to bring the world of Old Russian literature back to life again." What sort of "unified building" was this, what kind of "ensemble" that claimed "the labor of dozens of generations of Russian 'men of letters'"? In Likhachev's reading, this ensemble was not (and could not have been) humanly fabricated or engineered; it was a cosmic and liturgical ensemble in which the divine and the human, the eternal and the temporal, were closely intertwined. As he writes, "The universe was a book written by the hand of God, and literature deciphered this world of signs. The sense of the world's importance and grandeur underlay literature." The close linkage of the divine and human was made manifest in the design of old churches. "The church," we read, "was a micro-world, but it was also a macro-man. It had a head (the dome), there was the neck of the drum, and shoulders. The windows were the church's eyes, . . . above the windows there were 'eyebrows' for visors." This was the kind of cosmic or symbolic holism captured in Old Russian literature: "A large world and a small world, the universe and man!" As Likhachev exclaims admiringly, "Everything was interlinked, everything was important, everything reminded man of the meaning behind his existence, of the grandeur of the world and the significance of man's destiny in it."[14]

The linkage of the divine and the human is replicated in the connection between the eternal and the temporal. Everything that happens in Old Russian literature, Likhachev observes, occurs on two levels: the temporal, bearing "the imprint of the uniqueness of an event" or story, and the eternal, reflecting the deeper "meaning." Although keenly drawn toward the transtemporal, Old Russian writers were not fond of abstract schemes and never neglected "the importance of the temporal." Although seen as "a manifestation of the eternal," the temporal as manifestation was crucial. The point is that the eternal, by itself, "has no events," no histories or stories; hence, it needs to be "illustrated by events or explained by an allegory or a parable." Thus, transtemporal meaning had to be revealed in temporal settings and more specifically in the interconnected fabric of history as a whole. "Old Russian writings," Likhachev states, "make up an epos relating the history of the universe and of Rus. They all complement each other in the picture they create of the world." In this tapestry, not a single literary work stands on its own. "Each story is a complete whole, but is nonetheless linked to others. Each is only one chapter in the world's history." In this manner, historical events are inhabited by a rhythm inserting them into a broader frame: "The movement of the temporal draws the immobility of the eternal into its flow."[15]

In Likhachev's presentation, Old Russian literature was held together by a common style and even by what he calls a "structural unity," the same kind of unity exhibited by ritual folklore and great historical epics. Literature at the time was woven into a single fabric thanks mainly to "its unity of themes" and "the identity of literary time with historical time." Coupled with the effacement of authorial individuality and the grandeur of chosen themes, this unity contributed in his view to a "distinctive type of magnificence" that was the "basic stylistic feature" of that literature. In many ways, due to its holistic character, this literature was similar to "a celebration of divine service," so that the reader was in some respect "like a man at prayer," reading a text as he would "gaze at an icon." All this does not mean that the literature was uniform or monochromatic. Precisely because of its holistic quality, it had need of contrasting attitudes, such as mockery, irony, and buffoonery. In Likhachev's words, "Magnificence also had need of a fool: the jester and buffoon stood in opposition to the court master of ceremonies." By flouting the courtly etiquette, the fool served to emphasize "the etiquette's magnificence." This only shows again that Old Russian literature (and medieval literature in general) was home to two contrasting principles or allegiances: the eternal and the temporal or "commonplace." Under the aegis of the former, literature was "filled with a sense of loftiness" and sharply distinguished from daily speech in both language and style. Under the second rubric, literature was more "simple, unassuming, and 'lower'" in terms of both language and attitude toward events. In this manner, Old Russian literature encompassed the whole range of human experience in the broad cosmic drama.[16]

An important feature of this literature—connected again with its holism—is the absence of narrowly nationalistic demarcations, boundaries drawn along ethnic lines. In Likhachev's words, "National boundaries in Old Russian literature were very hazily defined." Most Old Russian literary works "belonged to Bulgarian and Serbian literature as well" and were written in "Old Church Slavonic," which in terms of its origin was identical to the "Old Bulgarian language," a tongue comprehensible to southern and eastern Slavs. In fact, the first three centuries of the period were a time, he says, "when the Old Ukrainian, Old Byelorussian, and Old Great Russian literatures were not yet distinguishable from each other." The division into Slavic nationalities occurred only later, after the Tatar–Mongol invasion in the mid–thirteenth century. Seen from this angle, Old Russian literature was the "fountainhood" of all Eastern Slavonic languages; many of its texts were written by people from diverse localities. On the whole, Russian literature during the medieval period was "not isolated from other literatures," nor was it "provincial." In Likhachev's words, early Russian literature was "European in its nature and, to a great extent, in its origin." An important feature of the literature—apart from the vagueness of boundaries— was the absence of "strictly defined delimitations between works and genres" or "between literature and other forms of artistic expression." All in all, this literature had "the soft, flexible structure always typical of a youthful organism, a 'childishness' which made it receptive and flexible, capable of further development."[17]

Precisely because of this flexibility, Old Russian literature underwent many subtle changes during the medieval period and more dramatic changes afterward. The process of change basically involved what sociologists call a steady drift toward differentiation coupled with renewed efforts at integration. As a result of this process, Likhachev says, "individual parts naturally broke away and began a life of their own; they became firmer, more tangible and distinctive." Thus, little by little, Old Russian literature lost "its initial unity and youthful shapelessness"; it broke apart along national lines as well as along thematic and generic lines. The two most important features that slowly matured and came to full fruition in the modern era were the individuation of writers and themes and the rise of the modern nation-state. For Likhachev, the modern nation-state has a deeply ambivalent status. On the one hand, in the Russian case the rise of the nation-state was a creative reaction to external dangers: the inroads of the Tatar–Mongol steppe people and later of foreign interventionism. To some extent, the emerging state also provided an antidote to the tendencies of progressive fragmentation and disintegration. On the other hand, the state was an *artifact,* a product of political engineering that could not possibly replace the earlier holistic fabric. In Likhachev's words, as a result of relentless centralization the state became "an especially powerful machine for the oppression of the people." This means that, in many ways, the state developed "at the expense of cultural development. . . . The building of the state absorbed all of the people's strength, thus drawing them away from other spheres of cultural activity."[18]

Fortunately, at least for a period of time, the state was not completely successful in curbing this activity. As indicated earlier, much cultural activity was now channeled in the direction of individuation (of writers and themes). Whereas during the medieval period "man was primarily a part of the hierarchical structure of society and the world," the increasing accent on individuality and personality in modern times tended to destroy "literary etiquette, stylistic monumentality, the sense of subordination to the whole, and the ceremonial style of literature." In Likhachev's account, personalized sympathy and individual compassion functioned as "the most powerful revolutionary principles in literature." Traditionally examined from a lofty pinnacle, the world was now presented to the reader through *one* individual's fate or sufferings. With this change, an entirely new style of literature came into being. The stress was now placed on *individual* stories: sometimes on heroic individuals conquering fate but more often on dissociated, disaffected, and alienated individuals. Literature, Likhachev says, "began to recognize the value of the human personality *outside* the system: a man who has lost everything, a man in a ragged dirty shirt and bast shoes, without money, social position or friends." With this shift of focus, the "ceremonial robes" of traditional texts dropped away: "Literature ceased to be a magnificent, but impersonal whole." An awareness grew up of "the unique value of the human personality—a value independent of man's social position, merits, or moral virtues."[19]

Post-Soviet Initiatives

As I see it, the modern world that emerged in the aftermath or from the ruins of Old Rus was for Likhachev a world of both grandeur and tragedy. It was grand because it brought to the fore the unique dignity and value of individuality. But it was also the harbinger of immense tragedies and catastrophes. Like the modern nation-state, modern culture for him was profoundly ambivalent and Janus-like: while signaling undeniably a great gain in individualized freedom, it also entailed a loss of meaningful coherence and solidarity. To be sure, traces of the traditional meaning structure were never completely lost. In part, the aim of *The Great Heritage* was to show the continued relevance of this structure in subsequent history. However, during the twentieth century most of these traces were brutally swept aside or driven underground. To repeat a statement quoted earlier from Likhachev's memoir, "My books are, in essence, memorial notes offered for the repose of Russia's soul" to show "the greatness of her tormented life."

However, what also emerges clearly from Likhachev's work and life is that the loss suffered in modernity cannot be made up with political or technological designs (which result only in gulags or concentration camps). Differently put: the holistic fabric of tradition cannot be recaptured by any totalizing strategy or totalitarian agenda because any manufactured totality necessarily excludes what defies manufacture and thus misses its goal. The twentieth century was replete with forms of totalitarianism—modes based on nationality or ethnicity (fascism), on economic class (communism), or on religious "fundamentalism" (clericofascism or theocracy). Vast cemeteries are filled with the bodies of their victims. Over long stretches of his life, Likhachev was also victimized by totalitarianism. What he learned through grim experience is that the unity of the "great heritage" cannot be regained through despotism or political fiat— through what Martin Heidegger called "machination" *(Machenschaft)*. The only way to be faithful to the past is by cherishing it as lost—by retrieving its recessed promise and carrying that promise forward into the future. The way forward is difficult because it requires a seasoning or "turning," a kind of homecoming through homelessness.

Likhachev's memoir, his "reflections on the Russian soul," is a declaration of love, and it is the only declaration of love that one should make to one's country. The poet Georg Trakl states that the soul is "a stranger on earth," which does not mean that it resides elsewhere but rather that it cannot be controlled, manipulated, instru-mentalized, or co-opted; it is "not for sale." In offering his reflections, Likhachev showed himself as a patriot but never a chauvinist or a devotee of national power or glory. Borrowing some recently fash-ionable terminology, one might call him a "rooted cosmopolitan"— that is, a thinker and writer nurtured by a distinctive history but open to broad horizons (which can never be dogmatically defined or politically manipulated). The opening chapter of *The Great Heritage* concludes with a stirring passage attesting to a rooted cosmopolitan outlook: "The world's cultural horizons are constantly expanding. . . . Humankind has freed itself of 'Eurocentrism' and an egocen-tric preoccupation with the present. A profound understanding of the culture of the past and the culture of other peoples serves to bring different eras and countries closer together. The world's unity is becoming increasingly tangible. The distance between cultures is decreasing, and there is less and less place in the world for national enmity and chauvinism."[20]

During the period of the Soviet regime, Likhachev's cosmo-politan and multicultural leanings were inevitably restricted by the effects of the Cold War. However, they emerged into full bloom after the demise of that regime in 1989. One year later, in November 1990, Likhachev delivered a major lecture in New York at Columbia Uni-versity. The lecture was presented under the auspices of the W. Aver-ell Harriman Institute for Advanced Study of the Soviet Union (the latter part of the name quickly being changed to "Russia"). The con-tent of the lecture, titled "The National Nature of Russian History," clearly demonstrated his "rooted cosmopolitanism," his ability to hold together his attachment to his homeland, and his openness to humanity at large.

Understandably, given almost half a century of Cold War, Likh-achev first of all tried to remove some prevailing misconceptions or prejudices. As he reminded his audience, to grasp the inner spirit or the "soul" of a country, it is necessary to attend not so much to its failures or derailments but to its best potential or its "better angels." "When compiling a history of any national art or literature, even a museum catalogue," he said, "we tend to emphasize the best, not the worst, focusing our attention on men of genius and their mas-terpieces." Thus, to give an example, we judge Italy "according to its achievements in the realm of painting, sculpture, architecture, spiritual life; not by less elevated matters." Hence, he added, "don't take it as braggadocio or nationalism, if I speak about the best in Russian culture, leaving out phenomena of negative or no value." This reminder was followed by comments of a broader philosophical character that are important for any cross-cultural endeavor: "I would like to call your attention to the fact that *evil* is always and everywhere the same, while *good* is various, individual." Therefore, "to understand something of a foreign culture, one must focus one's attention on the greatness of that culture, its accomplishments, rather than on its departures from these heights."[21]

Turning to the broadest cross-cultural horizons, Likhachev raised the issue of East–West relations: "Does Russia belong to the East, or to the West?" Behind this issue there lurk further questions: "What is 'the East'? What is 'the West'? Are there any borders on the map between the East and the West?" For Likhachev, the customary distinction between East and West does not make any sense, especially if we attend to the important fact that Russia "occupies vast expanses and is inhabited by numerous peoples of both the Western and Eastern types." Even during the medieval period, "the old state of Rus was multinational from the very start; so were its surroundings." And this did not change in later periods. For Likhachev, Russia's position in history has been shaped by "her position among other nations, small and great—some three hundred of them." In this condition, Russia served "as a vast 'bridge,' chiefly cultural, for these peoples. Hence the multinational character of her culture." This character was further enhanced during the eighteenth and nineteenth centuries. The flourishing of Russian culture during these centuries, Likhachev observed, "benefitted from the efforts of people of many nationalities, in Moscow and especially in Petersburg, where the population was multinational from the start." Against this background, the question whether Russian culture belongs to the East or the West is, for him, "evanescent. This culture belongs to dozens of peoples of both the East and the West, and this multinational soil has nurtured our culture, in all its idiosyncratic detail."[22]

In his lecture, Likhachev did not ignore or conceal some darker sides of Russian history, especially the frequent oppression and persecution of minorities or subjugated peoples. Basically, he attributed these dark features to the nation-state and the power wielded by state elites. Although inspired by deep humanistic and (in some sense) universalistic values and meant to serve as "a link between Europe and Asia," he stated, Russia at some points was also "the cruelest oppressor of other nationalities—first and foremost of its own, central Russian people"—which is one of "the most tragic of historical paradoxes." For Likhachev, this paradox was to a great extent the result of "an age long confrontation of people and state" as well as of a certain "polarization of the Russian character," with its urge "for both freedom and power." These dark derailments, in his view, can be overcome only by a widening of education and a steady deepening of culture both at home and in the world. His lecture ended with the plea for "the creation of a pan-European university," in which there would be "national colleges where people would associate with one another, and thus learn tolerance." Ultimately, he added, such a pan-European university could and should be "transformed into a world university, for all humankind."[23]

During the final decade of his life, Likhachev sought to practice and expand his "rooted cosmopolitanism" by working for both a strengthening and uplifting of Russian culture and an opening of that culture to the world. His book *The Great Heritage* pays a fine tribute to the best in Russian culture and literature and its contribution to civic virtue. This literature, he writes, "was always a civic-minded literature. It was always the people's conscience, so to speak. . . . It educated people and strove to reorganize life in a just and equitable fashion."[24] The desire for a just and equitable life was not limited, however, to Russia but had a cosmopolitan cast. At the beginning of this chapter, I mentioned Miklós Kun's comment that Likhachev finally "took the helm of the ship of Russian culture and steered it to a hopefully better world."

To the very end, Likhachev acted on his convictions. In 1999, shortly before his death, he wrote a letter welcoming an exchange program between local and national leaders of Russia and the United States: "With the start of perestroika, the Cold War era took flight. Not estrangement and distrust, but cooperation and friendship began to determine relations between Russia and America . . . I am certain that the mutual interest that inevitably arises among Americans and Russians will force them to communicate more often and more productively in order to understand each other's way of life and thoughts."[25]

Sixteen years have passed since this letter and Likhachev's death. Global tensions and geopolitical rivalries are steadily increasing; some people speak already of "Cold War II." In this situation, it is vitally important to remember Dimitry Likhachev and his efforts to steer us all toward a better, more equitable, and peaceful world.

9

Freedom as Engaged Social Praxis

Lessons from D. P. Chattopadhyaya

Those who have faith and good will find through pure
work their freedom.
                                            —*Bhagadvad Gita* (3:30)

Ever since the Enlightenment, Western culture has presented itself
emphatically as a culture of freedom. Constitutional documents and
charters celebrate the importance of human freedom and individual
liberty, sometimes to the point of erecting the entire constitutional
structure on this foundational premise. Needless to say, self-
presentation of this kind feeds on an opposition or contrasting foil.
Thus, when America presents itself quite specifically as the "land
of the free," there is at least the implication that other countries or
societies are marked by a lesser degree of freedom and perhaps by
unfreedom. This contrast, to be sure, is not entirely of a modern
vintage. As we know, ancient Greek and Roman cultures defined
themselves largely in terms of the dichotomy between civilized and
"barbarian" peoples—with barbarian peoples being basically characterized by their unfreedom or servile submission to despotic rule.
Over the centuries, this legacy congealed into the doctrine of "Ori-
ental" or "Asian" despotism, a doctrine that functioned for a long
time as a staple in Western political thought.

    Based on dubious assumptions, the described legacy is bound

to be troubling or offensive to reflective intellectuals everywhere, particularly in non-Western societies. Among the many aspects neglected by the doctrine is the multiplicity of possible conceptions of freedom when viewed from both a historical and a cross-cultural perspective. There is, hence, an evident need today to take a broad-gauged and fair-minded look at these conceptions, with the aim of assessing their distinctive merits and shortcomings. One of the most probing and insightful assessments in this domain has been offered by the Indian philosopher Debi Prasad Chattopadhyaya (b. 1933), longtime chairman of the Indian Council of Philosophical Research and more recently director of the Center for the Study of Civilizations in Delhi. One of the noteworthy features of Chattopadhyaya's life work has been his ability to combine a distinguished academic career in leading Indian and Western universities with thoughtful social and political engagement. As a philosopher, he has produced an impressive array of important texts ranging from the philosophy of science to ethics, but his social-political engagement has also been evident in his service as a Union cabinet minister and as governor of the state of Rajashtan. In 2010, he was awarded a Distinguished Life-Time Achievement Award by the Indian Council of Philosophical Research in Delhi.

In part because of his dual commitment to philosophical insight and social-political practice, Chattopadhyaya has been able to make an important contribution to the central topic of this book: the freedom–solidarity nexus. One of the chief premises of his work is that public freedom is not an exclusively Western monopoly, just as philosophical reflection on freedom (like philosophy as such) is not a Western prerogative. By extricating the practice of freedom from the confines of Western-style individualism, he was also able to show that it depends on social and cultural contexts—that is, on some measure of social solidarity. As he writes in one of his major texts, *Knowledge, Freedom, and Language*, "I think that the concept of freedom is central to the proper understanding of the individual's place in the world," but different social and cultural contexts color the meaning(s) of the term *freedom*.[1] In this chapter, I review Chattopadhyaya's discussion of different meanings of freedom as presented chiefly in that text, moving from a basically Western-style conception (freedom as self-liberation) to an important Hindu and

Buddhist conception (freedom as liberation from self) and finally to a late-modern or "postmodern" socialist conception (freedom as engaged social praxis). By way of conclusion, I briefly indicate the contemporary relevance of the discussion.

Freedom as Self-Liberation

In modern Western culture, freedom stands in the crucible of science, free will, and social responsibility or connectedness. The title of Chattopadhyaya's book *Knowledge, Freedom, and Language* clearly is indebted to this crucible—which, in a very broad sense, can be related to Kant's famous three critiques. As Chattopadhyaya notes, freedom in the modern West emerged basically as a rebellion against or emancipation from unexamined religious and metaphysical dogmas—dogmas enshrined at the time in autocratic forms of political domination. The engine of liberation or emancipation was initially or in the first instance "reason" or rationality and only secondarily human willing or spontaneity. The meaning of reason, however, remained for a long time ambivalent. In Chattopadhyaya's account, modern reason can be traced distantly to classical, especially Platonic, rationalism—although ancient rationalism was distinctly more metaphysical: "The essence of the European model, as I see it, is rooted in the Platonic view that reason in its pure form can truly and infallibly grasp the whole of reality, all its nooks and corners, without a remainder." What happened during the Renaissance and the early Enlightenment period was that reason was stripped of its cosmic-transcendental ambitions and tailored to the dimension of a human-centered or "anthropological" capacity—that is, the dimension of a cognitive-rational subjectivity standing over against the world (of which the Cartesian cogito is the prototype).[2]

Despite this reductive or tailoring effort, however, reason's broader ambitions were not completely curbed. Throughout much of the seventeenth and eighteenth centuries, concentration on human reason was conceived not so much as the negation of a higher divine purpose but rather precisely the gateway to a more accurate and reliable perception of a hidden master plan of the world. Given that both human reason and nature were assumed to be divinely structured or ordained, rational-scientific inquiry, properly pursued, could still hope to find the secret passageway to the deeper layers of cosmic order. This hope persisted even when nature began to be seen as a mechanical clockwork and reason to be approximated to mathematics or algebra (a *mathesis universalis*). As Chattopadhyaya comments, the "book of nature" remained "the first and most important book to be read for attaining the highest possible knowledge." Descartes, despite his radical skepsis, basically reached the same conclusion—namely, as Chattopadhyaya puts it, "that the book of nature can be clearly and distinctly, that is, scientifically, read only by the grace of a veracious or non-deceiving God." Thus, what prevailed at the time was a rationalism (cum empiricism) whose boundaries toward metaphysics were hazy and ill defined. The result, Chattopadhyaya adds, was a curious amalgam: "the emergence of naturalism, on the one hand, and deism, on the other."[3]

In a highly perceptive and erudite manner, *Knowledge, Freedom, and Language* traces the historical permutations of this amalgam through the writings of Newton, Spinoza, Leibniz, and Locke. What increasingly came to the fore in these permutations was an intrinsic dilemma or fissure afflicting the European Enlightenment: the realization that the relentlessly pursued scientific discovery of the laws of nature was liable to jeopardize the goal of human freedom and self-determination, which had been the initial impulse fueling the dawn of European modernity. Precisely to the degree that the metaphorical "book of nature" was replaced by a comprehensive natural-scientific determinism, pressure was placed not only on inscrutable divine providence but also on the conception of a self-propelled or undetermined human freedom. As Chattopadhyaya writes in a passage evocative of Max Horkheimer and Theodor Adorno's work *Dialectic of Enlightenment*,

The leading spirits of the European Enlightenment were working under some basic perceptions which did not prove easily reconcilable. First, they all sincerely believed that scientific knowledge based on experimental reasoning and expressible in mathematical language had to be taken very seriously. Secondly, deeply impressed by the law-governed characters of the universe, they were earnestly, almost desperately, searching for similar, at least comparable, sets of laws in the realm of human society. Their second concern invited some basic difficulties for them. They could not see how exactly the paradigm of scientific lawfulness could be transferred to social life without seriously impairing the ideal of individual freedom—the ideal which many of them . . . seriously defended as the most powerful argument against despotism.

What happened was that the unbounded expansion of scientific knowledge was purchased at a price comparable to the bargain of the sorcerer's apprentice: the progressive "disenchantment" of nature boomeranged by casting a disenchanting shadow on human life and initiative.[4]

Faced with this dilemma, European thinkers were driven to choose one of two options: either to accept the natural determinism of human will—a course followed by nineteenth-century positivism and its offshoots—or else to transcendentalize human freedom by placing it beyond the bounds of nature. The latter path was pursued most prominently and most nobly by Immanuel Kant, who proceeded to anchor the moral law in the "noumenal" freedom of human consciousness. As can readily be seen, this move did not so much overcome as radicalize the Cartesian subject–object (or mind–matter) division by further "spiritualizing" or internalizing freedom and thus by driving freedom more deeply into the inner recesses of subjectivity (and thus into a kind of "worldlessness," to use Hannah Arendt's term). To be sure, Kant still wrestled with both sides of the equation, but by tilting the balance in one direction. In Kant's philosophy, Chattopadhyaya observes, "the rationality of human will is independent of the rationality or intelligibility of nature." Viewed from another angle, however, nature's intelligibility owes its "main characters" to human reason, but human reason does not owe its own rationality to nature or the natural universe.[5]

For Chattopadhyaya, Kant's work constituted the "high water mark of the age of Enlightenment." The main spokesman of that age, in Chattopadhyaya's view, tried to achieve three things: to vindicate science, to ground moral freedom, and to search for a viable social order. In his imposing opus, Kant sought to accomplish all three by projecting rationality onto the "starry skies" as well as on morality and society. Yet in his rationalist eagerness he may have overreached himself and "invented light of reason where it was not." In a phrase again reminiscent of Horkheimer and Adorno, Chattopadhyaya concludes: "The age of Enlightenment does not mean all light and no darkness. Most of its chapters, to extend the metaphor, are grey."[6]

Freedom as Liberation from Self?

The discussion of modern Western freedom—more specifically, the freedom embroiled in the crucible of the Western Enlightenment—is followed in Chattopadhyaya's text by a close review of the conception of freedom as found in classical Indian and Buddhist thought. Crudely speaking, one might say that freedom in the modern West was anchored in a metaphysical subject–object scheme: a scheme in which humans were first projected as autonomous purveyors and masters of the natural universe and finally driven back into the inner core of private subjectivity in a disenchanted world. On the whole, classical Eastern thought pursued a different path that, undercutting the metaphysical (Cartesian) scheme, sought to liberate humans from both external and internal bondage—that is, both from material determinism and subjective self-enclosure or solipsism.

Given its different character and orientation, this path could not—as in the Western model—rely centrally on "reason" or rational-scientific inquiry and certainly not on human rationality seen as an instrument of self-aggrandizement and world appropriation. Without bypassing or negating reason (broadly understood), classical Indian and Buddhist thought tended to invoke more the resources of reflective-poetic thinking and symbolic expression—as well as sometimes of the disclosive potential of silence (as the antipode of propositional claims). Chattopadhyaya writes that the spirit of the Western Enlightenment was freedom, which was said "to be attainable by [rational] knowledge. But one must not think that there are no other paths as well leading to that ideal." As experience teaches, a person can be "wise and virtuous" without formal scientific training and gain insight without Western-style rationality. Thus, the ancient Rig-Vedic "poet-philosophers" of India read in their own way the "book of nature" and, in doing so, were able to "liberate" themselves from illusions and from the bondage induced by ignorance and ill will.[7]

Basically, the divine pantheon celebrated by the Vedic seers was not so much the target of cognitive-propositional knowledge as the emblem of a poetic world disclosure, revealing a reality where transcendence and immanence were intimately meshed. In Chattopadhyaya's words, the array of Vedic gods and divinities represented primarily "the powers of light, energy, and fertility"; simultaneously, they were "the symbols of needs, protection, and elevation or inspiration." Over time, the Vedic deities evolved into a "synonym for the life-breath" itself, metaphorical stand-ins for the "infinite and inexhaustible source of light and life, things and thoughts" that could assume such different names as "Agni," "Indra," and "Varuna" for "different beings according to their cravings, responding to their prayers." Contemplation of and participation in the higher reality animated by the divine pantheon were assumed to yield genuine freedom in the sense of a liberation from selfish desires and cognitive delusions.[8]

The Vedic tradition was modified but not radically changed or transformed by later Upanishadic teachings. Upanishadic texts basically integrated the Vedic deities into a more recessed spiritual matrix, the supreme *brahman*, which again was understood as encompassing or at least interlacing immanence and transcendence as well as selfhood and otherness. In Chattopadhyaya's words, "The Upanishadic view of moral life is not to be understood as logical-conceptual in a narrow sense. It rather requires one to open oneself up to the higher forces of light and delight of the universe." This means that the individual self (*jiva*) must realize that it cannot find true fulfillment and liberation "without the help of other fellow beings" and without the help and caring attention of *brahman* signaling the complex interrelation of all things.[9]

In opposition to the modern Western fascination with sharp conceptualization and the subjection of nature to propositional claims, ancient Indian thought was more elusive and reticent—and in any case averse to any kind of domineering rationality. Although not disdainful of language, classical thought often placed itself at the boundary of language or at the interstices of the "said" and the "unsaid"; it gestured toward a depth dimension of language, where the latter harbors or makes room for silence. "To say," Chattopadhy-aya writes, "that the highest stage of realization is a stage of endless ecstasy (*purnananda*) or of perfect freedom (*vimukti*) does not make the matter, intellectually [conceptually] speaking, very clear." This is why, at the border of the effable and the ineffable, classical thought often took recourse to metaphors and symbols, employing such images as "evaporation of camphor in air," "dissolution of a lump of salt into water," and "convergence of the jar-bound sky (*ghataka-sha*) and the unbounded sky (*patakasha*)." The classical ambivalence between saying and unsaying persisted in the long line of Vedantic and post-Vedantic thinkers, which prominently included such lumi-naries as Shankara, Mishra, and Ramanuja.[10]

Unable to assert cognitively or conceptually either the complete coincidence of the individual human (*jiva*) and the divine or their absolute distance or separation, these thinkers were constrained to navigate a precarious path between self-maintenance and self-abandonment—that is, between the active-purposive pursuit of the divine and the attainment of liberation through contemplative releasement from such pursuit. Thus, although insisting on the pri-macy of contemplation (*jñana*) over self-propelled seeking, Shankara also acknowledged the need for moral action and practical devotion (*bhakti*). Conversely, although privileging self-conscious and "inde-pendent" human striving, Ramanuja simultaneously recognized the divine as the inner wellspring (not merely the goal) of this search. As Chattopadhyaya observes, "Shankara's view of knowledge maxi-mally exploits the notion of identity—identity of the knower and the known—and scrupulously avoids their discursive association. But he, like Ramanuja, recognizes the necessity of worship, prayer and also *bhakti* for salvation from worldly bondage." Hence, in both cases, *jñana* is neither antithetical nor alien to *bhakti*: "both can take the soul to the same goal of supreme realization" or liberation.[11]

Transposed into a somewhat different key, with perhaps greater emphasis on unsaying than saying, elements of classical Indian thought were continued and elaborated by Buddhism. As is well known, the central motive of the Buddha's teaching is liberation from suffering, a suffering induced by ignorance and self-centered or clinging desire. In his famous "eightfold path," the Buddha delin-eated the road leading from the initial understanding of the cause

of suffering to the final stage of blissful freedom or nirvana. However, in pointing or rather gesturing toward nirvana, the Buddha
remained (and had to remain) ambivalent regarding the character
and role of the human self: whether nirvana was the achievement
of a goal-seeking self (*atman*) or it signaled in effect the cessation of
and liberation from self (*anatman*).

For the Buddha, Chattopadhyaya notes, the liberated self is "like
an extinguished lamp," an image expressed in such phrases as "blow-
ing out" or "cooling down" and in the synonymous use of such terms
as *sheenlessness, disappearance,* and *liberation.* However, when the
lamp is literally extinguished, who or what can still be claimed to
be liberated or blissful? Hence, Chattopadhyaya adds, the Buddha's
teaching here was "figurative," for the Buddha was keenly aware that
figurative expression is "the only possible approximation available to
the normal human mind for the understanding of the unspeakable
nature of *nirvana*." A similar difficulty affects the prominent Buddhist notion of *sunya* or *sunyata,* meaning emptiness and sometimes
likened to "speckless space or windless air." Here again, understanding has to proceed circumspectly. When radically separated from
ordinary or "full" reality and the normal flux of things, emptiness
is liable to be converted into something distinct in itself (or to be
objectified). Hence, its meaning can be approximated only through
a series of negations or else through figurative speech. In Chattopadhyaya's words,

> Perhaps, because of its intrinsic indefinability, the Buddha
> did not think it fit even to try to define this enigmatic nega-
> tion of every phenomenon. To affirm that *nirvana* is eternal
> or to state that it is a temporal process . . . is equally unten-
> able. The real truth of the matter is not itself a position, still
> less a third position, trying to reconcile the said two posi-
> tions. Both affirmation and denial of any position are two
> equally distorted ways of theoretization: Buddha's is not a
> theory, not a position [without being a negative theory or
> nihilism].[12]

The intrinsic and insuperable ambivalence of Buddhist teachings was highlighted with unmatched force and clarity by the great

Madhyamika philosopher Nagarjuna. Faithful to the "middle path" adumbrated by the Buddha himself, the Madhyamika school steered a kind of "dialectical" course between affirmation and negation, being and nonbeing. Without endorsing a reductive relativism, this approach emphasized the "relationality" or relational connection of all beings while denying the absoluteness of any essential self-nature (or any distinct entity as such). A particularly telling or revealing term employed by the school was *empty self-nature* (*svabhavasunya*), a term that, as Chattopadhyaya notes, was meant to indicate that the emptiness of every being is due precisely to "its essential relational character." It was in the writings of Nagarjuna that this dialectical, or aporetic, view of things found its most powerful articulation. Reflecting on the ultimate nature of reality, Nagarjuna took recourse to a "tetralemma"—that is, a series of four mutually deconstructive sentences: nirvana is not a positive entity (*bhava*); nirvana is not a negative entity (*abbhava*); nirvana is not both positive and negative; nirvana is neither something positive nor something negative.[13]

For Chattopadhyaya, it would be "rash" to conclude from these statements that Nagarjuna simply dismissed logic or cognitive rationality; what he did instead was to pursue rationality to its limit, forcing it to disclose its own aporia: "The proper use of logic, the Madhyamika points out, lies in *showing* the limits of logic." Only through a firm reliance on reason can the truth seeker finally "see for himself the flaws and faults of the logical formulation of the so-called 'knowledge' of the highest truths, of *nirvana* for example." By accepting aporia as a virtue, Madhyamika Buddhism left room for open-ended inquiry, thereby rejoining insights of early Western philosophical thought. "The Madhyamikas like Nagarjuna are bound to remind one of the Socratic method followed by Plato in his dialogues," states Chattopadhyaya. "The seemingly discursive 'fault-finding' is in reality rooted in, and oriented toward, truth-seeking" and genuine liberation.[14]

Freedom as Social Praxis

Having reviewed the conceptions of freedom in Western modernity and classical India, what lessons can one plausibly derive from these varying accounts, especially for our contemporary situation?

Clearly, the two accounts rely on different premises and follow divergent, perhaps even opposite, trajectories. Despite these divergences, however, one can also detect a subterranean linkage: in their different ways, both the dilemmas of Western Enlightenment and the aporias of classical India point to the elusive and even enigmatic character of human freedom. In classical Indian Vedanta, freedom was wedged between transcendent knowledge and individual desire or striving, and Madhyamika Buddhism located it in the interstices of self-being and non-self-being, presence and absence. In the case of Western modernity, freedom signified first of all a self-propelled appropriation and cognitive mastery of nature—an outreach that in the end jeopardized human agency by radically internalizing or privatizing its role.

Chattopadhyaya is lucidly eloquent in portraying the latter process. "The most important component of the European Enlightenment," he writes, was "reason and reason-based knowledge," a reason that was "praised for its discursive functions, associated with the marvels of experimental sciences, and put to classificatory, measurable, and system-making uses." Buoyed by the advances of natural science, "the European felt—for the first time and perhaps with some justification—that he could now successfully penetrate into the secrets of the universe and . . . conquer the world physically as well." The underlying engine of these advances was the cogito or cognitive "I think," which succeeded in "largely freeing itself from the dogmatic and dying institutional moorings of theology" and in "humbling religion." In the pursuit of world conquest or appropriation, however, something unexpected happened: the initial impulse of liberation "started yielding the pride of place to the concept of a rational order" governed by scientific determinism. In the end, under the increasing pressures of science and social conventions, "the self got somewhat smothered" (or was driven into world alienation).[15]

One lesson driven home by this story—and actually by the accounts of both Western and Asian freedom—has to do with the limitation of discursive-propositional language and more specifically with the limited competence of cognitive rationality in deciphering the "book of nature" as well as the complex textuality of human lives. It is in the context of a critique of propositional language that Chattopadhyaya draws attention to the teachings of Martin Heidegger and Hans-Georg Gadamer. As he notes with particular reference to *Being and Time,* communication for Heidegger is never a mere "information-conveying process" but rather involves "an experience of co-sharing." In the conversation between *Dasein* and co-*Dasein,* communication comprises both what is "talked about" and the "talking itself," and in fact "the two are hardly distinguishable."[16]

Moreover, besides oral and nonoral communication, there is for Heidegger the important dimension of silence, which is not outside but a part of language: "It may look like a dark and rugged island encircled by a boundless and bottomless sea, but in fact it is always supported by submarine firm territory of unheard and unspoken language." A similar insight may be gleaned from *Truth and Method,* where Gadamer speaks of an "inner dimension" of language and a hidden "dialectic of words." For Gadamer, Chattopadhyaya comments, language has "a life of its own," which first of all becomes "manifest and articulated in speech." Looked at from the reverse side, however, speech derives its meaning from language itself, which comprises silence as a "built-in" component: "If language is a plenum, uninterrupted continuum, it is so under the aspect of meaningfulness and not definable in terms of words, however large their number might be and however complex their syntax. The whole to which a word belongs contains in it meaningful slices of silence which interweave words but themselves are not words."[17]

Another, still more important lesson in the present context concerns the status and meaning of human freedom itself. As it appears from the previous accounts, freedom cannot be grasped in cognitive-propositional terms—under the rubric of the familiar subject–object scheme—without either being surrendered to external determinism or being reduced to private solipsism. In other words, freedom's aporetic status does not yield to a cognitive-theoretical solution offered in a spectatorial stance; its enigma can be resolved, if at all, only in a participatory stance or the mode of social action—through an action that is not willfully self-centered but rather self-transcending in the direction of social solidarity. In the Indian classical tradition, this kind of action was prominently thematized in the *Bhagavad Gita,* which celebrates self-transcending or nonattached praxis (karma yoga) as an eminent passageway to freedom.

In the modern Indian context, no one has more ably and persuasively embodied this praxis in public life than the Mahatma Gandhi. It is thus perhaps not surprising that D. P. Chattopadhyaya turned his attention increasingly to the Gandhian legacy. As he writes in a later essay titled "Gandhi on Freedom and Its Different Facets," Gandhi's conception of freedom rested on a "philosophical-cum-religious assumption" in the sense that, for him, individuals "exist in God" and hence are wayfarers on the paths to self-realization that simultaneously transgress the self. Humans, in this view, are indeed "makers of their own destiny," but not in a self-centered or solipsistic way that would violate the sacred "relationality" of all beings.[18] Students and colleagues in India and throughout the world owe D. P. Chattopadhyaya a profound debt of gratitude for all his manifold insights and especially for alerting readers again to the Mahatma's legacy.

10

Freedom and Solidarity (Again)

Reimagining Social Democracy

The present volume has from the start revolved around the difficult relation—sometimes viewed as antithesis—between freedom and solidarity, between individual independence and social interdependence or community. The opening chapters introduced the issue on a somewhat difficult philosophical level, invoking especially the teachings of Friedrich Nietzsche and Martin Heidegger. What the chapters mainly tried to show was that properly reconciling freedom and solidarity requires an innovative or pioneering move, a paradigm shift that transgresses the modern (Western) focus on "subjectivity" or the Cartesian *ego cogito*. Subsequent chapters explored the implications of this transgressive move in the areas of democratic theory, market relations, human rights, and conscientious resistance or dissent. Descending to the level of personal lived experience, additional chapters presented exemplary case studies of attempts to manage the freedom–solidarity nexus in different cultural contexts (moving from German Protestantism to Russian orthodoxy to Indian social thought). What was not offered at any point was a handy formula or catchy label to designate the intended aim. Given the innovative and exploratory character of the inquiry, great care must be taken not to allow the aim to congeal into an ideological doctrine or program.

Nevertheless, innovation is never ab ovo or without precedent. It would be foolish to claim utter novelty in a domain where human thought has valiantly labored for some time, guided by the desire to avoid social conformism or totalitarianism, on the one hand, and individual solipsism or narcissism, on the other. In fairness, one needs to recognize that during the past century and a half numerous proposals have been advanced designed to connect freedom and solidarity in such a manner as to safeguard the integrity of both. The great precursor of these efforts was Hegel's *Philosophy of Right*, which combined free initiative in civil society with the cultivation of civic virtues (*Sittlichkeit*) in a constitutional regime.[1] In subsequent developments, however, the Hegelian edifice was split apart, leaving as *disjecta membra* an increasingly radicalized individualism (cum capitalism) and an increasingly oppressive collectivism (along national or class lives) locked in relentless battle. It was inevitably not long before social theorists or intellectuals perceived the hopelessness of the situation or the dead-end character of the antithesis. Numerous proposals were introduced to tackle the dilemma, and various labels were chosen to designate the remedy—labels ranging from *liberal socialism* to *social liberalism* and *social democracy*. What matters are not so much these labels themselves as their intended content; moreover, as indicated, labels must not congeal into stereotypes. For my own purposes here, I prefer the notion "social democracy"—provided that the notion intends a regime grounded in free and equal human initiatives held together by laws and civic virtues oriented toward justice and the common good.

In this chapter, I proceed somewhat chronologically, moving from earlier to later and recent proposals. As it happens, these proposals originated mainly in European and American contexts, although parallels in other contexts can readily be found. One of the early initiatives in this field came from the American philosopher (and lapsed Hegelian) John Dewey. Given that Dewey is widely recognized as "the" philosopher of modern democracy, I start my account with him, while also paying attention to some of his important contemporaries. In a second step, I move to more recent initiatives in political philosophy, including a highly innovative proposal connecting creative hermeneutical interpretation with an unorthodox socialist or Communist agenda. By way of conclusion, I offer some of my own reflections on the freedom–solidarity symbiosis.

Dewey and Some Contemporaries

When invoking Dewey and his legacy today, one almost instantly encounters the question "Why?"—a query that is indicative of our present intellectual condition. More than that of any other American philosopher, Dewey's work is surrounded by a thick cloud of misreadings, especially the treatment of him as a shallow pragmatist bent on reducing all truth to efficiency or "what works." Aided and abetted even by some of his followers, this misreading inevitably rendered his work suspect or else quaintly obsolete in the eyes of a "more rigorous" approach—termed "analytical philosophy"—that emerged in America in the mid–twentieth century. This reputation of shallowness is aggravated by another feature of his work: its undeniable (quasi-Hegelian) "wholeness," which contrasts with the relentless polarization of contemporary social and intellectual life (evident in the Cold War and a succession of "culture wars"). Thus, trying to get access to Dewey's thought involves an uphill struggle—but a struggle made manageable by the nonesoteric and humane character of his writings.[2]

Dewey's work is sprawling and many faceted, dealing with a great number of topics. For present purposes, I select two of his writings that seem particularly instructive: *The Public and Its Problems* (1927) and *Individualism Old and New* (1930). The former text aimed to portray democracy as a public community held together by shared laws and (still more importantly) by engaged interactions, experiences, and aspirations. In line with Hegel's teachings, Dewey did not neglect the role of free individual initiatives in civil society; however, this is only part of the story. As he wrote, "All deliberate choices and plans are indeed the work of single human beings," but completely "false conclusions" have been drawn from this premise. From the angle of an excessively individualistic liberalism, the state or the public appears as nothing but "a fiction, a mask for private drives for power and position." From the same angle, society itself has been "pulverized into an aggregate of unrelated wants and wills." As a result, the public or the state is conceived either as total oppression or else as a massive collectivism smothering individual lives; differently put, it appears "either as a monster to be destroyed or as a Leviathan to be cherished." For Dewey, these developments signal a complete perversion of the idea of individual freedom; what has taken the place of this idea is an ideology: individualism or liberalism as an "ism" or dogmatic creed.[3]

What this creed neglects is the relationality of human conduct and indeed of all things in the world. "Electrons, atoms and molecules exemplify the omnipresence of conjoint behavior," Dewey writes. The same goes for social life: "Individuals still do the thinking, desiring and purposing, but *what* they think is the consequence of their behavior upon that of others and that of others upon themselves." Recognition of this relationality is particularly important in the state and the public sphere because of the broad range of the consequences of public interactions. Whereas interactions in the family and civil associations affect only a limited group of people, the state with its public sphere is distinguished by being the nodal point of all interactions in a given society. It is as a result of constant and persistent interactions that something like a "common interest" comes into being—that is, the realization that "all those affected by the consequences [of actions] are perforce concerned in the conduct of all those who along with themselves share in bringing about the results." It is in this way that a community not only of "interests" but of experiences, sentiments, and aspirations is generated that is (or should be) the nourishing backdrop of policies and decisions. To this community—which at times may be latent—Dewey gives the name "the public"; when the community adopts formal governmental institutions and structures, it turns into a "political state."[4]

As one should note, celebration of community, for Dewey, does not in any way imply a rejection of individual freedom, provided the latter is properly construed: not as a dogma or solipsistic creed but as a synonym for creative action and interaction. The penultimate chapter of *The Public and Its Problems* is a paean to community, even a "Great Community," which has irked (and continues to irk) libertarian absolutists. As we read there, "The clear consciousness of a communal life, in all its implications, constitutes the idea of democracy." This idea, moreover, is not static but involves a constant striving and progression—namely, "the search for conditions under which the Great Society may become a Great Community." As Dewey makes clear, this goal by no means violates the modern yardsticks of "liberty, equality, and fraternity." In fact, removed from social solidarity, these yardsticks become "hopeless abstractions" or shibboleths. In that case, liberty is denuded into arbitrary selfish whim, and equality becomes "a creed of mechanical sameness" and a recipe for "mediocrity." When reconnected with communal solidarity, however, human individuality unfolds freely as the "secure release and fulfillment of personal potentialities which take place only in rich and manifold association with others." Likewise, equality comes to denote "the unhampered share which each individual member of the community has in the consequences of associated action." As one can see, community or solidarity here is not equivalent to a stifling collectivism or conformism; moreover, its character is not only "physical and organic" but ethical and transformative and imbued with symbolic meaning. Dewey concludes this chapter with these words: when the Great Society becomes a Great Community, "democracy will come into its own, for it is a name for a life of free and enriching communion. It had its seer in Walt Whitman."[5]

Individualism Old and New traces the transformation and steady decline of individual life in modern Western societies, and especially in America, from a synonym for a "free and enriching communion" to an increasingly selfish and atomistic solipsism. In early American society, especially during the time of the open "frontier," individuals still lived in close contact with nature and in almost spontaneous solidarity with fellow pioneers seeking to tame the wilderness. The situation demanded a combination of individual courage and mutual dependence and trust. Those days, however, are long gone. As Dewey asks (rhetorically), "Where is the wilderness which now beckons creative energy and affords untold opportunity to initiative and vigor?" He answers: "The wilderness exists in the movie and the novel, and the children of the pioneers . . . enjoy pioneer life idly in the vicarious film." The fact is that society has entirely changed. "Anthropologically speaking," Dewey states, "we are living in a money culture; its cult and rites dominate." In this situation, the older idea of creative individuality has been eroded and replaced by the model of acquisitive agents operating in corporate structures. The inner spirit or "spiritual factor" animating the older idea—the accent on "free association and intercommunication"—has been "crowded out," making room for the rise of social Darwinism. As a result, Dewey notes, "instead of the development of individualities which [the tradition] prophetically set forth, there is a perversion of the whole ideal of individualism to conform to the practices of a pecuniary culture. It has become the source and justification of inequalities and oppression."[6]

Dewey's text is sharply critical of the changed condition in America (and in many Western societies) precisely because of its damaging effects on both individual freedom and sociality. "An economic individualism of motives and aims," he writes, "underlies our present corporate mechanisms, and undoes the individual." This loss of individuality is conspicuous and pervasive "because our civilization is so predominantly a business civilization." To this extent, one can speak of a "lost individual" in the midst of atomistic social structures because "the loyalties which once held individuals, which gave them support, direction and unity of outlook on life, have well-nigh disappeared." For Dewey, as stated earlier, society is a network of interactions, and individuality, no matter how creative or unique, can find its place and meaning only in this network: "Assured and integrated individuality is the product of definite social relationships and publicly acknowledged functions." Judged by this standard, even the most privileged corporate leaders—captains of finance and industry—are socially lost "because of the lack of a shared meaning of finance and industry" in civilization as a whole. The lack of sociality and solidarity is compensated by an intensified and nearly frantic pursuit of private gain (outside the bonds of social recognition). In Dewey's words, "The absence of a sense of social value is made up for by an exacerbated acceleration of the activities that increase private advantage and power." However, as in Hegel's master–slave relation, the triumph of financial mastery cannot fill the void of shared sociality. Anticipating recent studies of the psychopathologies of financial oligarchs, Dewey writes: "If there is any general degree of inner contentment on the part of those who form our pecuniary oligarchy, the evidence is sadly lacking. As for the many [the 99 percent], they are impelled hither and yon by forces beyond their control."[7]

Dewey's book is scathing in its critique of the reigning pecuniary culture and its lack of responsible social solidarity. He does not hesitate to invoke the idea of "socialism" as an antidote, albeit in a very unorthodox and uncoercive sense. The idea, he acknowledges, is still taboo for many: "The myth is still current that socialism desires to use political means in order to divide wealth equally among all individuals" and that hence it is opposed to progress and creative initiative. But there are other, more emancipatory meanings of the term *socialism*. "Those are many," Dewey states, "who believe that socialism of some form is needed to realize individual initiative and security on a wide scale. They are concerned about the restriction of power and freedom to a few in the present regime." Instead of being an obstacle, socialism can also be an ally in the struggle for social freedom among the multitude of people presently oppressed by the "pecuniary oligarchy." To be sure, Dewey is fully aware of the danger of collectivism and its offshoots of oppressive conformism and mindless mediocrity. "Conformity," he states, "is a name for the absence of vital interplay" in social relations, for "the arrest and benumbing of communication." Conformity's corollary, uniformity, is "a symptom of an inner void." Hence, the remedy for social ills envisaged by Dewey is a regime that might be called "liberal socialism" or "social liberalism," but preferably "social democracy"—that is, a regime where all members enjoy freedom in solidarity. His text describes the remedy in these terms: "a society in which daily occupations and relationships will give independence and substantial living to all who share in its ongoing interactions." Here is a more forceful declaration: "We are in for some kind of socialism, call it by whatever name you please. . . . [It involves] the choice between a socialism that is public and one that is capitalistic."[8]

In the preceding discussion, Dewey was singled out as a prominent—perhaps the most prominent—proponent of a symbiosis of freedom and solidarity bypassing rigid partisan agendas. There was no claim of the absolute uniqueness of his thoughts; in fact, his outlook was shared by a number of his contemporaries, both in America and abroad. For present purposes, a brief glance at some parallel intellectual orientations in Europe seems in order. In England, a broad movement of liberal socialism can be traced from the school of "new liberals" comprising T. H. Green, L. T. Hobhouse, and John Hobson to the ethical socialism of R. H. Tawney and the members of the Fabian Society, especially George Bernard Shaw and Sidney and Beatrice Webb. What linked members of these groups together was critique of the prevailing identification of liberty with financial wealth and privilege and the concomitant curtailment of the creative potentials of the industrial working class. In Germany, one can point to the "ethical socialism" of Eduard Bernstein and the proponents of a "social market economy" (Werner Sombart, Friedrich Naumann, and others). A particularly rich development of liberal socialism or social liberalism can be found in Italy. There, inspired by some of the German thinkers, Carlo Rosselli formulated an official political program called "liberal socialism" (*socialismo liberale*). In a book of the same title, Rosselli championed the idea of a mixed economy that would include both public and private property, limit cut-throat competition, and strengthen economic collaboration. Although supportive of a broadly socialist framework, his text strongly condemned conventional socialism's tendency to decay into totalitarian repression (a decay replicated by fascism in Italy and Germany). Rosselli's lead was continued by a number of other Italian public intellectuals, including Sandro Pertini and especially Guido Calogero, who in 1940 issued the "Manifesto of Liberal Socialism."[9]

Recent Political Philosophy

Following World War II, the time was ripe for a thorough rethinking of freedom and solidarity and their mutual relation. Such rethinking, however, was hampered by two main developments: first, the emergence of the Cold War, which sequestered freedom and solidarity into two rival worldviews, thus tendentially reducing them to geopolitical mantras; and second, the large-scale retreat of academic philosophy (at least in the West) from political and ethical domains in favor of the cultivation of knowledge theory (epistemology) and logic.[10] In the long run, however, obstacles of this kind could not withstand the pressure of concrete experiences and events. Having witnessed the horrors of totalitarian oppression manifest in the Holocaust, the Gulag, and Pol Pot, people almost everywhere had a profound thirst for freedom and the ability to shape their personal and communal lives in creative ways. At the same time, a sequence of serious economic crises, often manipulated by financial elites, drove home to most people the perversion of freedom into the property of a privileged minority and the erosion of solidarity under the impact of rampant social inequality. These and similar factors contributed to the steady resurgence of political philosophy (coupled with political economy) in recent decades, a resurgence of which I want to give some examples.

A prominent thinker who paid renewed attention to the freedom–solidarity issue was Richard Rorty, often considered Dewey's heir apparent. The latter treatment is not entirely fortuitous given obvious parallels. Like Dewey, Rorty was opposed to an abstract "intellectualism" divorced from concrete lived experience; again like his mentor, he stressed the role of continuous experimental learning. In other respects, however, the parallel is limited or dubious. Deviating from his mentor's "holism" or insistence on connections, Rorty's writings opened up a series of gaps or dichotomies, especially the gaps between public and private life, knowledge and opinion (*episteme* and *doxa*), and "objectivity" and subjective sentiment. These gaps predictably took their toll on the freedom–solidarity nexus. In a major move, Rorty transformed Dewey's pragmatism into a political and ethical relativism—a move that tendentially pushed freedom in the direction of arbitrary whim. Dislodged from concrete social structures and institutions, solidarity became a matter of private personal choice anchored in empathy. As he wrote in his well-known book *Contingency, Irony, and Solidarity* (1989), the latter term, *empathy,* does not so much imply any transpersonal nexus but a private and entirely optional state of feeling. In turn, the term *solidarity* does not denote an interpersonal or public state of mutual recognition but simply "the ability to see more and more traditional differences (of tribe, religion, race, customs, and the like) as unimportant when compared with similarities with respect to pain and humiliation."[11]

Another prominent (and more public-spirited) thinker is Chantal Mouffe, well known for her effort to rescue politics (or "the political") from its submergence in socioeconomic categories. In one of her early books, penned with Ernesto Laclau, Mouffe critiqued the monolithic and totalitarian character of Soviet communism, especially its repression of internal difference and dissent. Generalizing this point, she extended her critique to forms of public "communitarianism" that sideline internal pluralism, thereby transforming solidarity into an oppressive uniformity. Critical strictures of this kind, however, did not prompt Mouffe to endorse the equation of politics with the pursuit of private self-interest. As she observed in *The Return of the Political* (1993), "Today, the liberal illusion that harmony could be born from the free play of private interests, and that modern society no longer needs civic virtue, has finally shown itself to be dangerous; it puts in question the very existence of the democratic process." The upshot of her dual remonstrations—inspired in part by classical "civic republicanism" and Hannah Arendt's notion of the "public sphere"—is the endorsement of an ethically engaged social democracy composed of free agents: "Our choice is not one between an aggregate of individuals without common public concern and a premodern community organized around a single substantive idea of the common good." Once political economy is added to this balanced mixture, the result is a "radical and plural democracy" that incorporates and brings to fruition the traditional socialist agenda. "Understood as a process of democratization of the economy, socialism is a necessary component of the project of genuine democracy. I believe there is an urgent need to advocate a 'liberal socialism.'"[12]

A further important theorist—inspired in many ways also by Arendt—is Craig Calhoun, longtime president of the Social Science Research Council and recently director of the London School of Economics. In a series of writings, Calhoun has explored the meaning of such terms as "community," "nationalism," "solidarity," and the "public sphere." In an instructive essay titled "Imagining Solidarity" (2002), he seeks to articulate a version of solidarity that—in Hegelian and Deweyan fashion—recognizes in equal measure the needs for democratic community and individual agency. "There is an important Hegelian relation at work here," he writes, "a dialectic of the whole and its parts. Without grasping this dialectic, we can understand neither of its terms—*community* and *individual*. We are especially apt to be misled into seeing them as opposites, rather than as terms that are complicit with each other." On the basis of this insight, he offers a (mild) critique of Jürgen Habermas's tendency to split asunder cultural identity and rational discourse instead of linking them in public action. A remedy for this defect, in Calhoun's view, can be found in Arendt's work, which treats public life as grounded in creatively "founding" actions and recognizes people as "radically plural: not necessarily similar [or atomistic], but bound to one another by promises that are explicit or implicit in their lives together." In combination, these features contribute a particularly rich and multifaceted character to Arendt's notion of the "public sphere," an arena where individual autonomy and public responsibility meet—sometimes contesting, sometimes complementing each other. Seen from this angle, Calhoun concludes, the "public sphere" is important and effective "not only through informing state policy, but also through forming culture," which means that "through the exercise of social imagination and the forging of social relationships" the public sphere comes to constitute "a form of social solidarity."[13]

As a final example of innovative political theorizing, I want to mention *Hermeneutic Communism* (2011), written jointly by Gianni Vattimo and Santiago Zabala. Both writers have established a broad reputation through their efforts to bring postmodern philosophical insights to bear on traditional conceptions or frameworks (from Christian theology to Enlightenment rationalism to the socialist agenda). The title *Hermeneutic Communism* can be read as a new, somewhat unusual version of the freedom–solidarity relation. According to this text, hermeneutics—as articulated by Nietzsche, Heidegger, and Gadamer—is basically the antithesis of traditional "metaphysics," the latter seen as a compact, dogmatically held worldview claiming to capture the world "as it is" (minus its latent potentialities). Whereas metaphysics is "the philosophy of the winners who wish to conserve the world as it is," the authors say, hermeneutics is attentive to the "possible/impossible," thus capturing "the thought of the weak in search of alternatives." In terms of solidarity, what links hermeneutics and undogmatic Marxism is chiefly a shared reaction to domination and suffering: they are "alternative responses for the 'losers' of history."[14]

Concluding Comments

Vattimo and Zabala's reflections lead me back to the opening chapters of the present book. In those chapters, relying mainly on the teachings of Nietzsche and Heidegger, I pleaded strongly in favor of new beginnings or departures and the need to move beyond traditional philosophical formulations of political concepts—especially the notions of freedom and solidarity. As I indicated, these new departures are necessary mainly (though not only) because of the derailment of these notions during recent centuries into compact "metaphysical" shibboleths: on the one hand, a narcissistic liberal individualism disdainful of social obligations; on the other hand, a totalizing collectivism neglectful of liberty and of social and cultural pluralism. To be sure, the derailment can be traced further back to the onset of Western modernity: the glorification of egocentric reason by Descartes and the transformation of Aristotelian experientialism into calculating modern science. As also mentioned earlier, the remedy for these misadventures cannot be found in a simple dismissal of modern freedom and solidarity but must be located in their sustained rethinking and reassessment—a reassessment that has been this book's main endeavor.

It may be appropriate now that I have traversed a series of chapters to recall or restate more precisely what is at issue for me in these deliberations. This has not been an exercise in "conceptual history," where one would examine in how many senses the terms *freedom* and *solidarity* have been used in various places at different points of history. My concern is also not purely instrumental or utilitarian in the sense of an inquiry designed to show how the practical application of one term can lead to the strengthening or flourishing of the other term. Thus, it is undeniably the case that the practice of solidarity among a group of people can lead to the achievement of political freedom that would not have been possible for individuals acting alone. Likewise, in a well-established regime held together by solidarity, the enjoyment of freedom by individuals or groups may be more secure. All these points I take for granted but leave aside. My concern is also not with a purely contingent or haphazard relationship—that is, a situation where freedom and equality, although normally unrelated, happen to come into temporary proximity like two planets in separate orbits.

Leaving aside purely conceptual or else accidental constellations, my concern in these pages has been basically existential and, in a sense, ontological. Here I can return to my discussion of Heidegger in the opening chapters. For Heidegger, the relation between self and others is not fortuitous or engineered but rather primary. His basic definition of human existence as "being-in-the-world" (with hyphens) means precisely that human *Dasein* is not self-sufficient or self-contained and that "world"—including all other beings—is *constitutive* for the very meaning of *Dasein*. There is no ready exodus or escape hatch. In Heidegger's words, we are "thrown" into the world, which, however, is not a prison but rather an open horizon inviting and requiring constant efforts to interpret and rethink what it means to "be." In this sense, human beings enjoy indeed a staggering creative freedom, a freedom that lifts them above "the world as it is," enabling them to perceive the world's potential. Yet in line with the "thrown" character of *Dasein*, creative interpretation never proceeds from scratch or from a tabula rasa but always in contact with the temporal and social conditions of the world (with its sedimented "prejudgments"). To this extent, the combination of hermeneutics and communism proposed by Vattimo and Zabala appears entirely plausible. Due to *Dasein*'s constitutive character of "co-being" (*Mitsein*), there is indeed an inescapable "communism" or solidarity among all beings. This feature, however, is crisscrossed and rendered porous by a creative interpretation that construes communality variously, orienting it in different directions.

What I want to add to this account—and this is my own interpretation—is a more distinctly ethical or ethical-ontological dimension. In my reading, human being-in-the-world implies not only a factual coexistence but also a bond of mutual ethical responsibility. By the very fact of its being co-constituted by world and other beings, *Dasein* owes to world and other beings the ethical duty of world maintenance—that is, of contributing to their well-being or flourishing. Heidegger thematizes this obligation under the rubrics *care* (*Sorge*) and *letting-be* (*Sein-lassen*). In numerous places, he presents careful "letting-be" as the primordial human praxis—that is, as the key to a properly human way of life.[15] To this extent, one might say that careful letting-be constitutes a "categorical" obligation (not so much in a Kantian sense as in an ontological sense). To be sure, such obligation can take different forms and occurs in many different settings or contexts. Primary contexts are the family, the local community, the larger society, and the world (seen as global community). No doubt, there are contexts or relationships that are purely voluntary or contingent; one thinks of social clubs, fraternities, business relations, and even some churches. However, some human relations are inescapable. Everyone is born into a family at a given place and time; everyone lives in a local and a larger community; everyone lives in the "world." Even though some communities (small and large) can be replaced or exchanged, one still ends up living in a community (small and large). Thus, wherever one turns, even the most "solitary" individual finds himself or herself enmeshed in bonds of ethical responsibility that he or she cannot shirk.[16]

The most precise question I wanted to raise in this book is this: Given the recognition of "categorical" ethical bonds or a "categorical" solidarity, is there still room for human freedom? Differently put: Is freedom compatible with a strong sense of solidarity and solidarity compatible with a strong sense of freedom? My basic answer is "yes" because both are constitutive of each other. Given the primordial character of "letting-be," *Dasein*, as being-in-the-world, cannot be genuinely free as long as others are oppressed, dominated, or exploited. To be sure, there are liable to be tensions between freedom and solidarity in various contexts. As previously indicated, freedom can decay into solipsism and solidarity into collectivism. In our time, the latter danger is particularly virulent, manifest in the worldwide upsurge of nationalistic or ethnocentric creeds fueling violent crowd behavior (often abetted by mass media). In these situations, we require individual leaders who are able to rise above the crowds' uniformity and venomous spirit. This is the meaning of Nietzsche's appeal to the "overman" and of Heidegger's invocation of "authentic" human freedom. To be sure, leadership here is (and must be) free of the taint of elitism because the leaders' objective is not to accumulate wealth or power for themselves but to serve their community's well-being. Differently put: their task is to rescue a community mired in abject desires by appealing from their lower instincts to their "better angels." Historical examples of such figures are Saint Francis of Assisi, Mahatma Gandhi, Nelson Mandela, Martin Luther King Jr., Bishop Desmond Tutu, and the Dalai Lama. Following John Dewey, one might also add the "seer" of a Great Community, Walt Whitman.

Notes

Introduction

1. Karl Jaspers, *The Origin and Goal of History,* trans. Michael Bullock (New Haven: Yale University Press, 1953), 1–3, 8.

2. Relying in part on Jaspers, Karen Armstrong has portrayed modernity and the Enlightenment as a "Second Axial Age," with a focus on such thinkers as Isaac Newton, Sigmund Freud, and Albert Einstein. The problem for her is how to recover insights of the first Axial Age in and through the second. See Karen Armstrong, *The Great Transformation: The Beginnings of Our Religious Traditions* (New York: Knopf, 2006). Compare Robert Bellah, *Religion in Human Evolution: From the Paleolithic to the Axial* Age (Cambridge, MA: Belknap Press of Harvard University Press, 2011); Robert Bellah and Hans Joas, eds., *The Axial Age and Its Consequences* (Cambridge, MA: Belknap Press of Harvard University Press, 2012); Johann P. Arnason, Shmuel N. Eisenstadt, and Björn Wittrock, eds., *Axial Civilizations and World History* (Leiden: Brill, 2005); and Yves Lambert, "Religion in Modernity as a New Axial Age: Secularization or New Religious Forms," *Sociology of Religion* 60 (1999): 303–310.

3. Jaspers, *The Origin and Goal of History,* 24, 81–83. In this study, Jaspers distinguished four watersheds or new beginnings: the onset of "prehistory," the rise of ancient civilizations, the Axial Age, and the scientific-technological age (24).

4. Jaspers himself was fully aware of this needed change of focus. As he states in a section of *The Origin and Goal of History* titled "The Faith of the Future," "No one can foretell what might be possible through the rejuvenation of the Churches. . . . Ecclesiastical faith is expressed in notions, ideas, dogmas and becomes creed [orthodoxy]. It is capable of forgetting its origin . . . and then must lose its strength. . . . Opposed to this is a metamorphosis of the mode of faith which is foreign to the Churches: Man, aware of his liberty, leaves his faith in suspension in an inexpressible general implication, and is decisive in his historicity, in the decisions of his personal life. . . . The question is whether the epoch, which has taught whole populations to read and to write for the first time, does not by this very fact afford new possibilities for a free faith that is undogmatic in its tenets, without diminution of earnestness and unconditionality" (224–225).

5. The notion of radical "paradigm shifts" is well known from the work of Thomas S. Kuhn; see especially *The Structure of Scientific Revolutions*, 2nd ed. (Chicago: University of Chicago Press, 1970). However, for Kuhn, such shifts were chiefly cognitive or epistemic in nature and did not involve a comprehensive change in social and political ways of life. The latter broad configuration is better captured in the notion of "social imaginaries." See, for example, Cornelius Castoriadis, *The Imaginary Institution of Society*, trans. Kathleen Blamey (Cambridge, MA: MIT Press, 1987), and Charles Taylor, *Modern Social Imaginaries* (Durham, NC: Duke University Press, 2004). For a broader existential conception of paradigm shifts, compare Barry Miller, *The Fullness of Being: A New Paradigm for Existence* (Notre Dame, IN: University of Notre Dame Press, 2002).

6. Axel Honneth captures well the pivotal status of freedom in modernity: "Among all the ethical values which have gained dominance or compete for supremacy in modern society, only *one* was capable of shaping decisively the modern institutional order: freedom in the sense of individual autonomy. . . . Since the days of Thomas Hobbes, the category of individual freedom must count—both substantively and logically—as one of the most determining and contested concepts of social modernity" (*Das Recht der Freiheit: Grundriss einer demokratischen Sittlichkeit* [Frankfurt: Suhrkamp, 2011], 35, 41 [my translation]). Honneth actually criticizes as a possible lapse into dangerous atavism any attempt to reconceive the modern notion of freedom.

7. Isaiah Berlin formulated the standard conceptions of "positive" and "negative" freedom in *Four Essays on Liberty* (London: Oxford University Press, 1969).

8. The classical text that discusses these developments is Theodor W. Adorno and Max Horkheimer, *Dialectic of Enlightenment*, trans. John Cumming (New York: Seabury Books, 1973). Compare Maurice Merleau-Ponty, *Adventures of the Dialectic*, trans. Joseph Bien (Evanston: Northwestern University Press, 1973).

9. On the process of "disembedding," see especially Karl Polanyi, *The Great Transformation: The Political and Economic Origins of Our Time* (Boston: Beacon Press, 1957); also, from a more religious angle, see Taylor, *Modern Social Imaginaries*, 49–67.

10. The beneficial role of freedom is sidelined, for example, in the prominent critiques of modernity advanced by Alasdair MacIntyre, Leo Strauss, and Eric Voegelin. See Alasdair MacIntyre, *After Virtue: A Study in Moral Theory*, 2nd ed. (Notre Dame, IN: University of Notre Dame Press, 1984); Leo Strauss, *Political Philosophy: Six Essays*, ed. Hilab Gildin (Indianapolis: Pegasus, 1975); Eric Voegelin, *Modernity without Restraint*, ed. Manfred Henningsen (Columbia: University of Missouri Press, 2000).

11. The standard analysis of this phenomenon is Hannah Arendt, *The Origins of Totalitarianism* (New York: Harcourt, Brace, 1951). To be sure, Arendt was far removed from simply equating fascist and Communist totalitarianism.

12. Maurice Merleau-Ponty, *The Visible and the Invisible, Followed by Working Notes*, ed. Claude Lefort, trans. Alphonso Lingis (Evanston: Northwestern University Press, 1968), 170. Merleau-Ponty adds that this world "is at bottom Being in Heidegger's sense, which is more than all painting, than all speech, than every 'attitude,' and which, apprehended by philosophy in its universality, appears as containing everything that will ever be said, and yet leaving us to say it" (170). See also Raimon Panikkar, *The Rhythm of Being: The Gifford Lectures* (Maryknoll, NY: Orbis Books, 2010), and *Invisible Harmony: Essays on Contemplation and Responsibility*, ed. Harry James Cargas (Minneapolis: Fortress Press, 1995).

13. Merleau-Ponty, *The Visible and the Invisible*, 159. The openness invoked here corresponds again closely to Heidegger's notion of *Offenheit* (openness) and *Erschlossenheit* (disclosedness). See Martin Heidegger, *Being and Time*, trans. John Macquarrie and Edward Robinson (New York: Harper & Row, 1962), sec. 7, p. 62, and sec. 16, pp. 105–106. On disclosure and its primacy over cognitive "validation," see also Nikolas Compridis, *Critique and Disclosure: Critical Theory between Past and Future* (Cambridge, MA: MIT Press, 2006), and my essay "Disclosure and Critique: Critical Reason and Its Horizons," in my book *Integral Pluralism: Beyond Culture Wars* (Lexington: University Press of Kentucky, 2010), 175–184.

14. Gilles Deleuze, *Difference and Repetition*, trans. Paul Patton (New York: Columbia University Press, 1994), 54, 199. In the background, there are echoes of Spinoza's distinction between *natura naturans* and *natura naturata*. More distant parallels can be drawn with the distinction between the "state of nature" and the "civil state" in the work of Thomas Hobbes and Jean-Jacques Rousseau.

15. Merleau-Ponty, *The Visible and the Invisible*, 250 (unless otherwise noted, emphasis in quotes from all sources is in the original). Merleau-Ponty is paraphrasing Martin Heidegger, *Unterwegs zur Sprache* (Tübingen: Mohr, 1959), 13; *Poetry, Language, Thought*, trans. Albert Hofstadter (New York: Harper & Row, 1971), 191.

16. For a detailed historical analysis of the concept of solidarity, see Hauke Brunkhorst, *Solidarity: From Civic Friendship to Global Legal Community*, trans. Jeffrey Flynn (Cambridge, MA: MIT Press, 2005).

17. The paradoxical character of solidarity and community life has been stressed especially by Jacques Derrida and Jean-Luc Nancy. See Jean-Luc Nancy, *The Inoperative Community*, ed. Peter Connor (Minneapolis: University of Minnesota Press, 1991), and my essay "An 'Inoperative' Global Community? Reflections on Nancy," in my book *Alternative Visions: Paths in the Global Village* (Lanham, MD: Rowman & Littlefield, 1998), 277–279.

18. See, for example, my book *The Other Heidegger* (Ithaca: Cornell University Press, 1993), and my essays "Resisting Totalizing Uniformity: Martin Heidegger on *Macht* and *Machenschaft*," in *Achieving Our World: Toward a Global and Plural Democracy* (Lanham, MD: Rowman & Littlefield, 2001), 189–209,

and "The Underside of Modernity: Adorno, Heidegger, and Dussel," *Constellations* 11 (2004): 102–120.

19. See my essay "Democracy without Banisters: Reading Claude Lefort," in my book *The Promise of Democracy: Political Agency and Transformation* (Albany: State University of New York Press, 2010), 187–193.

20. See especially the following works by Michael Sandel: *Public Philosophy: Essays on Morality in Politics* (Cambridge, MA: Harvard University Press, 2006); *Justice: What's the Right Thing to Do?* (New York: Farrar, Straus and Giroux, 2009); and *What Money Can't Buy: The Moral Limits of Markets* (New York: Farrar, Straus and Giroux, 2012).

1. Twilights and New Dawns

1. Friedrich Nietzsche, *Beyond Good and Evil: Prelude to a Philosophy of the Future*, trans. Walter Kaufmann (New York: Random House, 1966), 45, 153.

2. Ibid., 52, 117.

3. Ibid., 10, 23–24. Cautiously guarding against reification, Nietzsche adds that maybe "one has even gone too far with this 'it thinks'—for even the 'it' contains an *interpretation* of the process" (24).

4. Ibid., 24–26, 28.

5. Ibid., 29, 123, 126. The last sentence bears a distant resemblance to the exaggerated celebration of "otherness" during the heyday of postmodernism.

6. Ibid., 20, 27.

7. Ibid., 201, 203–204, 206.

8. Ibid., 203.

9. Ibid., 117, 138–139, 215.

10. Ibid., 245. The poem in this context also appeals to the "friend Zarathustra, the guest of guests." One can acknowledge, of course, a certain tension between democracy and meritocracy, but without accepting their radical opposition.

11. Ibid., 5, 203. Although recognizing certain variations in the meaning of "power," Nietzsche does not sufficiently distinguish between power, empowerment, force, and strength. For these distinctions, see Hannah Arendt, "On Violence," in *Crises of the Republic* (New York: Harcourt Brace Jovanovich, 1970), 142–145.

12. Friedrich Nietzsche, *The Will to Power*, ed. Walter Kaufmann, trans. Walter Kaufmann and R. J. Hollingdale (New York: Random House, 1967), 3–4. (For some reason, the subtitle—although mentioned in the preface—is omitted in this edition.)

13. Ibid., 347, 401, 457, 501.

14. The crucial text here is Martin Heidegger, "Letter on Humanism," in *Martin Heidegger: Basic Writings*, ed. David F. Krell (New York: Harper & Row, 1977), 189–242. For Heidegger's intense struggle to come to terms with

and distance himself from Nietzsche, see his four-volume work *Nietzsche,* ed. David F. Krell (New York: Harper & Row, 1979). In a simplified way, one might say that Heidegger moved from Nietzsche to Hölderlin.

15. Martin Heidegger, *Sein und Zeit,* 11th ed. (Tübingen: Niemeyer, 1967), 98, 116–117 (my translation); *Being and Time,* trans. John Macquarrie and Edward Robinson (New York: Harper & Row, 1962), sec. 21, p. 131, and sec. 25, pp. 151–152.

16. Heidegger, *Sein und Zeit,* 20; *Being and Time,* sec. 6, p. 41.

17. Heidegger, *Sein und Zeit,* 20–22; *Being and Time,* sec. 6, pp. 41–43.

18. Heidegger, *Sein und Zeit,* 22–23; *Being and Time,* sec. 6, pp. 43–44. The only tradition that Heidegger exempts to some extent from the patina of mere traditionalism is Kant's philosophy, but even in this case some unreflected patina prevails because of Kant's indebtedness to the Cartesian *ego cogitans.*

19. Heidegger, *Sein und Zeit,* 27–29; *Being and Time,* sec. 7, pp. 49–51. Heidegger at this point launches into an intricate discussion of the difference between semblance (*Schein*) and appearance (*Erscheinung*) as well as between two types of appearance—a discussion that I bypass here.

20. Heidegger, *Sein und Zeit,* 34–35; *Being and Time,* sec. 7, pp. 58–59.

21. Heidegger, *Sein und Zeit,* 36–37; *Being and Time,* sec. 7, pp. 60–61.

22. Heidegger, *Sein und Zeit,* 37–38; *Being and Time,* sec. 7, pp. 61–62. In these statements, Heidegger obviously tried to reconcile the "being-question" with Husserl's "transcendental phenomenology" of essences. As he came to see later, however, the statements conceded too much to Husserl's transcendentalism.

23. For Heidegger's struggle with Nietzsche, see note 14 for this chapter. Regarding *Machenschaft,* see my essay "Resisting Totalizing Uniformity," in *Achieving Our World: Toward a Global and Plural Democracy* (Lanham, MD: Rowman & Littlefield, 2001), 189–209.

24. The term *en-owning* was used in the first English translation of *Beiträge;* see Martin Heidegger, *Contributions to Philosophy (From Enowning),* trans. Parvis Emad and Kenneth Maly (Bloomington: Indiana University Press, 1999).

25. Martin Heidegger, *Beiträge zur Philosophie (Vom Ereignis),* ed. Friedrich-Wilhelm von Herrmann, vol. 65 of *Gesamtausgabe* (Frankfurt-Main: Klostermann, 1989), 3, 10 (my translation). For a more recent English translation, see Martin Heidegger, *Contributions to Philosophy (Of the Event),* trans. Richard Rojcewicz and Daniéla Vallege-Neu (Bloomington: Indiana University Press, 2012), 5, 10–11. The translators bring two dubious terms together when they write that the reflections in *Beiträge* "attempt to let themselves be *appropriated* by the event" (suggesting a heteronomous takeover) but add: "What 'essence' and 'event' come to mean in the course of these ponderings is up to the reader to decide" ("Translators' Introduction," xv–xvi). I prefer to let *Ereignis* stand, although occasionally I find the term *advent* suitable.

26. Heidegger, *Beiträge,* 3–5; *Contributions,* 5–7. As Heidegger adds, "In the

context of transitional thinking, the first beginning remains decisive as the first and yet is overcome as beginning. For this thinking, the profound respect for the first beginning . . . must go together with the disrespect implicit in another questioning and way of speaking" (*Beiträge*, 6; *Contributions*, 7). Heidegger's comments imply a strong warning against attempts to fabricate or engineer paradigm shifts or a new "Axial Age" through manifestoes, platforms, or marching orders (all of which are manifestations of *Machenschaft* and will to power).

27. Heidegger, *Beiträge*, 34–36, 52–53; *Contributions*, 28–30, 43 (the term *Verhaltenheit* is here translated as "restraint"). In a political vein, Heidegger adds that reticence is the opposite of "that self-certainty which is the inner core of 'liberalism' which pretends to guarantee free human development, based on the gospel of external progress. From this angle, 'world-view' (*Weltanschaung*), 'personality,' 'genius' and 'culture' are the 'values' which are to be actualized" (*Beiträge*, 53; *Contributions*, 43).

28. Heidegger, *Beiträge*, 169, 172–173; *Contributions*, 133, 135–136. Heidegger adds that all merely negative reactions "end up remaining in the confines of metaphysics. This is true of all biologisms and naturalisms," including exuberant types of "life philosophy" (*Beiträge*, 173; *Contributions*, 136). In some passages, Nietzsche's thought is portrayed as such a "life philosophy" (*Beiträge*, 362–364; *Contributions*, 286–287).

29. Heidegger, *Beiträge*, 227–228; *Contributions*, 179–180.

30. Heidegger, *Beiträge*, 307, 311, 395–397, 401, 409–411; *Contributions*, 243, 246–247, 313–315, 318, 324–326. Heidegger does not elaborate on the possibility of a new community engendered by the "future ones." The reason, one can conjecture, is clear: the Nazi abuse of the idea of community through their advocacy of "folkish community" ("one folk, one Reich, one führer"). For Heidegger's sharply critical comments on "folk" (*Volk*), see *Beiträge*, 42–43, 98–99, 319–320, 398–400; *Contributions*, 34–35, 77–78, 253–254, 316–317.

31. Martin Heidegger, *Das Ereignis*, ed. Friedrich-Wilhelm von Herrmann, vol. 71 of *Gesamtausgabe* (Frankfurt-Main: Klostermann, 2009), 75, 79, 84, 101 (my translation). For the critique of "will to power" and "will to will," see especially pages 105, 115–117. In the text, the "transition" is facilitated by recollection of the "ontic-ontological difference" (*Unterschied*) (121–135). On *Ereignis*, see 181–185; on pain and refusal, 235–245.

32. Martin Heidegger, *Über den Anfang*, ed. Paola-Ludovika Coriando, vol. 70 of *Gesamtausgabe* (Frankfurt-Main: Klostermann, 2005), 9–10, 15–17, 19, 107 (my translation). The two wartime texts were followed in 1944 by *Die Stege des Anfangs* (Paths of the beginning) and *Zum Ereignis-Denken* (On thinking *Ereignis*).

2. Letting-Be Politically

1. See my essay "Heidegger and Politics: Some Lessons," in my book *The Other Heidegger* (Ithaca: Cornell University Press, 1993), 15–48; Victor Farias,

Heidegger and Nazism, trans. Paul Burrell and Gabriel R. Ricci (Philadelphia: Temple University Press, 1989); Tom Rookmore and Joseph Margolis, eds., *The Heidegger Case: On Philosophy and Politics* (Philadelphia: Temple University Press, 1992); Richard Wolin, ed., *The Heidegger Controversy: A Critical Reader* (New York: Columbia University Press, 1991); Philippe Lacoue-Labarthe, *Heidegger, Art, and Politics: The Fiction of the Political*, trans. Chris Turner (Oxford: Blackwell, 1990); and Jürg Altwegg, ed., *Die Heidegger Kontroverse* (Frankfurt-Main: Athenäum, 1988).

2. On interpretations of Heidegger's work in the direction of either an extreme voluntarism or extreme fatalism (or both), see Jürgen Habermas, *Philosophical-Political Profiles*, trans. Frederick G. Lawrence (Cambridge, MA: MIT Press, 1983), 57–58, and Christian Graf von Krockow, *Die Entscheidung: Eine Untersuchung über Ernst Jünger, Carl Schmitt, Martin Heidegger* (Stuttgart: Enke, 1958).

3. Martin Heidegger, *Sein und Zeit*, 11th ed. (Tübingen: Niemeyer, 1967), 42–46, 53–57 (my translation); *Being and Time*, trans. John Macquarrie and Edward Robinson (London: SCM, 1962), sec. 9 and 12, pp. 67–71, 78–84.

4. Heidegger, *Sein und Zeit*, 267–269, 295–298; *Being and Time*, sec. 54, 60, pp. 312–314, 341–345. For an instructive discussion of the relation of freedom and "resoluteness," see Charles M. Sherover, "Heidegger and Practical Reason," in *Phenomenology: Dialogues and Bridges*, ed. Ronald Bruzina and Bruce Wilshire (Albany: State University of New York Press, 1982), 23–36.

5. Martin Heidegger, "Vom Wesen der Wahrheit," in *Wegmarken* (Frankfurt-Main: Klostermann, 1967), 81–82 (my translation); for an English translation, see "On the Essence of Truth," in *Martin Heidegger: Basic Writings*, ed. David F. Krell (New York: Harper & Row, 1977), 125–126.

6. Heidegger, "Vom Wesen der Wahrheit," 83, 87; "On the Essence of Truth," 127, 130. For Heidegger, the disclosure of the truth of Being carries with it the possibility of concealment and distortion and thus the possibility of "untruth" or the "nonbeing of truth" (*Unwesen der Wahrheit*). As he writes, "Because truth is in essence freedom, historical *Dasein*—in letting beings be— can also *not* let beings be what they are and as they are; in this case, beings are concealed and distorted. Thus, semblance becomes dominant, and with it the non-being of truth" ("Vom Wesen der Wahrheit," 86; "On the Essence of Truth," 130).

7. Heidegger, "Vom Wesen der Wahrheit," 84–86; "On the Essence of Truth," 128–130.

8. Martin Heidegger, *Vom Wesen der menschlichen Freiheit: Einleitung in die Philosophie*, ed. Hartmut Tietjen, vol. 31 of *Gesamtausgabe* (Frankfurt-Main: Klostermann, 1982).

9. Ibid., 21–22, 24–25, 28–29, 137–139 (my translation).

10. Ibid., 134–135, 198–199, 209–210, 300–302. As Heidegger adds, "To let an encounter with beings happen and to comport oneself to beings in a mode

of openness or disclosedness is possible only on the basis of freedom. Thus, *freedom is the condition of possibility of the disclosure of the Being of beings and of the understanding of Being*" (303).

11. Martin Heidegger, *Schellings Abhandlung über das Wesen der menchlichen Freiheit* (1809), ed. Hildegand Feick (Tübingen: Niemeyer, 1971), 10–11 (my translation). Regarding this text, see also my essay "Heidegger on Ethics and Justice," in *The Other Heidegger*, 106–131, and Parvis Ernad, "Heidegger on Schelling's Conception of Freedom," *Man and World* 8 (1975): 152–172.

12. Heidegger, *Schellings Abhandlung*, 83, 90–95, 104–105.

13. See Martin Heidegger, *Beiträge zur Philosophie (Vom Ereignis)*, ed. Friedrich-Wilhelm von Herrmann, vol. 65 of *Gesamtausgabe* (Frankfurt-Main: Klostermann, 1989), and *Besinnung*, ed. Friedrich-Wilhelm von Herrmann, vol. 66 of *Gesamtausgabe* (Frankfurt-Main: Klostermann, 1997).

14. Martin Heidegger, "Di Frage nach der Technik," in *Vorträge und Aufsätze*, part I (Pfullingen: Neske, 1967), 22–25 (my translation); "The Question Concerning Technology," in *Martin Heidegger: Basic Writings*, 305–307.

15. Martin Heidegger, "Bauen Wohnen Denken," in *Vorträge und Aufsätze*, part II (Pfullingen: Neske, 1967), 22–23 (my translation); "Building Dwelling Thinking," in *Martin Heidegger: Basic Writings*, 326–327.

16. See, for example, Emmanuel Levinas, *Humanism of the Other*, trans. Nidra Poller (Urbana: University of Illinois Press, 2003), and *Entre Nous: On Thinking-of-the-Other*, trans. Michael B. Smith and Baslana Harshav (New York: Columbia University Press, 1988); from another angle, see Jürgen Habermas, *Postmetaphysical Thinking*, trans. Frederick Lawrence (Cambridge, MA: MIT Press, 1987).

17. See Heidegger, *Sein und Zeit*, 53–62, 63–95; *Being and Time*, sec. 12–13 and 14–20, pp. 78–90, 91–127.

18. Heidegger, *Sein und Zeit*, 42–46, 67–72, 83–88; *Being and Time*, sec. 4, pp. 32–35, and sec. 9, 15, and 18, pp. 67–71, 95–101, 114–122.

19. Heidegger, *Sein und Zeit*, 114–125; *Being and Time*, sec. 25 and 26, pp. 150–163.

20. Heidegger, *Sein und Zeit*, 117–120; *Being and Time* sec. 26, pp. 153–156.

21. Heidegger, *Sein und Zeit*, 120–125; *Being and Time* sec. 26, pp. 156–163.

22. Heidegger, *Sein und Zeit*, 126–128; *Being and Time* sec. 27, pp. 163–165.

23. Heidegger, *Sein und Zeit*, 128–130; *Being and Time* sec. 26, pp. 165–168.

24. Heidegger, *Sein und Zeit*, 295–298; *Being and Time*, sec. 60, pp. 341–345.

25. Heidegger, *Sein und Zeit*, 238–245, 250–253; *Being and Time*, sec. 47–48, 50, 52, pp. 281–290, 293–295.

26. Heidegger, *Sein und Zeit*, 238–240, 260–267; *Being and Time*, sec. 47, 53, pp. 281–284, 304–311.

27. Martin Heidegger, *Metaphysische Anfangsgründe der Logik*, ed. Klaus Held, vol. 26 of *Gesamtausgabe* (Frankfurt-Main: Klostermann, 1978), esp. "Leitsätze," 172–177 (my translation). For an English version, see *The Meta-*

physical Foundations of Logic, trans. Michael Heim (Bloomington: Indiana University Press, 1984).

28. Martin Heidegger, *Einleitung in die Philosophie,* ed. Otto Saame and Ina Saame-Speidel, vol. 27 of *Gesamtausgabe* (Frankfurt-Main: Klostermann, 1996), 118–119, 134–135, 141, 145–148 (my translation). In the latter quotation, Heidegger clearly distances himself from the dominant sociological conceptions of *gemeinschaft* and *gesellschaft.* Compare Ferdinand Tönnies, *Community and Society (Gemeinschaft und Gesellschaft),* trans. Charles P. Loomis (New York: Harper & Row, 1963).

29. Martin Heidegger, "Letter on Humanism," in *Martin Heidegger: Basic Writings,* 197, 221.

30. Martin Heidegger, *Zollikoner Seminare,* ed. Medard Boss (Frankfurt-Main: Klostermann, 1987), 145, 151 (my translation). For an English version, see *Zollikon Seminars: Protocols, Conversations, Letters,* trans. Franz Mayr and Richard Akay (Evanston: Northwestern University Press, 2001). Compare also my essay "Heidegger and Psychotherapy," in my book *Between Freiburg and Frankfurt* (Amherst: University of Massachusetts Press, 1991), 210–237.

31. See in this context my essay "Cosmopolitanism: In Search of Cosmos," in my book *Being in the World: Dialogue and Cosmopolis* (Lexington: University Press of Kentucky, 2013), 30–46.

32. See in this context my essays "Resisting Totalizing Uniformity: Martin Heidegger on *Macht* and *Machenschaft,*" in my book *Achieving Our World: Toward a Global and Plural Democracy* (Lanham, MD: Rowman & Littlefield, 2001), 189–209, and "The Underside of Modernity: Adorno, Heidegger, and Dussel," *Constellations* 11 (2004): 102–120.

33. Martin Heidegger, "Der Spruch des Anaximander," in *Holzwege,* 4th ed. (Frankfurt-Main: Klostermann, 1963), 343 (my translation). For an English translation, see "The Anaximander Fragment," in *Early Greek Thinking,* trans. David F. Krell and Frank A. Capuzzi (New York: Harper & Row, 1984), 13–58.

34. Heidegger, *Beiträge,* 28, 179 (my translation). For an English version, see *Contributions to Philosophy (From Enowning),* trans. Parvis Emad and Kenneth Maly (Bloomington: Indiana University Press, 1999).

35. Heidegger, *Besinnung,* sec. 12 and 24, pp. 40–42, 98 (my translation). For an English version, see *Mindfulness,* trans. Parvis Ernad and Thomas Kalary (New York: Continuum International, 2006).

36. Martin Heidegger, " . . . dichterisch wohnet der Mensch . . . ," in *Vorträge und Aufsätze,* part 2, 76–78; for an English translation, see " . . . Poetically Man Dwells . . . ," in *Poetry, Language, Thought,* trans. Albert Hofstadter (New York: Harper & Row, 1971), 228–229. As Heidegger writes in one of his later essays, only when openness and care prevail will human beings be able "to dwell poetically and properly humanly (*menschlich*) on this earth."

3. The Promise of Democracy

1. The symposium was held at the University of Westminster, London, November 3, 2012. Meant for oral presentation, the style of this chapter differs from the rest.

2. Sheldon Wolin, "Fugitive Democracy," in *Democracy and Difference: Contesting the Boundaries of the Political*, ed. Seyla Benhabib (Princeton: Princeton University Press, 1996), 38, 43. Compare in this context a statement by Maurice Merleau-Ponty: "A society is not the temple of value-idols that figure on the front of its monuments or in its constitutional scrolls; the value of a society is the value it places upon human relations. . . . To understand and judge a society, one has to penetrate its basic structure to the human bond upon which it is built; this undoubtedly depends upon legal relations, but also upon forms of labor, ways of loving, living, and dying" (*Humanism and Terror*, trans. John O'Neill [Boston: Beacon Press, 1969], xiv).

3. See in this context my book *The Promise of Democracy: Political Agency and Transformation* (Albany: State University of New York Press, 2010). The presentation in this chapter offers glosses on some chapters in this book.

4. See, for example, Ernst Kantorowicz, *The King's Two Bodies: A Study in Medieval Political Theology* (Princeton: Princeton University Press, 1957).

5. John Dewey, "Creative Democracy—the Task before Us," in *John Dewey, the Later Works, 1925–1953*, vol. 14, ed. Jo Boydston (Carbondale: Southern Illinois University Press, 1988), 226. This view is echoed by Sheldon Wolin when he writes that "democracy is a project concerned with the political potentiality of ordinary citizens, that is, with their possibilities for becoming political beings through the self-discovery of common concerns and modes of action for realizing them" ("Fugitive Democracy," 31).

6. See Ernesto Laclau and Lilian Zac, "Minding the Gap: The Subject of Politics," in *The Making of Political Identities*, ed. Ernesto Laclau (London: Verso, 1994), 11–39.

7. Martin Heidegger, "Letter on Humanism," in *Martin Heidegger: Basic Writings*, ed. David F. Krell (New York: Harper & Row, 1977), 193. Compare also Heidegger's terse statement in *Being and Time*: "Higher than actuality stands *possibility*. We can understand phenomenology only by grasping it as a possibility" (*Being and Time*, trans. John Macquarrie and Edward Robinson [New York: Harper & Row, 1962], sec. 2, p. 63).

8. Martin Heidegger, *Einleitung in die Philosophie*, ed. Otto Saame and Ina Saame-Speidel, vol. 27 of *Gesamtausgabe* (Frankfurt-Main: Klostermann, 1996), 173–178, 183–184 (my translation).

9. Hannah Arendt, *The Human Condition: A Study of the Central Dilemmas Facing Modern Man* (Chicago: University of Chicago Press, 1958), 50, 159–163, 173, 184. To some extent, Arendt corrected the individualistic bias in some of her later writings inspired by Kant's *Critique of Judgment*; see, for example, Hannah Arendt, *Lectures on Kant's Political Philosophy*, ed. Ronald

Beiner (Chicago: University of Chicago Press, 1982), and *Responsibility and Judgment,* ed. Jerome Kohn (New York: Schocken Books, 2003).

10. For the notion of "event" as disruption or irruption in recent French philosophy, see Claver Boundja, *Philosphie de l'événement* (Paris: Harmattan, 2003), and Alain Badiou, *Logique des mondes: L'être et l'événement* (Paris: Editions du Seuil, 2006). For Heidegger's different perspective, see *Beiträge zur Philosophy (Vom Ereignis),* ed. Friederich-Wilhem von Hermann, vol. 65 of *Gesamtausgabe* (Frankfurt-Main: Klostermann, 1994), 9–11, 30–33; for one translation of this work, see *Contributions to Philosophy (Of the Event),* trans. Richard Rajcewicz and Daniéla Vallega-Neu (Bloomington: Indiana University Press, 2012). Regarding the notion of *"democracie à venir,"* see Jacques Derrida, *Rogues: Two Essays on Reason,* trans. Pascale-Anne Brault and Michael Naas (Stanford, CA: Stanford University Press, 2005), esp. xii–xv.

11. Romand Coles, *Gated Politics: Reflections on the Possibility of Democracy* (Minneapolis: University of Minnesota Press, 2005), 178.

12. Stephen White, *Political Theory and Postmodernism* (Cambridge: Cambridge University Press, 1991), 1–2, 72.

13. Claude Lefort, *Democracy and Political Theory,* trans. David Macey (Minneapolis: University of Minnesota Press, 1988), 225; see also 9–12, 217–226.

14. Martin Heidegger, "What Is Metaphysics?" in *Martin Heidegger: Basic Writings,* 105.

15. Ernesto Laclau and Chantal Mouffe, *Hegemony and Socialist Strategy: Towards a Radical Democratic Politics,* trans. Winston Moore and Paul Commack (London: Verso, 1985), 51–62, 122–133. See also Ernesto Laclau, *New Reflections on the Revolution of Our Time* (London: Verso, 1980), and *Emancipation(s)* (London: Verso, 1996).

16. In Chantal Mouffe's case, the issue is attenuated because she changes Lefort's ontic-ontological distinction between politics and polity into an ontic-empirical difference between competing political forces ("the political") and the ensemble of groups in a public community ("politics"). In this manner, the radicality of Laclau's perspective is mitigated, but the status of the ensemble (whether it is simply the result of political antagonism) remains unclear. See, for example, Chantal Mouffe, *On the Political* (London: Routledge, 2005), 8–34.

17. Hannah Arendt, "On Violence," in *Crises of the Republic* (New York: Harcourt Brace Jovanovich, 1972), 177.

18. Recent times have seen strenuous efforts (partially successful) to reintroduce the voice of religion into public discourse. See, for example, Robert Booth Fowler, *Religion and Politics in America* (Boulder: Westview Press, 2004); John T. S. Madeley, ed., *Religion and Politics* (Burlington, VT: Ashgate, 2003). The later Heidegger's attention to the voice of poetry from Hölderlin to Trak and Rilke is well known; see, for example, Martin Heidegger, *Poetry, Language, Thought,*

trans. Albert Hofstadter (New York: Harper & Row, 1971). See also Michael Oakeshott, "The Voice of Poetry in the Conversation of Mankind," in *Rationalism in Politics, and Other Essays* (New York: Basic Books, 1962), 197–247.

19. For an instructive argument along these lines, see Hans-Georg Gadamer, "On the Possibility of a Philosophical Ethics," in *Hermeneutics, Religion, and Ethics*, trans. Joel Weinsheimer (New Haven: Yale University Press, 1999), 18–36.

20. Mahatma Gandhi, *Satyagraha* (Ahmedabad: Navajivan, 1958), 6; compare Thomas Pantham, "Beyond Liberal Democracy: Thinking with Mahatma Gandhi," in *Political Thought in Modern India*, ed. Thomas Pantham and Kenneth L. Deutsch (New Delhi: Sage, 1986), 340–341.

21. As is well known, a central category in Heidegger's philosophy is "care" (*Sorge*), a term whose meaning covers a broad spectrum ranging from "anxiety" and "worry" to "taken care of" (*Besorgen*) and "caring for" or "solicitude" (*Fürsorge*). On the level of solicitude, caring can be manipulative (by taking over the other's care) or liberating (by assisting the other's care for meaning). The "affective" dimension of human *Dasein* is captured in the emphasis on modes of "tuning" (*Stimmung, Befindlichkeit*), which can range from being "out of tune" to being "in tune." See Martin Heidegger, *Sein und Zeit*, 11th ed. (Tübingen: Niemeyer, 1967), 134–140 (my translation); *Being and Time*, sec. 5, pp. 172–173 (where *Stimmung* is misleadingly translated as "state-of-mind"), and sec. 6, pp. 235–241. On the "embodied" character of democracy, additional insights can be gleaned from Merleau-Ponty's work, especially *Adventures of the Dialectic*, trans. Joseph Bien (Evanston: Northwestern University Press, 1973), and *Humanism and Terror*.

22. On this "searching democracy," see my book *In Search of the Good Life: A Pedagogy for Troubled Times* (Lexington: University Press of Kentucky, 2007).

23. Friedrich Nietzsche, *Thus Spoke Zarathustra*, part 3, "The Other Dancing Song," in *The Portable Nietzsche*, ed. Walter Kaufmann (New York: Viking Press, 1968), 339. Compare in this context Theodor Adorno's statement that dialectical materialism "involves the feeling of 'all pain and all negativity' of the oppressed other, the damaged life which is one of the moving forces of dialectical thinking" (*Negative Dialectics*, trans. E. B. Ashton [New York: Seabury Press, 1979], 202). According to Simon Jarvis, dialectical materialism for Adorno is "not primarily a metaphysical doctrine but a 'practice of thinking' that seeks 'the end of suffering'" ("Adorno, Marx, Materialism," in *The Cambridge Companion to Adorno*, ed. Tom Huhn [Cambridge: Cambridge University Press, 2004], 84). Compare also Raymond Geuss, "Suffering and Knowledge in Adorno," *Constellations* 12 (2008): 3–20.

4. Markets and Democracy

1. Michael J. Sandel, *What Money Can't Buy: The Moral Limits of Markets* (New York: Farrar, Straus and Giroux, 2012), 3–6, 12.

2. Ibid., 8–10.

3. Karl Polanyi, *The Great Transformation: The Political and Economic Origins of Our Time* (1944; reprint, Boston: Beacon Press, 2001). As economist Fred Block writes in his introduction to this reprint of Polanyi's book, "Polanyi argues that creating a fully self-regulating market economy requires that human beings and the natural environment be turned into pure commodities, which assures the destruction of both society and the natural environment. . . . The logic underlying this argument rests on Polanyi's distinction between real and fictitious commodities. For Polanyi the definition of a commodity is something that has been produced for sale on a market. By this definition land, labor, and money are fictitious commodities because they were not originally produced to be sold on the market" (xxv). For Polanyi's own statements to this effect, see pages 75–76.

4. On the history of economics, see, for example, Jacob Viner, *Essays on the Intellectual History of Economics* (Princeton: Princeton University Press, 1991), and David M. Levy and Sandra Peart, *The Secret History of the Dismal Science* (Ann Arbor: University of Michigan Press, 2001).

5. Adam Smith, *The Theory of Moral Sentiments* (1759), ed. Knud Haakenssen (Cambridge: Cambridge University Press, 2002). Regarding the Scottish Enlightenment, see Thomas Ahnert and Susan Manning, eds., *Character, Self, and Sociability in the Scottish Enlightenment* (New York: Palgrave, 2011); James Buchan, *Crowded with Genius: The Scottish Enlightenment* (New York: HarperCollins, 2003); and the discussion of Hume in Alasdair MacIntyre, *After Virtue: A Study in Moral Theory*, 3rd ed. (Notre Dame, IN: University of Notre Dame Press, 2007), 47–56.

6. John Rae, *Life of Adam Smith* (New York: Kelley, 1895), 5.

7. Adam Smith, *The Wealth of Nations*, 2 vols., Glasgow ed. (Oxford: Clarendon Press, 1976), 2:79, 177.

8. Noam Chomsky, *Class Warfare: Interviews with David Barsamian* (Monroe, ME: Common Courage Press, 1996), 27. These comments are in agreement with Karl Polanyi's view that "Adam Smith, it is true, treated material wealth as a separate field of study. . . . [But] for all that, wealth was for him merely an aspect of the life of a community, to the purposes of which it remained subordinate" (*The Great Transformation*, 116). The statement stands in stark contrast to widespread portrayals that Smith was a dogmatic defender of laissez-faire capitalism and supply-side economics.

9. Angus Sibley, *The "Poisoned Spring" of Economic Libertarianism* (Washington, DC: Pax Romana, 2011), 56.

10. Carl Menger, *Principles of Economics*, trans. James Dingwall and Bert F. Hoselitz (New York: New York University Press, 1976), 171.

11. Ludwig von Mises, *Human Action* (New Haven: Yale University Press, 1949), 2, 680, 840, 884; see also Ludwig von Mises, *Die Gemeinwirtschaft* (1922), translated as *Socialism* by Jacques Kahane (New Haven: Yale University Press, 1951), 458.

12. Friedrich von Hayek, *The Fatal Conceit* (London: Routledge, 1988), 13, 63. See also Hayek's works *The Constitution of Liberty* (London: Routledge and Kegan Paul, 1960), 11; *The Road to Serfdom* (London: Routledge and Kegan Paul, 1944); and *The Mirage of Social Justice*, vol. 2 of *Law, Legislation, and Liberty* (Chicago: University of Chicago Press, 1976), 126. From here the road is not far to works by Ayn Rand such as *Atlas Shrugged* (New York: Random House, 1957) and *The Virtue of Selfishness* (New York: New American Library, 1964) or to the so-called Tea Party movement. Compare also Robert H. Frank, *The Darwin Economy: Liberty, Competition, and the Common Good* (Princeton: Princeton University Press, 2012).

13. Sibley, *The "Poisoned Spring" of Economic Libertarianism*, 194–198.

14. The most prominent economist of the Chicago School was Milton Friedman (1912–2006). According to Sibley, the distinctiveness of the Chicago School resides in a further ascent to abstractness: "Economics has definite, universal mechanical laws, like those of Newtonian physics; economic behavior . . . is based on self-interest and can be modeled and predicted mathematically" (*The "Poisoned Spring of Economic Libertarianism,"* 73). The Austrian School still resisted this move toward economic "science" and econometrics; see on this point Friedrich von Hayek, *The Counter-Revolution of Science* (Glencoe, IL: Free Press, 1952).

15. Robert Scheer, *The Great American Stickup* (New York: Nation Books, 2010), 2–3.

16. Paul Krugman, *The Return of Depression Economics and the Crisis of 2008* (New York: Norton, 2009), 193, 196. Krugman adds, "Some people say that our economic problems are structural, with no quick cure available; but I believe that the only important structural obstacles to world prosperity are the obsolete doctrines that clutter the minds of men" (131).

17. Joseph Stiglitz, foreword to Polanyi, *The Great Transformation*, vii–x, xv.

18. Joseph E. Stiglitz, *Freefall: America, Free Markets, and the Sinking of the World Economy* (New York: Norton, 2010), xvi–xvii, xx–xxi, 1, 27. Stiglitz comments in the chapter "Reforming Economics," "As we peel back the layers of 'what went wrong,' we cannot escape looking at the economics profession. . . . Economics had moved—more than economists would like to think—from being a scientific discipline into becoming free market capitalism's biggest cheerleader. If the United States is going to succeed in reforming its economy, it may have to begin by reforming economics" (238).

19. Ibid., xii, xxii, 274. In Stiglitz's view, such a rethinking of premises is particularly called for in the present situation of geopolitical transformation when America has to resort to the power of argument rather than to the argument of power: "The newly emerging global balance of power means that the United States will not be able to dictate the terms of the emerging world order. If it is to lead, it must be through moral suasion, by example, and by the force of its arguments" (342).

20. Gar Alperovitz, *America beyond Capitalism: Reclaiming Our Wealth, Our Liberty, and Our Democracy* (Hoboken, NJ: Wiley, 2005), ix.

21. James Gustave Speth outlines some of these ideas in his article "America the Possible: A Manifesto," *Orion Magazine,* March–April 2012 (http://orionmagazine.org/index.php/articles/article/668/). One additional idea in the manifesto is the transformation of foreign policy: from "American exceptionalism" to America as a "normal nation," from hard power to soft power. The article ends with this important statement: "That [envisaged] system won't be yesterday's socialism, but it won't be today's American capitalism either. . . . It is a moment of democratic possibility."

22. Alperovitz's and other speakers' addresses can be accessed at http://neweconomicsinstitute.org/videos.

23. Alperovitz, *America beyond Capitalism,* 234–235.

24. Sibley, *The "Poisoned Spring" of Economic Libertarianism,* 168–171, 173–178. At the University of Notre Dame, where I have served on the faculty, the Economics Department used to be prominent for emphasizing Catholic social teachings; however, under the influence of neoliberalism, that department was abolished and replaced by a new department specializing in "econometrics." These and similar developments support Stiglitz's argument in favor of a new and reformed discipline of economics.

25. Herman E. Daly and John B. Cobb Jr., *For the Common Good: Redirecting the Economy toward Community, the Environment, and a Sustainable Future,* 2nd ed. (Boston: Beacon Press, 1994), 6, 14, 382–383. There is some similarity between the position adopted in this study and that of so-called Ordo Liberalism—although the latter seems to be closer to the Austrian School. On this point, see Sibley, *The "Poisoned Spring" of Economic Libertarianism,* 67–68.

26. Michael J. Sandel, *Justice: What's the Right Thing to Do?* (New York: Farrar, Straus and Giroux, 2009), 19–20, 260–261. For another discussion of ethical theories leading to a similar conclusion, see Alasdair MacIntyre, *Three Rival Versions of Moral Enquiry: Encyclopedia, Genealogy, and Tradition* (Notre Dame, IN: University of Notre Dame Press, 1990).

27. Sandel, *What Money Can't Buy,* 14, 202–203.

28. Block, introduction to Polanyi, *The Great Transformation,* xxxvii. Compare in this context Lisa L. Martin, "Polanyi's Revenge," *Perspectives on Politics* 11 (March 2013): 177–183. The essay reviews, among other texts, Joseph Stiglitz, *The Price of Inequality: How Today's Divided Society Endangers Our Future* (New York: Norton, 2012).

5. Rights and Right(ness)

1. Raimon Panikkar, "Is the Notion of Human Rights a Western Concept?" *Diogenes,* no. 120 (1982): 77–78. The essay is an expanded and revised version of Panikkar's presentation at the "Entretiens de Dakar" meeting in Senegal in

1982. The meeting was preceded by a UNESCO symposium in Bangkok in December 1979 under the title "Meeting of Experts on the Place of Human Rights in Cultural and Religious Traditions." See *Final Report*, SS-79/CONF. 607/10 (Paris: UNESCO, February 6, 1980).

2. Panikkar, "Is the Notion of Human Rights a Western Concept?" 80, 88. For Hobbes's formula, see *Leviathan* (London: Dent & Sons, 1953), part I, chap. 14, p. 73; for Locke's formula, see *Two Treatises of Civil Government* (London: Dent & Sons, 1953), book 2, chap. 2, p. 119.

3. Panikkar, "Is the Notion of Human Rights a Western Concept?" 79–85.

4. Ibid., 95–96.

5. Ibid., 97–99. A similar notion of self-preservation can also be found in the philosophy of Spinoza (in contradistinction to that of Hobbes). See in this context my essay "Nature and Divine Substance: Spinoza," in my book *Return to Nature? An Ecological Counterhistory* (Lexington: University Press of Kentucky, 2011), 11–32.

6. Panikkar, "Is the Notion of Human Rights a Western Concept?" 100.

7. Ibid., 75, 77, 100–101. Compare in this context Raimon Panikkar, *Myth, Faith, and Hermeneutics* (New York: Paulist Press, 1979).

8. Panikkar, "Is the Notion of Human Rights a Western Concept?" 90, 102. See also Raimon Panikkar, *The Cosmotheandric Experience: Emerging Religious Consciousness,* ed. Scott Eastham (Maryknoll, NY: Orbis Books, 1993). Regarding personhood, Panikkar adds, "In drawing the distinction between individual and person I would put much more content in it than a French moral philosophy would do nowadays" ("Is the Notion of Human Rights a Western Concept?" 91). The reference is apparently to Emmanuel Mounier, *Personalism,* trans. Philip Mairet (Notre Dame, IN: University of Notre Dame Press, 1970). To be sure, the notion of personalism is associated with numerous other thinkers, such as Max Scheler and Cardinal Karol Wojtyla (later Pope John Paul II).

9. As Robert N. Bellah has observed in a critical vein, filial piety and hierarchical rank order in ancient China "became absolutes," with the model of parental authority eventually spilling over into all other relationships (*Beyond Belief: Essays on Religion in a Post-traditional World* [New York: Harper & Row, 1976], 94–95). For a proposal to add citizen relations to the classical five relationships, see my essay "Confucianism and the Public Sphere: Five Relationships Plus One," in my book *Peace Talks—Who Will Listen?* (Notre Dame, IN: University of Notre Dame Press, 2004), 152–171.

10. Regarding these attitudes, see Fred Dallmayr and Zhao Tingyang, eds., *Contemporary Chinese Political Thought: Debates and Perspectives* (Lexington: University Press of Kentucky, 2012).

11. Tu Weiming, *Confucian Thought: Selfhood as Creative Transformation* (Albany: State University of New York Press, 1985), 144–146.

12. Ibid., 81, 88, 133, 137. Compare also Wing-tsit Chang, "Chinese and

Western Interpretations of *Jen* (Humanity)," *Journal of Chinese Philosophy* 2 (1975): 122.

13. Tu Weiming, "Epilogue: Human Rights as a Confucian Moral Discourse," in *Confucianism and Human Rights*, ed. William Theodore de Bary and Tu Weiming (New York: Columbia University Press, 1998), 299, 302–303. In this context, Tu stresses these core contributions of Confucian teachings: "the perception of the person as a center of relationships rather than simply as an isolated individual; the idea of society as a community of trust rather than merely a system of adversarial relationships; and the belief that human beings are duty-bound to respect their family, society, and nation" (and world) (299).

14. Ann Elizabeth Mayer, *Islam and Human Rights: Tradition and Politics*, 3rd ed. (Boulder: Westview Press, 1999), 39, 41, 45, 55.

15. A. K. Brohi, "The Nature of Islamic Law and the Concept of Human Rights," *PLD Journal* 35 (1983): 150, qtd. in Mayer, *Islam and Human Rights*, 221. Brohi's article also strongly denounces the Western focus on "individualism," replacing it with a stress on organic communalism and "collectivity."

16. Mayer, *Islam and Human Rights*, 51.

17. In addition to rational philosophy, one also needs to mention the more recessed legacy of Sufism and its many sectarian manifestations. As Ann Elizabeth Mayer notes (in my view correctly), "If the adherents of rationalist and humanistic currents had attained greater political power and influence, such thinkers might have oriented Islamic thought in ways that would have created a much more propitious climate for the early emergence of human rights ideas" (*Islam and Human Rights*, 43).

18. Chandra Muzaffar, "From Human Rights to Human Dignity," in *Debating Human Rights: Critical Essays from the United States and Asia*, ed. Peter Van Ness (New York: Routledge, 1999), 26, 28–30.

19. See Chandra Muzaffar, *Rights, Religion, and Reform: Enhancing Human Dignity through Spiritual and Moral Transformation* (London: Routledge Curzon, 2002), 25. Compare Chandra Muzaffar, *Global Ethic or Global Hegemony* (London: Asean Academic Press, 2005), and Chandra Muzaffar, ed., *Human Wrongs* (Penang, Malaysia: Just World Trust, 1996).

20. Abdullahi An-Na'im, introduction to *Human Rights in Cross-Cultural Perspectives: A Quest for Consensus*, ed. Abdullahi An-Na'im (Philadelphia: University of Pennsylvania Press, 1992), 2–4. See also An-Na'im's essays "The Cultural Mediation of Rights," in *The East Asian Challenge for Human Rights*, ed. Joanne R. Bauer and Daniel A. Bell (Cambridge: Cambridge University Press, 1999), 147–168, and "Islamic Foundations for Religious Human Rights," in *Religious Human Rights in Global Perspectives*, ed. John Witte Jr. and Johan van der Vyver (Dordrecht: Martinus Nijhoff, 1966), 337–360. Other leading Muslim thinkers involved in efforts of reinterpretation are Hassan Hanafi, Nasr Hamid Abu Zaid, Muhammad Arkoun, Mohammed al-Jabri, and Abdolkarim Soroush. See in this context my essays "Islam and Democracy: Reflections on

Abdolkarim Soroush," in *Dialogue among Civilizations: Some Exemplary Voices* (New York: Palgrave Macmillan, 2002), 167–184, and "Opening the Doors of Interpretation: In Memory of Abu Zayd and Mohammed al-Jabri," in *Being in the World: Dialogue and Cosmopolis* (Lexington: University Press of Kentucky, 2013), 177–194.

21. Theodor W. Adorno, *Minima Moralia: Reflections from the Damaged Life*, trans. E. F. N. Jephott (London: Verso, 1978).

22. Henry Rosemont Jr., "Human Rights: A Bill of Worries," in Bary and Tu, *Confucianism and Human Rights*, 57, 60; Chandra Muzaffar, *Human Rights and the World Order* (Penang: Just World Trust, 1993), 39; Smitu Kothari and Harsh Sethi, introduction to *Rethinking Human Rights*, ed. Smitu Kothari and Harsh Sethi (Delhi: Lokayan, 1989), 9–11.

23. Kothari and Sethi, introduction to *Rethinking Human Rights*, 9.

6. "Man against the State"

1. Friedrich Nietzsche, *Thus Spoke Zarathustra*, in *The Portable Nietzsche*, ed. Walter Kaufmann (New York: Viking Press, 1968), 160.

2. Ibid., 162, 163. Max Weber used the phrase "specialists without spirit" in "Die Protestantische Ethik und der Geist des Kapitalimus," in *Gesammelte Aufsätze zur Religionssoziologie,* vol. 1 (Tübingen: Mohr, 1988), 204. Compare in this context George Orwell, *1984: A Novel* (New York: New American Library, 1943), and Virgil Gheorghiu, *The Twenty-Fifth Hour,* trans. Rita Elden (New York: Knopf, 1950).

3. Nietzsche, *Thus Spoke Zarathustra*, 160, 163, 174.

4. For some of Herbert Spencer's major works, see *Social Statics* (1851; reprint, London: Schalkenbach Foundation, 1970); *Essays: Moral, Political, and Speculative,* 3 vols. (1868–1874; reprint, London: Williams and Norgate, 1901); *The Study of Sociology* (1873; reprint, Ann Arbor: University of Michigan Press, 1969); *The Principles of Ethics,* 2 vols. (1879–1893; reprint, Indianapolis: Liberty Classics, 1978); *The Principles of Sociology,* 3 vols. (1876–1896; reprint, New York: Appleton, 1903).

5. Herbert Spencer, *The Man versus the State,* ed. Donald Macrae (Baltimore: Penguin Books, 1969), 148, 174–175.

6. Ibid., 164, 173, 176–177.

7. See, for example, Richard Hofstadter, *Social Darwinism in American Thought* (Boston: Beacon Press, 1955), and Raymond Williams, "Social Darwinism," in *Herbert Spencer: Critical Assessments,* ed. John Offer (New York: Routledge, 2000), 186–199.

8. Spencer, *Man versus the State*, 181.

9. William Graham Sumner, *What Social Classes Owe to Each Other* (New York: Harper and Row, 1883). Compare also William Graham Sumner, *Social Darwinism: Selected Essays of William Graham Sumner,* ed. Stow Persons

(Englewood Cliffs, NJ: Prentice Hall, 1969). One of the prominent later heirs of Spencer and Sumner is the Russian American writer Ayn Rand, whose writings have exerted a major influence in recent times on American libertarians, especially the Tea Party variety.

10. Ludwig von Mises, *Human Action* (New Haven: Yale University Press, 1949), 840. The Ludwig von Mises Institute, established in 1982 in Auburn, Alabama, is strongly under the influence of Spencer's *Man versus the State*. For additional discussion of the Austrian School, see chapter 7.

11. Henry David Thoreau, *Essay on Civil Disobedience*, in *The Portable Thoreau*, ed. Carl Bode (New York: Penguin Books, 1975), 109–110.

12. Ibid., 111.

13. Ibid., 112–113.

14. Ibid., 113, 119–120, 122, 136.

15. Erik H. Erikson, *Gandhi's Truth: On the Origin of Militant Nonviolence* (New York: Norton, 1993), 397. For Erikson, the ethical-spiritual motif of *satyagraha* is missed in many translations, where it is given as "passive resistance," "nonviolent resistance," and "militant nonviolence."

16. Mahatma Gandhi, *Satyagraha* (Ahmedabad: Navajivan, 1958), 6. Compare Indira Rothermund, "Gandhi's *Satyagraha* and Hindu Thought," in *Political Thought in Modern India*, ed. Thomas Pantham and Kenneth L. Deutsch (New Delhi: Sage, 1986), 297–306, and my essay "*Satyagraha*: Gandhi's Truth Revisited," in my book *Alternative Visions: Paths in the Global Village* (Lanham, MD: Rowman and Littlefield, 1998), 105–121.

17. Mahatma Gandhi, *India's Case for Swaraj* (Ahmedabad: Yeshanand, 1932), 369. See also Thomas Pantham, "Beyond Liberal Democracy: Thinking with Mahatma Gandhi," in Pantham and Deutsch, *Political Thought in Modern India*, 340–341.

18. Parel's comment is given in Mahatma Gandhi, *Hind Swaraj*, ed. Anthony J. Parel (Cambridge: Cambridge University Press, 1997), 81 n. 158.

19. Albert Camus, *The Rebel: An Essay of Man in Revolt*, trans. Anthony Bower (New York: Vintage Books, 1956), 6–8. As Camus adds in an existentialist vein (showing the influence of Heidegger, Jean-Paul Sartre, and others), "Man is the only creature who refuses to be what he is. The problem is to know whether this refusal can only lead to the destruction of himself and of others, whether all rebellion must end in the justification of universal murder" (11).

20. Ibid., 15–17, 22.

21. Recent disclosures of total global surveillance systems maintained by some countries clearly reveal a striving for "a technological world empire" animated by a "religion of secular technology." The total collection and storage of all communications in the world aims at the achievement of total knowledge as a corollary of total or absolute power. In religious terms, the systems emulate God's omniscience and omnipotence—while completely sidelining divine benevolence, grace, and charity.

22. Camus, *The Rebel*, 175, 180, 249–251.

23. Ibid., 281, 283–285. Camus's arguments proceed from a secular-humanist perspective, but many of his views can also be stated in Christian religious terms, as Gabriel Marcel did in *Man against Mass Society* (first published in 1952, one year after Camus's book). As Marcel states there, "It would be necessary to show that the idea of being creative [or free] always implies the idea of being open toward others: that openness I have called intersubjectivity. . . . The freedom which we have to defend is not the freedom of Prometheus defying Jupiter; it is not the freedom of a being who would exist or would claim to exist *by himself.* . . . Freedom is nothing unless, in a spirit of complete humility, it recognizes that it has a vital connection with grace [extended to all]" (*Man against Mass Society*, trans. G. S. Fraser [Chicago: Regnery, 1962], 24, 247).

24. Plato, *The Apology*, in *Great Dialogues of Plato*, ed. Eric H. Warmington and Philip G. Rouse, trans. W. H. D. Rouse (New York: New American Library, 1956), 437 (32A). As Plato adds, "It is necessary that one who really and truly fights for the right, if he is to survive even for a short time, shall act as a private man, not as a public man." Perhaps this comment can be read as counseling not a retreat into individual privacy but an engagement in "civil society" (to use the modern term).

25. Plato, *Criton*, in *Great Dialogues of Plato*, 454 (49B). The dialogue puts these words into the mouth of "the Laws": "As things are, if you depart from this life, you will depart wronged not by us, the Laws [the idea of justice], but by human beings only" (459, 54E).

26. On the resistance to the Nazis inside Germany, see, for example, Peter Hoffmann, *German Resistance to Hitler* (Cambridge, MA: Harvard University Press, 1988), and *The Second World War: German Society and Resistance to Hitler* (Cambridge: Cambridge University Press, 1994); and Gerd Wunder, *Die Schenken von Stauffenberg* (Stuttgart: Müller and Graeff, 1972).

27. Dietrich Bonhoeffer, *Ethics*, in *Dietrich Bonhoeffer Works*, vol. 6, ed. Clifford Green, trans. Reinhard Krauss, Douglas W. Scott, and Charles C. West (Minneapolis: Fortress Press, 2005), 244. Compare Dietrich Bonhoeffer, *Letters and Papers from Prison*, in *Dietrich Bonhoeffer Works*, vol. 8, ed. John W. de Gruchy, trans. Isabel Best et al. (Minneapolis: Fortress Press, 2010).

28. Camus, *The Rebel*, 279. As Camus adds, "Between two holocausts, scaffolds are installed in underground caverns where executioners celebrate their new cult of silence. What cry would ever trouble them?"

29. Friedrich Nietzsche, "From *The Wanderer and His Shadow*," in *The Portable Nietzsche*, 72.

7. Faith and Communicative Freedom

1. Joachim Gauck, Antrittsrede: "Nicht den Ängsten folgen, sondern dem Mut," March 23, 2012, http://www.bundespräsident.de/Reden (my translation).

2. Ibid.

3. For the reference to Luther's formula, see Joachim Gauck, *Winter im Sommer—Frühling im Herbst, Erinnerungen*, 6th ed. (Munich: Pantheon, 2011), 340. As Gauck adds there, "Freedom and responsibility demand a continuous adaptation and constitute a permanent challenge" (337, my translation). As we know, Pope John XXIII (1958–1963) adopted Luther's formula (*ecclesia semper reformanda*) in some of his official statements and writings.

4. Compare in this context my essays "Religious Freedom: Preserving the Salt of the Earth," in my book *In Search of the Good Life: A Pedagogy for Troubled Times* (Lexington: University Press of Kentucky, 2007), 205–219, and "Religion and the World: The Quest for Justice and Peace," in my book *Integral Pluralism: Beyond Culture Wars* (Lexington: University Press of Kentucky, 2010), 85–101.

5. "Theological Declaration of Barmen," in Wolfgang Huber, *Folgen christlicher Freiheit: Ethik und Theorie der Kirche im Horizont der Barmer Theologischen Erklärung* (Neukirchen-Vluyn: Neukirchner, 1983), chap. 1, 15–21 (my translation). For an English translation, see "Theological Declaration of Barmen," in Arthur C. Cochrane, *The Church's Confession under Hitler* (Philadelphia: Westminster Press, 1962), 237–242, http://www.sacred-texts.com/chr/barmen.htm. The Barmen Declaration has not lost its relevance today, especially in view of efforts to enlist or instrumentalize Christian faith in the service of nationalist or geopolitical agendas.

6. Huber, *Folgen christlicher Freiheit*, 25, 29 (my translation).

7. Bonhoeffer and Niemöller are discussed in ibid., 29–30, 47. Niemöller is quoted in Karl Kupisch, *Quellen zur Geschichte des deutschen Protestantismus von 1945 bis zur Gegenwart* (Göttingen: Musterschmidt, 1971), part 1, p. 44 (my translation).

8. Huber, *Folgen christlicher Freiheit*, 36, 59. In his interpretation of Barth, Huber seems to be close to Paul Tillich, who at one point found "dialectical theology" insufficiently dialectical.

9. Ibid., 41, 155.

10. Ibid., 26, 54. Perhaps more than in Europe, this avoidance of the economic domain is glaringly evident in the United States, where liberal progressivism (including liberal Protestantism) has encouraged the growth of a "health and wealth gospel" in which the relation between Christianity and capitalism is seen as entirely unproblematical.

11. Ibid., 29, 46, 49.

12. Ibid., 49, 118. Huber adds that "the idea of freedom as communicative freedom is grounded in the notion of God who as Christ approaches humans in free love and thus liberates them to an identity actualized in acts of communicative existence" (118). At a later point, we read, "Christian freedom has the character of a freedom that surrenders itself—that is, as a loving or communicative freedom" (210).

13. Wolfgang Huber, *Im Geist der Freiheit: Für eine Ökumene der Profile* (Freiburg: Herder, 2007), 9–10 (my translation). Compare in this context my book *Integral Pluralism*; the chapter "The Dignity of Difference" in my book *Small Wonder: Global Power and Its Discontents* (Lanham, MD: Rowman & Littlefield, 2005), 209–217; and my essay (dealing with relations between Western and Eastern/Orthodox Christianity) "The Humility of the Faithful, the Harmony of Faiths," *Thirty Days* (*Trenta Giorni*), special issue (2008): 80–81.

14. Huber, *Im Geist der Freiheit*, 11–15. In my view, ecumenical efforts are promising only on the level of practices and not (or much less) on the level of doctrines and beliefs. The chief practice where ecumenism is still blocked but most desirable is the sharing of the Eucharist (Abendmahl).

15. Ibid., 73–77, 79.

16. Ibid., 90–96.

17. Ibid., 39–44. As Huber makes clear, the state's so-called neutrality cannot mean laïcist indifference because the state in modern democracies is meant to encourage or foster the free exercise of religion. Hence, he prefers the phrase "supportive neutrality" employed by the German constitutional court.

18. Ibid., 61–65, 109–128. Compare in this context my essay "Post-secularity and (Global) Politics: A Need for Radical Redefinition," in my book *Being in the World: Dialogue and Cosmopolis* (Lexington: University Press of Kentucky, 2013), 137–150.

19. Huber, *Im Geist der Freiheit*, 54–55. Huber adds that "solidarity does not arise from the market" (56).

20. Ibid., 104–106. Huber actually refers approvingly to an agreement reached between Catholic and Protestant theologians in 1992 on the relation between faith and "works" and thus on the central issue of "justification" (*Rechtfertigung*) (111). As is well known, partially as a result of Alasdair MacIntyre's book *After Virtue* (1984), there has been a strong revival of "virtue ethics," which, although relying mainly on Aristotle, today finds resonance in East Asian, Indian, and even Islamic traditions of ethics. See, for example, Stanley Hauerwas and Charles Pinches, *Christians among the Virtues* (Notre Dame, IN: University of Notre Dame, 1997).

21. Wolfgang Huber, *Von der Freiheit: Perspektiven für eine solidarische Welt* (Munich: Beck, 2012), 8–9 (my translation).

22. Ibid., 58–59, 63.

23. Huber, *Im Geist der Freiheit*, 148.

24. See, for example, Stanley Hauerwas, *A Community of Character: Toward a Constructive Christian Social Ethic* (Notre Dame, IN: University of Notre Dame Press, 1981), and *In Good Company: The Church as Polis* (Notre Dame, IN: University of Notre Dame Press, 1995); John B. Cobb Jr., *Reclaiming the Church* (Louisville: J. Knox Press, 1997).

25. Charles Taylor, *Varieties of Religion Today: William James Revisited* (Cambridge, MA: Harvard University Press, 2002), 93–94. Taylor's study offers

a critique of James's notion of personal religion as "the feelings, acts and experiences of individual men in their solitude" (7). For this formulation, see William James, *The Varieties of Religious Experience: A Study in Human Nature*, 36th impression (New York: Longmans, Green, 1928), 28–29. For a discussion of both James and Taylor, see my essay "Postsecular Faith: Toward a Religion of Service," in *Integral Pluralism*, 67–83.

26. Huber, *Im Geist der Freiheit*, 149–150, 157. Compare in this context John W. Wright, ed., *Postliberal Theology and the Church Catholic* (Grand Rapids, MI: Baker Academic, 2012).

27. Huber, *Von der Freiheit*, 10. See also Michael Theunissen, *Hegels Lehre vom absoluten Geist als theologisch-politscher Traktat* (Berlin: Aldine de Gruyter, 1970), and *Der Andere* (Berlin: Aldine de Gruyter, 1965), translated by Christopher Macann as *The Other* (Cambridge, MA: MIT Press, 1984). Compare my essay "Dialogue and Otherness: Theunissen," in my book *Critical Encounters: Between Philosophy and Politics* (Notre Dame: University of Notre Dame Press, 1987), 209–244.

28. Huber, *Von der Freiheit*, 87–89, 169–170. See also Karl-Otto Apel, *Transformation den Philosophie*, 2 vols. (Frankfurt: Suhrkamp, 1973), translated by Glyn Adey and David Frisby as *Towards a Transformation of Philosophy* (London: Routledge & Kegan Paul, 1980), and Jürgen Habermas, *Erläuterungen zur Diskursethik* (Frankfurt: Suhrkamp, 1991), translated by Ciaran Cronin as *Justification and Application: Remarks on Discourse Ethics* (Cambridge, MA: MIT Press, 1993). Compare Seyla Benhabib and Fred Dallmayr, eds., *The Communicative Ethics Controversy* (Cambridge, MA: MIT Press, 1990), and my article "Apel's Transformation of Philosophy," in *Critical Encounters*, 101–125.

29. Huber, *Von der Freiheit*, 89–90. Compare Charles Taylor, *The Ethics of Authenticity* (Cambridge, MA: Harvard University Press, 1992), where Taylor sensibly occupies a middle ground between the "knockers" and the "boosters" of modernity; Franklin I. Gamwell, *The Divine Good* (San Francisco: Harper, 1990), and *Existence and the Good* (Albany: State University of New York Press, 2011); and my book *In Search of the Good Life*.

30. Huber, *Von der Freiheit*, 175–176.

31. Gauck, "Nicht den Ängsten folgen."

8. Between Holism and Totalitarianism

1. These comments were prepared for the Thirteenth International Likhachev Conference (also called Likhachev Readings), St. Petersburg, May 16–17, 2013.

2. Miklós Kun, introduction to Dimitry S. Likhachev, *Reflections on the Russian Soul: A Memoir*, trans. Bernard Adams (New York: Central European University Press, 2000), viii, xiii.

3. Ibid., viii.

4. Ibid., ix.

5. Likhachev, *Reflections on the Russian Soul*, 25.

6. Ibid., 26–27.

7. Ibid., 62–63.

8. Kun, introduction to Likhachev, *Reflections on the Russian Soul*, viii.

9. Likhachev, *Reflections on the Russian Soul*, 63–65.

10. Ibid., 65–67.

11. Ibid., 68–69, 71.

12. Ibid., 65.

13. Dimitry Likhachev, *The Great Heritage: The Classical Literature of Old Rus*, trans. Doris Bradbury (Moscow: Progress, 1981), 7, 9.

14. Ibid., 10–11.

15. Ibid., 14–16.

16. Ibid., 19–20.

17. Ibid., 5–6, 21–23.

18. Ibid., 23, 26.

19. Ibid., 26–27, 30–31.

20. Ibid., 31.

21. Dimitry Likhachev, *The National Nature of Russian History* (New York: Columbia University Press, 1990), 9–10.

22. Ibid., 10–12, 14–15.

23. Ibid., 14, 19.

24. Likhachev, *The Great Heritage*, 343; Kun, introduction to Likhachev, *Reflections on the Russian Soul*, xiii.

25. Dimitry Likhachev, letter to the Open World Leadership Center, March 15, 1999, http://www.openworld.gov/about/11.php?sub=2331ang-1 (accessed March 20, 2013, but the letter is no longer accessible at this address).

9. Freedom as Engaged Social Praxis

This chapter is a strongly revised version of an essay that first appeared in my book *Dialogue among Civilizations* (New York: Palgrave Macmillan, 2002). Although that essay focuses on freedom alone, the present revision shifts the accent to the freedom–solidarity relation.

1. D. P. Chattopadhyaya, *Knowledge, Freedom, and Language: An Interwoven Fabric of Man, Time, and World* (Delhi: Motilal Banarsidass, 1989), 279.

2. Ibid., 241. Chattopadhyaya himself seems to subscribe to such a reduced or chastised version of reason when he describes himself as an "anthropological rationalist" (in opposition to a speculative transcendentalist) (15). However, as is clear from this book and other writings, his conception of rationalism is flexible enough to embrace many diverse forms of reasoning or thinking, just as his view of being human is not narrowly anthropocentric but makes room for different ways of being-in-the-world (as attested by his numerous references

to Heidegger and Gadamer). Compare in this context his book *Individuals and Worlds: Essays in Anthropological Rationalism* (New Delhi: Oxford University Press, 1976).

3. Chattopadhyaya, *Knowledge, Freedom, and Language*, 242.

4. Ibid., 244, 246.

5. Ibid., 251. For Arendt's notion of "worldlessness" or "world alienation," see *The Human Condition* (Chicago: University of Chicago Press, 1958), 230–233.

6. Chattopadhyaya, *Knowledge, Freedom, and Language*, 255–256.

7. Ibid., 258–259.

8. Ibid., 259–260.

9. Ibid., 260–261.

10. Ibid., 261–262.

11. Ibid., 263.

12. Ibid., 270–271. Regarding the significance and profound sense of the Buddha's silence, see Raimon Panikkar, *The Silence of God: The Answer of the Buddha* (Maryknoll, NY: Orbis Books, 1989). For a comparison of Western (ego-based) freedom and Buddhist (ego-transcending) freedom, see Charles Taylor, "Conditions of an Uncoerced Consensus on Human Rights," in *The East Asian Challenge for Human Rights*, ed. Joanne R. Bauer and Daniel A. Bell (Cambridge: Cambridge University Press, 1999), 124–144.

13. Chattopadhyaya, *Knowledge, Freedom, and Language*, 275–276.

14. Ibid., 277.

15. Ibid., 268.

16. Ibid., 295–296. Chattopadhyaya refers to Martin Heidegger, *Sein und Zeit*, 11th ed. (Tübingen: Niemeyer, 1967) (*Being and Time*, trans. John Macquarrie and Edward Robinson [London: SCM Press, 1962], sec. 161), and Hans-Georg Gadamer, *Truth and Method*, 2nd rev. ed., trans. Joel Weinsheimer and Donald G. Marshall (New York: Crossroad, 1989), 415–416.

17. Chattopadhyaya, *Knowledge, Freedom, and Language*, 299.

18. D. P. Chattopadhyaya, "Gandhi on Freedom and Its Different Facets," in *Environment, Evolution, and Values* (Delhi: Motilal Banarsidass, 1993), 203–204.

10. Freedom and Solidarity (Again)

1. In my book *G. W. F. Hegel: Modernity and Politics*, rev. ed. (Lanham, MD: Rowman & Littlefield, 2002), I present the German philosopher precisely in this light.

2. For a discussion of Dewey's "holism," see my essay "Democratic Action and Experience: Dewey's 'Holistic' Pragmatism," in my book *The Promise of Democracy: Political Agency and Transformation* (Albany: State University of New York Press, 2010), 43–65.

3. John Dewey, *The Public and Its Problems,* new ed. (1927; Athens: Ohio University Press, 1954), 21–22.

4. Ibid., 24–25, 34–35.

5. Ibid., 147, 149–151, 184.

6. John Dewey, *Individualism Old and New* (Amherst, NY: Prometheus Books, 1999), 5, 9, 40.

7. Ibid., 26–27, 30. Regarding psychopathologies, see Zygmunt Bauman, *Globalization: The Human Consequences* (Cambridge: Polity Press, 1998).

8. Dewey, *Individualism Old and New,* 40, 42–44, 50, 58. A "capitalistic" type of socialism may be described as one where the winnings are privatized and the losses socialized. Dewey's text pays tribute to Karl Marx as the "prophet" of economic development, but Dewey criticizes Marx for depending too much on "psychological economic premises" and for anticipating too little emerging "technical advances" (50–51). He also has little sympathy for Russian Bolshevism (42).

9. See, for example, Noel W. Thompson, *Political Economy and the Labour Party: The Economics of Democratic Socialism, 1884–2005,* 2nd ed. (New York: Routledge, 2006); Manfred B. Steger, *The Quest for Evolutionary Socialism* (Cambridge: Cambridge University Press, 2006); Matt Carter, *T. H. Green and the Development of Ethical Socialism* (Charlottesville, VA: Imprint Academic, 2003); Stanislao G. Pugliese, *Carlo Rosselli: Socialist Heretic and Antifascist Exile* (Cambridge, MA: Harvard University Press, 1999).

10. To be sure, there were illustrious exceptions to this trend, including John Rawls, *A Theory of Justice* (Cambridge, MA: Harvard University Press, 1971); Charles Taylor, *Hegel* (Cambridge: Cambridge University Press, 1975); and Alasdair MacIntyre, *After Virtue: A Study in Moral Theory* (Notre Dame: University of Notre Dame Press, 1981). In Germany, there was the revival of the Frankfurt School under the leadership of Jürgen Habermas.

11. Richard Rorty, *Contingency, Irony, and Solidarity* (Cambridge: Cambridge University Press, 1989), 192. See also Rorty's essay "Solidarity or Objectivity?" in *Post-analytic Philosophy,* ed. John Rajchman and Cornel West (New York: Columbia University Press, 1984), 3–19. I have criticized some of Rorty's departures from Dewey in my book *The Promise of Democracy* (63). For an even stronger critique along these lines, see Richard Bernstein, "One Step Forward, Two Steps Backward: Rorty on Liberal Democracy and Philosophy" and "Rorty's Liberal Utopia," in *The New Constellation: The Ethico-political Horizons of Modernity/Postmodernity* (Cambridge, MA: MIT Press, 1992), 230–257, 258–292.

12. Chantal Mouffe, *The Return of the Political* (New York: Verso, 1993), 25, 65, 90. See also Ernesto Laclau and Chantal Mouffe, *Hegemony and Socialist Strategy: Towards a Radical Democratic Politics,* trans. Winston Moore and Paul Cammack (London: Verso, 1985), as well as my essays "Postmodernism and Radical Democracy: Laclau and Mouffe on 'Hegemony'" and "The Return of

the Political: On Chantal Mouffe," both in *The Promise of Democracy*, 99–115, 195–203. As these pieces show, there is considerable synergy between Mouffe and myself (marred only by her fondness for Carl Schmitt).

13. Craig Calhoun, "Imagining Solidarity: Cosmopolitanism, Constitutional Patriotism, and the Public Sphere," *Public Culture* 14 (Winter 2002): 154, 159, 163. Compare in this context Jürgen Habermas, *The Structural Transformation of the Public Sphere: An Inquiry into a Category of Bourgeois Society*, trans. Thomas Burger and Frederick Lawrence (Cambridge, MA: MIT Press, 1989); Hannah Arendt, *The Human Condition* (Chicago: University of Chicago Press, 1958), and *Crises of the Republic* (New York: Harcourt Brace Jovanovich, 1972); Craig Calhoun, "Plurality, Promises, and Public Spheres," in *Hannah Arendt and the Meaning of Politics*, ed. Craig Calhoun and John McGowan (Minneapolis: University of Minnesota Press, 1997), 232–259; Nancy Fraser, "Rethinking the Public Sphere," in *Habermas and the Public Sphere*, ed. Craig Calhoun (Cambridge, MA: MIT Press, 1992), 109–142; and my essay "Action in the Public Realm: Arendt Between Past and Future," in *The Promise of Democracy*, 83–97.

14. Gianni Vattimo and Santiago Zabala, *Hermeneutic Communism: From Heidegger to Marx* (New York: Columbia University Press, 2011), 2, 110. Despite its aloofness from Hegelian dialectics, this text does not endorse violent, unilateral uprisings—that is, "revolutionary positions at the service of power." As the authors state, "Communism and hermeneutics or, better, 'hermeneutic communism' leaves aside both the [neoliberal] *ideal of development* and also the general call for revolution. Unlike Alain Badiou, Antonio Negri, and other contemporary Marxist theorists, we do not believe that the twenty-first century calls for revolution because the forces of the politics of description [that is, realism] are too powerful, violent, and oppressive to be overcome through a parallel insurrection: only such a weak thought as hermeneutics can avoid violent ideological revolts and therefore defend the weak" (3). Remarkably insightful are the text's comments on Heidegger: "He discredited communism, along with capitalism and democracy, not because of his early sympathies for Nazism but rather because of his need to overcome metaphysics" (4).

15. See in this context my essay "Agency and Letting-Be: Heidegger on Primordial Praxis," in *The Promise of Democracy*, 67–81.

16. In this respect, I find particularly appealing Confucian ethics, which starts not from absolute universal maxims but from concrete human relationships (that is, from the ground up). Compare in this context Kwong-loi Shun and David B. Wang, *Confucian Ethics: A Comparative Study of Self, Autonomy, and Community* (Cambridge: Cambridge University Press, 2004), and my essay "Confucianism and the Public Sphere: Five Relationships Plus One?" in my book *Peace Talks: Who Will Listen?* (Notre Dame: University of Notre Dame Press, 2004), 152–171. On the compatibility of Confucianism

with Deweyan-style democracy, see, for example, David L. Hall and Roger T. Ames, *The Democracy of the Dead: Dewey, Confucius, and the Hope for Democracy in China* (La Salle, IL: Open Court, 1999), and Sor-hoon Tan, *Confucian Democracy: A Deweyan Reconstruction* (Albany: State University of New York Press, 2003).

Index

'Abduh, Muhammad, 109
absurdism, 128
action theory, 68–69
Adorno, Theodor, 111, 172–174
ahimsa, 78, 126
al-Farabi, 109
Allen, Douglas, xv
Alperovitz, Gar, 90–92
Ambedkar, B. R., 102
anarchism, 117
Anaximander, 62
An-Na'im, Abdullahi, 111
antagonism, 72
anthropocentrism, 11, 27, 45, 61,
    100–103, 107–111
anthropocosmic vision, 108
anthropology, 98
antiessentialism, 73
Antigone, 132
anti-idealism, 18
anti-rationalism, 8
Apel, Karl-Otto, 150–151
appropriation, 35
Arab Spring, 65
Arendt, Hannah, 69, 75, 173, 192
argumentation, 76
aristocracy, 67, 71
Aristotle, 18, 29, 31, 67, 69–70, 76,
    81, 94, 116, 148, 194
atheism, 67
atomism, 22; of soul, 22
Austrian School, 83–84, 97, 121

authenticity, 41–424, 58, 111
autocracy, 97, 115–116
autonomy, 3–5, 21, 39–40, 46, 94, 149
Axial Age, xiii, 12, 94, 112

Bacon, Francis, xii, 2, 81
Bakhtin, Mikhail, 154
Barmen Declaration, 13, 133, 137–
    142, 145, 217n5
Barth, Karl, 13, 133, 137, 140
being-toward-death, 55–56
being-with, 52–53, 55–59
Bentham, Jeremy, 117–119
Berdyaev, Nikolai, 13, 153–154
Berlin, Isaiah, 85, 139
Bernstein, Eduard, 189
Bhagavad Gita, 100, 169, 180
Bonhoeffer, Dietrich, xv, 12–13, 133,
    137–139
Boss, Medard, 59
Buddha, 176–178
Buddhism, 171, 176–178
Bulgakov, Sergei, 13, 154
bureaucracy, 122

Calhoun, Craig, 192
Calogero, Guido, 190
Camus, Albert, 12, 116, 127–131,
    134, 216n23
capital, 4, 121; social, 88
capitalism, xii, 4, 83, 121, 184;
    financial, 93

care, 41, 51, 77, 195, 208n21
Catholic social teachings, 92, 145,
    211n24
causality, 46–47, 50; of nature, 46
causation, 41, 47
chaos, 7
chaosmos, 7
Chattopadhyaya, D. P., 14, 170–181
chauvinism, 61, 135, 165
Chicago School, 83
Chomsky, Noam, 83
church, 136, 139–140, 144–147;
    established, 138; evangelical, 150;
    of freedom, 150; Russian, 156, 160
civilization, 188
Cobb, John B., 93, 150
co-being, 50, 57, 70, 195
Cold War, xii, 165–168, 185, 190
Coles, Romand, 71
collectivism, 40, 59–60, 63, 91–93,
    184–189, 195–196
communalism, 9
communism, xii, 5, 164, 195;
    hermeneutic, 15, 193
communitarianism, xiv, 5, 51, 63,
    150, 191
community, 115, 130, 186; civic, 122
Comte, Auguste, 117–120
conformism, xiv, 124, 187
Confucianism, 104–105
conscience, 55–56
contract, 99, 119–120; social, 99
cosmology, 98
cosmopolitanism, 165; rooted, 165
cosmotheandric vision, 11, 104
correspondence, 43
critical theory, 13, 151
culture war, 185

Dalai Lama, 196
Daly, Herman, 93

Darwin, Charles, 117, 120
decisionism, 41
deconstruction, xiii, 8, 26, 28–30, 60,
    71
Deleuze, Gilles, 7
democracy, 9–10, 24, 27, 65–80, 95,
    97, 122–124, 185–186; agonistic,
    73; caring, 10, 65, 77; deliberative,
    75; intellectual, 158; modern,
    9, 18, 67, 75, 97; promise of, 9,
    65–66, 75; social, 183–184, 189,
    192
"democracy to come," 70
deontology, 94, 151
Derrida, Jacques, xiii, 63, 70–73
Descartes, René, xi, 2–3, 18–21, 27,
    29, 41, 58–61, 68, 81, 85, 128,
    171–172, 194
despotism, 40, 116, 97, 164, 169, 173
determinism, 21, 172–173, 179
Dewey, John, 9, 14–15, 66–70, 76, 97,
    184–191, 196
dharma, 101–103, 105, 113
Dharmashastras, 100
dialogue, 103
dictatorship, 158
difference, 49; ontic-ontological, 32
differentiation, 162
disclosedness, 55
disclosure, 50
disembedding, 4
dissent, 115, 130, 183
domination, 62, 171
dualism, 41, 140
Durkheim, Émile, 150
dwelling, 63

Earl of Shaftesbury, 82
econometrics, 84
economics, 80–91, 141, 149;
    capitalist, 87; depression, 87;

laissez-faire, 80; market, 79–80; modern, 93; neoclassical, 83, 121; neoliberal, 95; trickle-down, 88
ecumenism, 143
egocentrism, 26, 35, 103, 165
embeddedness, 5
emotionalism, 77
empathy, 53
empiricism, 118, 172
emptiness, 178
empty space, 72
enframing, 62
Enlightenment, 3–4, 18, 29, 117, 169, 171–174, 179. *See also* Scottish Enlightenment
epistemology, 22, 67, 190
equality, 8
Ereignis, 33–36, 71, 201n25
Erikson, Erik, 125–126
essence, 73
essentialism, 24, 74
ethics, 94, 131, 170; public, 148; relational, 104; virtue, 94
Eurocentrism, 165
event, 34
everydayness, 51–55
evolutionism, 117, 120
existence, 52–53
existentialism, 18, 51, 58, 73; spiritual, 158

Fabian Society, 189
Falk, Richard, xv
fascism, 61, 129, 164, 190
faith, 135–137, 142, 144, 147; Christian, 139; private, 142; religious, 141
fatalism, 41, 48–49
finitude, 56
Francis of Assisi, 196
fraternity, 8

free being, 44–45
freedom, xiii, 3, 13, 19, 39–48, 50–51, 55–59, 62–69, 77, 88, 115–118, 135, 139–145, 148–157, 169–171, 183–184, 189–190, 194; communicative, 13–14, 135–136, 143–149; creative, 195; culture of, 151, 169; democratic, 12; denial of, 60; economic, 83–85; from/ of self, 14; human, 5, 8, 172, 179–180; individual, 82, 173, 185, 188; modern, 5, 11–13; negative, 4, 6, 44–45, 86; noumenal, 173; ontology of, 49; positive, 4, 6, 44–45; religious, 142, 146; responsible, 149; social, 189; Western, 136, 174; of will, 21
free enterprise, 105, 121
free will, 21, 43, 48–49, 171
free world, 40
friendship, 105
fundamentalism, 107, 164; theocratic, 107

Gadamer, Hans-Georg, 76, 141, 180, 193
Galileo, Galilei, 2
Galtung, Johan, xv
Gamwell, Franklin, 151
Gandhi, Mahatma, xiv–xv, 12, 15, 66, 77–78, 102, 113, 116, 125–127, 131, 181, 196
Gauck, Joachim, 135–136, 151–152
globalization, 143, 147
Great Community, 186–187
Green, T. H., 189
Guizot, François, 83

Habermas, Jürgen, 75–76, 150–151, 192
Hamann, Johann G., 76

Hauerwas, Stanley, 150
Hayek, Friedrich, 84–86
hedonism, 19
Hegel, Georg W. F., 149–150, 184–185, 188, 192
hegemony, 73
Heidegger, Martin, xiii, 7–9, 17–20, 27–38, 40–63, 68–73, 76, 164, 179–183, 193–196
Herder, Johann G., 76
herd mentality, 25–26
hermeneutics, 18, 30–32, 193; of Dasein, 33; diatopical, 103
heteronomy, 21, 45
Hindutva, 102
historicality, 28–29
Hobbes, Thomas, xi–xii, 12, 99, 115–117, 119, 149
Hobhouse, L. T., 189
Hobson, John, 189
holism, 5, 12, 102, 153, 160, 191
Honneth, Axel, 198n6
Horkheimer, Max, 172, 174
Huber, Wolfgang, 13, 136–152
humaneness, 106, 113
humanism, 68, 100, 108–109
humanities, 81, 153
Hume, David, 82
Husserl, Edmund, 8, 27, 30–32, 51–53, 70, 201n22
Hutcheson, Francis, 82
hypermodernism, 72

Ibn Rushd, 109
Ibn Sina, 109
identity, 73, 75; politics of, 73
immanence, 41, 137, 175
imperialism, 110
individualism, 11–14, 18, 26, 40, 54, 99–102, 110, 116, 163, 170, 184; atomistic, 13; economic, 188;

exaggerated, 86; liberal, 193; radical, 91
individuality, 164
industrialism, 118
inequality, 80–83, 89, 106, 121, 147; social, 147, 190
injustice, 123–126, 132, 147
integration, 162
intellectualism, 76, 191
intelligentsia, 154; Russian, 154–156
internationalism, 59, 61
interpretation, 21, 31
intersubjectivity, 52–53

Jacobi, F. H., 48
Jaspers, Karl, 1–3, 70
jihadism, 75
justice, 86, 94, 98, 109, 113, 126–128, 131–132, 136, 139, 151–152; economic, 147; interhuman, 130; social, 86, 132, 136, 141–149

Kant, Immanuel, 41, 45–47, 51, 95, 144–145, 149–151, 171, 173
Kapur, Jagdish, xv
Keynes, John Maynard, 90
Kierkegaard, Søren, 42
King, Martin Luther, Jr., xiv, 113, 196
Köchler, Hans, xv
Kothari, Smitu, 112
Krugman, Paul, 87
Kun, Miklós, 153–156, 167

labor, 83–84; division of, 83
Laclau, Ernesto, 68, 73, 191
language, 175–180
Lefort, Claude, 9, 66, 71–72
Leibniz, G. W., 75–172
letting-be, 44–45, 69, 77, 195–196
liberalism, xii, 40, 60–63, 100, 116–117, 185, 202n27; British, 118;

laissez-faire, 4, 10–12, 84; social, 184, 189–190
libertarianism, 12, 60–63, 84, 94, 116, 131
liberty, xi, 85; economic, 86; negative, 18, 85, 139; positive, 139; social, xiv
Likhachev, Dimitry, 13, 153–168
Locke, John, xi, 12, 83, 100, 117–119, 172
Luther, Martin, 136, 140–141

Machenschaft, 33, 37–38, 164
Machiavelli, Niccolo, 67
machination, 164
MacIntyre, Alasdair, xiv–xv
Mandela, Nelson, xiv, 113, 196
market, 79–80, 85; economic, 102; fundamentalism, 89, 95; self-regulating, 89; social, 189; triumphalism, 79–80, 84, 87, 95
Marxism, 15, 84, 105, 193
Mayer, Ann Elizabeth, 108–109
mediocrity, 25–27, 186, 189
Meister Eckhart, 38
Menger, Carl, 84
Merleau-Ponty, Maurice, 6, 9, 71, 206n2
metaphysics, 28, 34–36, 144, 193; dogmatic, 145; end of, 36; modern, 37; overcoming of, 7, 36; traditional, 7, 18, 27, 76, 193
Mises, Ludwig von, 84–86
modernity, xi–xii, 2–3, 21, 37, 80, 99, 10–4, 146, 164, 172, 178; crisis of, 5; liberal, 137; Western, 4, 29, 45, 62, 81, 97–102, 117, 141, 173, 194
monadology, 57
monarchy, 67, 71
monologue, 74, 130
moralism, 76

morality, 19, 149; collective, 157; master, 23; overcoming of, 19; slave, 23
Mouffe, Chantal, 72–73, 191–192, 207n16
multiculturalism, 100, 143
Muzaffar, Chandra, xv, 110–112
mysticism, 49

Nagarjuna, 178
Nandy, Ashis, xvi
Napoleon, 129
nationalism, 59, 61, 166
nation-state, 162–164, 167
naturalism, 172
nature, xi, 81, 172, 179; book of, 179; control of, xi, 179; domination of, 141, 179; state of, 141, 179
Naumann, Friedrich, 189
neocolonialism, 110
neoconservatism, 61
neoliberalism, 10, 63, 79, 86–87, 89–91
neo-Protestantism, 142–149
neutrality, 85
Newton, Isaac, 12
Niebuhr, Reinhold, 133
Niemöller, Martin, 139
Nietzsche, Friedrich, xiii–xiv, 7–8, 17–24, 27, 33, 36, 78, 115–116, 129, 134, 157, 183, 193, 196
nihilism, 25, 38, 127–129, 177; European, 26; perfect, 26
nobility, 24–25
nonviolence, 216
nothingness, 72

Oakeshott, Michael, 76
oligarchy, 65
ontology, 29, 31–32; fundamental, 47; phenomenological, 33

openness, 6
otherness, 50; absolute, 51

Panikkar, Raimon, 6, 98–108, 111
pantheism, 48
paradigm, xi–xii, 6, 22–23, 26–28,
    34, 93, 98–99, 107; dominant,
    33; modern, 11; shift, 3, 6–7, 14,
    17, 33, 91, 105, 108–111, 183;
    Western, 11, 100
Parel, Anthony, 127
particularity, 73–75
Pasternak, Boris, 13, 154
peace, 151
person, 103, 107, 163, 212n8
phenomenology, 18, 27, 30–32, 70;
    transcendental, 33
philosophy, 19, 45, 98, 170;
    analytical, 185; critical, 45;
    Greek, 109, 144; Islamic, 109;
    Kantian, 45; of mind, 68; moral,
    19; synthetic, 118; transactional,
    149; transformation of, 19
Physiocrats, 82
Picasso, Pablo, xvi
Plato, 24, 29, 67, 171
pluralism, 75, 145, 191–193;
    religious, 143
Polanyi, Karl, 10, 80, 88, 95, 209n3
polis, 116
politicization, 137
positivism, 22, 117, 173
postmetaphysics, 35
postmodernism, 50–51, 71
potentiality, 66–68
power, 167, 189
pragmatism, 191
praxis, 14, 68–69, 76, 169, 171, 195;
    primordial, 69; social, 14, 169,
    178
privatization, 137, 139

professionalism, 60
progress, 121–123
property, 120, 142; private, 118–119,
    141, 149
Protestantism, 137, 183; professing, 137
publicity, 54, 59, 70
public opinion, 59
public realm, 69, 146, 186, 192

Quesnay, François, 82

racism, 61
Ramanuja, 176
rank order, 23
rationalism, 108–109, 171–172,
    193
rationality, 75, 145–146, 171, 174–
    175, 178–179
Rawls, John, 75
realism, 24
reason, 171, 174, 178–179
rebellion, 128
Reformation, 4
reformism, 136
Reid, Thomas, 82
relativism, 191
Renaissance, 4, 171
resistance, 124, 130–132
resolution, 55
revaluation, 7, 18–26
rights, 10–11, 97–113; human, 10–11,
    97–113; individual, 97; natural,
    119–120
rightness, 128
Rorty, Richard, 190–191
Rosemont, Henry, Jr., 112
Rosselli, Carlo, 190
Rousseau, Jean-Jacques, xi, 72
routinization, xi
rupture, 70
Ruskin, John, 125

Salafism, 67
Sandel, Michael J., 79–81, 92–95
Sartre, Jean-Paul, 54, 58
satyagraha, 77, 125–127
Scheer, Robert, 87
Scheler, Max, 53
Schelling, Friedrich, 47–49
Scholasticism, 29
science, 22
scientism, 18
Scottish Enlightenment, 82–83
secularism, xi, 107, 141
secularization, 146
security, 62
self, 107; relational, 107
self-interest, 119, 136
self-transcendence, 14
Sethi, Harsh, 112
Shankara, 176
Shaw, George Bernard, 189
Sibley, Angus, 84–87, 92
Smith, Adam, 10, 81–84, 93
social contract, 39, 58
Social Darwinism, 12, 116, 120–122,
    130–131, 187
socialism, xii, 40, 84–85, 121, 188–
    189, 192; authentic, 8–9; liberal,
    xvi, 184, 189–190, 192
sociology, 117; interactive, 149
Socrates, 116, 126, 131
solidarity, xii–xiv, 8, 13–15,
    40, 50, 54–58, 62, 86, 116,
    128–132, 135–136, 149, 154,
    164, 180, 183–184, 186–188,
    190–196
solipsism, 58–61, 174, 183, 187, 196
solicitude, 42, 54–57, 77
solitude, 44, 53, 129
Sombart, Werner, 189
Sorokin, Pitirim, 154
sovereignty, 60

Spencer, Herbert, 12, 116–120, 122–
    123, 128
Spengler, Oswald, 1
Spinoza, Benedict, 48, 67, 172
spirit, 29
spiritualization, 1–2
spontaneity, 46, 171
Stalin, Joseph, 129
state, 115–116, 138–139, 144–146,
    162–163, 185–186; modern, 138;
    political, 186; terrorism, 129
statism, 118
Stauffenberg, Count von, 12, 133
Stiglitz, Joseph, 88–90
subjectivism, 59, 61
subjectivity, xii, 29, 58–59, 171–174,
    183; transcendental, 51
Sumner, William Graham, 121
sunyata, 177
surveillance, 115, 134
survival, 120
sympathy, 82

Tawney, R. H., 189
Taylor, Charles, xvi, 150–151
technology, 3, 37, 49
theocentrism, 108
theocracy, 164
theology, 13; Christian, 193;
    dialectical, 13, 133, 137, 140;
    negative, 67; process, 67
Theunissen, Michael, 150
Thoreau, Henry David, 12, 115–116,
    122–125, 127, 131
Tolstoy, Leo, 125
totalitarianism, xv, 12–13, 97, 132–
    134, 136–137, 142, 153, 164, 190
Toynbee, Arnold, 1
tradition, 19, 28, 45, 164
traditionalism, 29, 105
Trakl, Georg, 164

transcendence, 41, 67, 137, 175
truth, 39, 43–47, 77–78, 139, 177,
  203n6
Tutu, Bishop Desmond, 196
Tu Weiming, xvi, 105–106

unfreedom, 169
Upanishads, 175
utilitarianism, 19, 94, 117–118

Vattimo, Gianni, 193, 195, 223n14
Vedanta, 176, 179
Vedas, 175
Vico, Giambattista, 76
virtue(s), 147–148; cardinal, 147;
  ethics, 94; evangelical, 147
voluntarism, 41

Wahhabism, 75

Webb, Beatrice, 189
Webb, Sidney, 189
Weber, Max, xi–xii
White Rose, 133
White, Stephen, 71
Whitman, Walt, 187, 196
wholeness, 185
Wilde, Oscar, 157
will, 37; to power, 25–27, 33, 62–63,
  157, 202n31; to will, 37
willpower, 50
Wing-tsit Chang, 106
Wittgenstein, Ludwig, 98
Wolin, Sheldon, 9, 65–66, 77
world disclosure, 175

Yusa, Michiko, xvi

Zabala, Santiago, 193, 195

www.ingramcontent.com/pod-product-compliance
Lightning Source LLC
Chambersburg PA
CBHW031546260326
41914CB00002B/293